T0271354

GENERALIZED VECTORIZATION, CROSS-PRODUCTS, AND MATRIX CALCULUS

This book presents the reader with new operators and matrices that arise in the area of matrix calculus. The properties of these mathematical concepts are investigated and linked with zero-one matrices such as the commutation matrix. Elimination and duplication matrices are revisited and partitioned into submatrices. Studying the properties of these submatrices facilitates achieving new results for the original matrices themselves. Different concepts of matrix derivatives are presented and transformation principles linking these concepts are obtained. One of these concepts is used to derive new matrix calculus results, some involving the new operators and others the derivatives of the operators themselves. The last chapter contains applications of matrix calculus, including optimization, differentiation of log-likelihood functions, iterative interpretations of maximum likelihood estimators, and a Lagrangian multiplier test for endogeneity.

Darrell A. Turkington is a professor of economics at the University of Western Australia. His numerous publications include articles in leading international journals such as the *Journal of the American Statistical Association*, the *International Economic Review*, and the *Journal of Econometrics*. He is also the author of *Instrumental Variables* (Cambridge University Press, 1985, with Roger J. Bowden), *Matrix Calculus and Zero-One Matrices: Statistical and Econometric Applications* (Cambridge University Press, 2002), and *Mathematical Tools for Economics* (2007). Professor Turkington received his PhD in theoretical econometrics from the University of California, Berkeley.

Generalized Vectorization, Cross-Products, and Matrix Calculus

DARRELL A. TURKINGTON

University of Western Australia

CAMBRIDGE
UNIVERSITY PRESS

Shaftesbury Road, Cambridge CB2 8EA, United Kingdom

One Liberty Plaza, 20th Floor, New York, NY 10006, USA

477 Williamstown Road, Port Melbourne, VIC 3207, Australia

314–321, 3rd Floor, Plot 3, Splendor Forum, Jasola District Centre, New Delhi – 110025, India

103 Penang Road, #05–06/07, Visioncrest Commercial, Singapore 238467

Cambridge University Press is part of Cambridge University Press & Assessment, a department of the University of Cambridge.

We share the University's mission to contribute to society through the pursuit of education, learning and research at the highest international levels of excellence.

www.cambridge.org
Information on this title: www.cambridge.org/9781107032002

First published 2013
First paperback edition 2014

A catalogue record for this publication is available from the British Library

Library of Congress Cataloging-in-Publication data
Turkington, Darrell A., author.
Generalized vectorization, cross-products, and matrix calculus /
Darrell A. Turkington.
pages   cm
Includes bibliographical references and index.
ISBN 978-1-107-03200-2 (hardback)
1. Matrices.   2. Vector analysis.   I. Title.
QA188.T8645   2012
515′.63–dc23   2012022017

ISBN   978-1-107-03200-2   Hardback
ISBN   978-1-107-44872-8   Paperback

Contents

v

Preface

This book can be regarded as a sequel to my previous book, *Matrix Calculus and Zero-One Matrices: Statistical and Econometric Applications*, which was published by Cambridge University Press in 2002 (with a paperback edition published in 2005). It largely concerns itself with the mathematics behind matrix calculus. Several new matrix operators and matrices are introduced in this book and their properties are studied. This forms the substance of the first three chapters of the book. Chapter 4 may be regarded as an application of some of these mathematical concepts. Chapter 5 gives new matrix calculus results pertaining to the new operators. The last chapter gives some applications of matrix calculus itself.

Aiming to have a self-contained book, I cannot avoid presenting some known theorems and definitions along with some results from my previous book.

The outline of the chapters in more detail follows: The first chapter introduces a new matrix operator, which I call a cross-product of matrices. It sums Kronecker products formed from two partitioned matrices. Generalized vecs and rvecs are presented. These matrix operators are generalizations of the vec and rvec operators, and come into their own when we are dealing with partitioned matrices.

Chapter 2 deals with well-known zero-one matrices such as selection matrices, permutation matrices, elementary matrices, and commutation matrices. A number of theorems are given involving commutation matrices and cross-products of matrices. This chapter also looks at zero-one matrices that the reader may not be as familiar with, namely generalized vecs and rvecs of the commutation matrix. These concepts were introduced in my previous book. The chapter builds on this work presenting many new theorems about generalized vecs and rvecs of the commutation matrix, and methods for finding results for these matrices from known results of the commutation matrix itself. This chapter introduces two new matrices whose properties are investigated. One is similar to the commutation matrix in that its submatrices are certain elementary matrices. The second, I call a 'twining matrix', a zero-one matrix that intertwines rows or columns of a given set of matrices. Its relationship to the commutation matrix is clearly shown.

Chapter 3 studies in some detail well-known matrices associated with matrix calculus, namely elimination and duplication matrices. The approach taken is to partition these matrices into interesting submatrices and study the properties of these submatrices. This facilitates the investigation as to how these peculiar matrices interact with other matrices, particularly Kronecker products. It also involves the introduction of new matrix operators whose properties in turn are studied.

Chapter 4 looks at four concepts of the derivative of a matrix with respect to another matrix that exists in the literature and develops transformation principles that allow an easy movement from a result obtained using one of the concepts to the corresponding results for the others. In doing so, extensive use is made of results obtained in the first two chapters.

Chapter 5 derives new matrix calculus results with reference to generalized vecs and cross-products of matrices, and shows how those results can be expanded into appropriate submatrices. The last section of this chapter gives some simple, but powerful, theorems involving the concept of the matrix derivative used in this book.

The final chapter presents applications of matrix calculus itself. It demonstrates how matrix calculus can be used to efficiently solve complicated optimization problems, but it is largely concerned with the use of matrix calculus in statistics and econometrics. It explains how matrix differentiation can be used in differentiating a log-likelihood function, involving as it usually does a symmetric covariance matrix, in obtaining the score vector and finally in obtaining the information matrix. This work calls on the theorems of the last section of Chapter 5.

The second part of Chapter 6 uses matrix calculus to obtain iterative interpretations of maximum likelihood estimators in simultaneous equation models in terms of econometric estimators. It looks at the computational convergence of the different interpretations. Finally, a new Lagrangian multiplier test statistic is derived for testing for endogeneity in such models.

Two institutions should be mentioned in the preface: First, my home university, the University of Western Australia, for allowing me time off from teaching to concentrate on the manuscript; second, Nuffield College

ONE

Mathematical Prerequisites

1.1 Introduction

This chapter considers elements of matrix algebra, knowledge of which is essential for discussions throughout this book. This body of mathematics centres around the concepts of Kronecker products and vecs of a matrix. From the elements of an $m \times n$ matrix $A = \{a_{ij}\}$ and a $p \times q$ matrix $B = \{b_{ij}\}$, the Kronecker product forms a new $mp \times nq$ matrix. The vec operator forms a column vector from the elements of a given matrix by stacking its columns one underneath the other. This chapter discusses several new operators that are derived from these basic operators.

The operator, which I call the cross-product operator, takes the sum of Kronecker products formed from submatrices of two given matrices. The rvec operator forms a row vector by stacking the rows of a given matrix alongside each other. The generalized vec operator forms a new matrix from a given matrix by stacking a certain number of its columns, taken as a block, under each other. The generalized rvec operator forms a new matrix by stacking a certain number of rows, again taken as a block, alongside each other.

Although it is well known that Kronecker products and vecs are intimately connected, this connection also holds for rvec and generalised operators as well. The cross-product operator, as far as I know, is being introduced by this book. As such, I present several theorems designed to investigate the properties of this operator. This book's approach is to list, without proof, well-known properties of the mathematical operator or concept in hand. However, I give a proof whenever I present the properties of a new operator or concept, a property in a different light, or something new about a concept.

1

1.2 Kronecker Products

Let $A = \{a_{ij}\}$ be an $m \times n$ matrix and B be a $p \times q$ matrix. The $mp \times nq$ matrix given by

$$
\begin{bmatrix}
a_{11}B & \cdots & a_{1n}B \\
\vdots & & \vdots \\
a_{m1}B & \cdots & a_{mn}B
\end{bmatrix}
$$

is called the **Kronecker product** of A and B, denoted by $A \otimes B$.

Well-known properties of Kronecker products are as follows:

$$A \otimes (B \otimes C) = (A \otimes B) \otimes C = A \otimes B \otimes C;$$
$$(A + B) \otimes (C + D) = A \otimes C + A \otimes D + B \otimes C + B \otimes D; \text{ and}$$
$$(A \otimes B)(C \otimes D) = AC \otimes BD \text{ provided AC and BD exist.} \quad (1.1)$$

The transpose of a Kronecker product is the Kronecker product of transposes

$$(A \otimes B)' = A' \otimes B'.$$

If A and B are non-singular, the inverse of a Kronecker product is the Kronecker product of the inverses

$$(A \otimes B)^{-1} = A^{-1} \otimes B^{-1}.$$

If A is an $n \times n$ matrix and B is an $p \times p$ matrix, then

$$\operatorname{tr}(A \otimes B) = \operatorname{tr}A.\operatorname{tr}B,$$

where the determinant of the Kronecker product is given by

$$|A \otimes B| = |A|^P.|B|^n.$$

Notice that generally, this operator does not obey the commutative law. That is, $A \otimes B \neq B \otimes A$. One exception to this rule is if a and b are column vectors, not necessarily of the same order, then

$$a' \otimes b = b \otimes a' = ba'. \quad (1.2)$$

This exception allows us to write $A \otimes b$ in an interesting way, where A is an $m \times n$ matrix and b is a column vector. Partition A into its rows so

$$
A = \begin{pmatrix} a^{1'} \\ \vdots \\ a^{m'} \end{pmatrix}
$$

where the notation we use for the ith row of a matrix throughout this book is $a^{i'}$. Thus, from our definition of a Kronecker product

$$A \otimes b = \begin{pmatrix} a^{1'} \otimes b \\ \vdots \\ a^{m'} \otimes b \end{pmatrix}.$$

By using Equation 1.2, we can write

$$A \otimes b = \begin{pmatrix} b \otimes a^{1'} \\ \vdots \\ b \otimes a^{m'} \end{pmatrix}.$$

As far as partitioned matrices are concerned, suppose we partition A into submatrices as follows:

$$A = \begin{pmatrix} A_{11} & \cdots & A_{1K} \\ \vdots & & \vdots \\ A_{L1} & \cdots & A_{LK} \end{pmatrix}.$$

Therefore, from our definition it is clear that

$$A \otimes B = \begin{pmatrix} A_{11} \otimes B & \cdots & A_{1K} \otimes B \\ \vdots & & \\ A_{L1} \otimes B & \cdots & A_{LK} \otimes B \end{pmatrix}. \tag{1.3}$$

Likewise, suppose we partition B into an arbitrary number of submatrices, say,

$$B = \begin{pmatrix} B_{11} & \cdots & B_{1r} \\ \vdots & & \vdots \\ B_{s1} & \cdots & B_{sr} \end{pmatrix}.$$

Then, in general,

$$A \otimes B \neq \begin{pmatrix} A \otimes B_{11} & \cdots & A \otimes B_{1r} \\ \vdots & & \vdots \\ A \otimes B_{s1} & \cdots & A \otimes B_{sr} \end{pmatrix}.$$

One exception to this rule can be formulated as follows: Suppose B is a $p \times q$ matrix and we write $B = (B_1 \ldots B_r)$, where each submatrix of B has p rows.

Furthermore, let a be any column vector, say $m \times 1$. Then,

$$a \otimes B = \begin{pmatrix} a_1(B_1 \ldots B_r) \\ \vdots \\ a_m(B_1 \ldots B_r) \end{pmatrix} = \begin{pmatrix} a_1 B_1 & \cdots & a_1 B_r \\ \vdots & & \vdots \\ a_m B_1 & & a_m B_r \end{pmatrix}$$

$$= (a \otimes B_1 \ldots a \otimes B_r). \tag{1.4}$$

Staying with the same partitioning of B, consider A a $m \times n$ matrix partitioned into its columns $A = (a_1 \ldots a_n)$. Therefore, using Equations 1.3 and 1.4, it is clear that

$$A \otimes B = (a_1 \otimes B_1 \ldots a_1 \otimes B_r \ldots a_n \otimes B_1 \ldots a_n \otimes B_r).$$

If, for example, B is partitioned into its columns, then $B = (b_1 \ldots b_q)$, so we can write

$$A \otimes B = (a_1 \otimes b_1 \ldots a_1 \otimes b_q \ldots a_n \otimes b_1 \ldots a_n \otimes b_q). \tag{1.5}$$

Another exception to the rule is $a' \otimes B$, where we now partition B as $B = (B'_1 \ldots B'_s)'$ and each submatrix has q columns. Therefore,

$$a' \otimes B = \begin{pmatrix} a' \otimes B_1 \\ \vdots \\ a' \otimes B_s \end{pmatrix}.$$

If A is $m \times n$, then

$$A \otimes B = \begin{pmatrix} a^{1'} \otimes B_1 \\ \vdots \\ a^{1'} \otimes B_s \\ \vdots \\ a^{m'} \otimes B_1 \\ \vdots \\ a^{m'} \otimes B_s \end{pmatrix}$$

where, as before, $a^{i'}$ refers to the ith row of A, $i = 1, \ldots, m$. If B is partitioned into its rows, then

$$A \otimes B = \begin{pmatrix} a^{1'} \otimes b^{1'} \\ \vdots \\ a^{1'} \otimes b^{p'} \\ \vdots \\ a^{m'} \otimes b^{1'} \\ \vdots \\ a^{m'} \otimes b^{p'} \end{pmatrix} \tag{1.6}$$

where $b^{j'}$ refers to this jth row of B, $j = 1, \ldots, p$.

Let x be a column vector and A a matrix. As a consequence of these results, the ith row of $x' \otimes A$ is $x' \otimes a^{i'}$, where $a^{i'}$ is the ith row of A, and the jth column of $x \otimes A$ is $x \otimes a_j$, where a_j is the jth column of A.

Another useful property for Kronecker products is this: Suppose A and B are $m \times n$ and $p \times q$ matrices respectively, and x is any column vector. Then,

$$A(I_n \otimes x') = (A \otimes 1)(I_n \otimes x') = A \otimes x'$$
$$(x \otimes I_p)B = (x \otimes I_p)(1 \otimes B) = x \otimes B,$$

where I_n is the $n \times n$ identity matrix.

We can use these results to prove that for a, a $n \times 1$ column vector and b a $p \times 1$ column vector,

$$(a' \otimes I_G)(b' \otimes I_{nG}) = b' \otimes a' \otimes I_G.$$

Clearly,

$$(a' \otimes I_G)(b' \otimes I_{nG}) = (a' \otimes I_G)(b' \otimes I_n \otimes I_G) = a'(b' \otimes I_n) \otimes I_G$$
$$= (1 \otimes a')(b' \otimes I_n) \otimes I_G = b' \otimes a' \otimes I_G.$$

Another notation used throughout this book is: I represent the ith column of the $n \times n$ identity matrix I_n by e_i^n and the jth row of this identity matrix by $e_j^{n'}$. Using this notation, a result that we find useful in our future work is given by our first theorem.

Theorem 1.1 *Consider the $n \times m$ matrix given by*

$$\begin{pmatrix} O & e_i^n & O \\ n \times (p-1) & & n \times (m-p) \end{pmatrix}$$

for $i = 1, \ldots, n$. Then,

$$I_n \otimes e_m^{p'} = \left(O \; e_1^n \; O \ldots O \; e_n^n \; O \right).$$

Proof: We have

$$I_n \otimes e_m^{p'} = \left(e_1^n \otimes e_p^{m'} \ldots e_n^n \otimes e_p^{m'} \right) = \left(e_p^{m'} \otimes e_1^n \ldots e_p^{m'} \otimes e_n^n \right)$$
$$= \left(O \; e_1^n \; O \ldots O \; e_n^n \; O \right). \qquad \blacksquare$$

1.3 Cross-Product of Matrices

Much of this book's discussions involve partitioned matrices. A matrix operator that I find very useful when working with such matrices is the cross-product operator. This section introduces this operator and presents several theorems designed to portray its properties.

Let A be an $mG \times p$ matrix and B be an $nG \times q$ matrix. Partition these matrices as follows:

$$A = \begin{pmatrix} A_1 \\ \vdots \\ A_G \end{pmatrix}, \quad B = \begin{pmatrix} B_1 \\ \vdots \\ B_G \end{pmatrix}$$

where each submatrix A_i of A is $m \times p$ for $i = 1, \ldots, G$ and each submatrix B_j of B is $n \times q$ for $j = 1, \ldots, G$. The **cross-product** of A and B denoted by $A\tau_{Gmn}B$ is the $mn \times pq$ matrix given by

$$A\tau_{Gmn}B = A_1 \otimes B_1 + \cdots + A_G \otimes B_G.$$

Notice the first subscript attached to the operator refers to the number of submatrices in the partitions of the two matrices, the second subscript refers to the number of rows in each submatrix of A, and the third subscript refers to the number of rows in each of the submatrices of B.

A similar operator can be defined when the two matrices in question are partitioned into a row of submatrices, instead of a column of submatrices as previously discussed. Let C be a $p \times mG$ matrix and D be a $q \times nG$ matrix, and partition these matrices as follows:

$$C = (C_1 \ldots C_G) \quad D = (D_1 \ldots D_G),$$

where each submatrix C_i of C is $p \times m$ for $i = 1, \ldots, G$ and each submatrix D_j of D is $q \times n$ for $j = 1, \ldots, G$. Then, the column cross-product is defined as

$$C\bar{\tau}_{Gmn}D = C_1 \otimes D_1 + \cdots + C_G \otimes D_G.$$

The operator τ is the relevant operator to use when matrices are partitioned into a 'column' of submatrices, where as $\bar{\tau}$ is the appropriate operator to use when matrices are partitioned into a 'row' of submatrices. The two operators are intimately connected as

$$(A\tau_{Gmn}B)' = A_1' \otimes B_1' + \cdots + A_G' \otimes B_G' = A'\bar{\tau}_{Gmn}B'.$$

In this book, theorems are proved for τ operator and the equivalent results for the $\bar{\tau}$ operator can be obtained by taking transposes.

Sometimes, we have occasion to take the cross-products of very large matrices. For example, suppose A is $mrG \times p$ and B is $nG \times q$ as previously shown. Thus, if we partition A as

$$A = \begin{pmatrix} A_1 \\ \vdots \\ A_G \end{pmatrix},$$

each of the submatrices in this partition is $mr \times p$. To avoid confusion, signify the cross-product between A and B, namely $A_1 \otimes B_1 + \cdots + A_G \otimes B_G$ as $A\tau_{G,mr,n}B$, and the cross-product between B and A, $B_1 \otimes A_1 + \cdots + B_G \otimes A_G$ as $B\tau_{G,n,mr}A$.

Notice that in dealing with two matrices A and B, where A is $mG \times p$ and B is $mG \times q$, then it is possible to take two cross-products $A\tau_{Gmm}B$ or $A\tau_{mGG}B$, but, of course, these are not the same. However, the following theorem shows that in some cases the two cross-products are related.

Theorem 1.2 *Let A be a $mG \times p$ matrix, B be a $ns \times q$ matrix, and D be a $G \times s$ matrix. Then,*

$$B\tau_{snm}(D' \otimes I_m)A = (D \otimes I_n)B \,\tau_{Gnm}A.$$

Proof: Write

$$D = (d_1 \ldots d_s) = \begin{pmatrix} d^{1'} \\ \vdots \\ d^{G'} \end{pmatrix}.$$

Then,

$$(D \otimes I_n)B = \begin{pmatrix} d^{1'} \otimes I_n \\ \vdots \\ d^{G'} \otimes I_n \end{pmatrix} B = \begin{pmatrix} (d^{1'} \otimes I_n)B \\ \vdots \\ (d^{G'} \otimes I_n)B \end{pmatrix}.$$

Partition A as

$$A = \begin{pmatrix} A_1 \\ \vdots \\ A_G \end{pmatrix}$$

where each submatrix A_i is $m \times p$. Then,

$$(D \otimes I_n)B \, \tau_{Gnm} A = (d^{1'} \otimes I_n)B \otimes A_1 + \cdots + (d^{G'} \otimes I_n)B \otimes A_G.$$

Now

$$(D' \otimes I_m)A = \begin{pmatrix} d_1' \otimes I_m \\ \vdots \\ d_s' \otimes I_m \end{pmatrix} A = \begin{pmatrix} (d_1' \otimes I_m)A \\ \vdots \\ (d_s' \otimes I_m)A \end{pmatrix}.$$

But,

$$\left(d_j' \otimes I_m\right)A = \left(d_{1j}I_m \ldots d_{Gj}I_m\right) \begin{pmatrix} A_1 \\ \vdots \\ A_G \end{pmatrix} = d_{1j}A_1 + \cdots + d_{Gj}A_G,$$

so when we partition B as

$$B = \begin{pmatrix} B_1 \\ \vdots \\ B_s \end{pmatrix}$$

where each submatrix B_i is $n \times q$, we have

$$
\begin{aligned}
B\tau_{snm}&(D' \otimes I_m)A \\
&= B_1 \otimes (d_{11}A_1 + \cdots + d_{G1}A_G) + \cdots + B_s \otimes (d_{1s}A_1 + \ldots d_{Gs}A_G) \\
&= B_1 \otimes d_{11}A_1 + \cdots + B_s \otimes d_{1s}A_1 \ldots B_1 \otimes d_{G1}A_G + \cdots + B_s \otimes d_{Gs}A_G \\
&= (d_{11}B_1 + \cdots + d_{1s}B_s) \otimes A_1 + \cdots + (d_{G1}B_1 \ldots + d_{Gs}B_s) \otimes A_G \\
&= (d^{1'} \otimes I_n)B \otimes A_1 + \cdots + (d^{G'} \otimes I_n)B \otimes A_G. \quad\blacksquare
\end{aligned}
$$

In the following theorems, unless specified, A is $mG \times p$ and B is $nG \times q$, and

$$A = \begin{pmatrix} A_1 \\ \vdots \\ A_G \end{pmatrix}, \quad B = \begin{pmatrix} B_1 \\ \vdots \\ B_G \end{pmatrix} \tag{1.7}$$

where each submatrix A_i of A is $m \times p$ and each submatrix B_j of B is $n \times q$, for $i = 1, \ldots, G$ and $j = 1, \ldots, G$. The proofs of these theorems are derived using the properties of Kronecker products.

Theorem 1.3 *Partition A differently as*

$$A = (C \ D \ldots F)$$

where each submatrix $C, D, \ldots, F$ has mG rows. Then,

$$A\tau_{Gmn}B = (C\tau_{Gmn}B \ D\tau_{Gmn}B \ldots F\tau_{Gmn}B).$$

Proof: From our definition,

$$A\tau_{Gmn}B = A_1 \otimes B_1 + \cdots + A_G \otimes B_G.$$

Writing $A_i = (C_i \ D_i \ldots F_i)$ for $i = 1, \ldots, G$, we have from the properties of Kronecker products that

$$A_i \otimes B_i = (C_i \otimes B_i \ D_i \otimes B_i \ldots F_i \otimes B_i).$$

The result follows immediately. ∎

Theorem 1.4 *Let A and B be $mG \times p$ matrices, and let C and D be $nG \times q$ matrices. Then,*

$$(A + B)\tau_{Gmn}C = A\tau_{Gmn}C + B\tau_{Gmn}C$$

and

$$A\tau_{Gmn}(C + D) = A\tau_{Gmn}C + A\tau_{Gmn}D.$$

Proof: Clearly,

$$\begin{aligned}(A + B)\tau_{Gmn}C &= (A_1 + B_1) \otimes C_1 + \cdots + (A_G + B_G) \otimes C_G \\ &= A_1 \otimes C_1 + \cdots + A_G \otimes C_G + B_1 \otimes C_1 + \cdots + B_G \otimes C_G \\ &= A\tau_{Gmn}C + B\tau_{Gmn}C.\end{aligned}$$

The second result is proved similarly. ∎

Theorem 1.5 *Let A and B be specified in Equation 1.7, let C, D, E, F be $p \times r, q \times s, r \times m,$ and $s \times n$ matrices, respectively. Then,*

$$(A\tau_{Gmn}B)(C \otimes D) = AC\tau_{Gmn}BD$$

and

$$(E \otimes F)(A\tau_{Gmn}B) = (I_G \otimes E)A\tau_{Grs}(I_G \otimes F)B.$$

Proof: Clearly,

$$
\begin{aligned}
(A\tau_{Gmn}B)(C \otimes D) &= (A_1 \otimes B_1 + \cdots A_G \otimes B_G)(C \otimes D) \\
&= A_1 C \otimes B_1 D + \cdots + A_G C \otimes B_G D \\
&= \begin{pmatrix} A_1 C \\ \vdots \\ A_G C \end{pmatrix} \tau_{Gmn} \begin{pmatrix} B_1 D \\ \vdots \\ B_G D \end{pmatrix} = AC\,\tau_{Gmn}\,BD.
\end{aligned}
$$

Likewise,

$$
\begin{aligned}
(E \otimes F)(A\tau_{Gmn}B) &= (E \otimes F)(A_1 \otimes B_1 + \cdots + A_G \otimes B_G) \\
&= EA_1 \otimes FB_1 + \cdots + EA_G \otimes FB_G \\
&= \begin{pmatrix} EA_1 \\ \vdots \\ EA_G \end{pmatrix} \tau_{Grs} \begin{pmatrix} FB_1 \\ \vdots \\ FB_G \end{pmatrix} \\
&= (I_G \otimes E)A\,\tau_{Grs}\,(I_G \otimes F)B. \qquad\blacksquare
\end{aligned}
$$

A standard notation that is regularly used in this book is

$A_{i.} = i$-th row of the matrix A
$A_{.j} = j$-th column of the matrix A.

For the next theorem, it is advantageous to introduce a new notation that we will find useful for our work throughout most chapters. We are considering A a $mG \times p$ matrix, which we have partitioned as

$$A = \begin{pmatrix} A_1 \\ \vdots \\ A_G \end{pmatrix}$$

where each submatrix A_i in this partitioning is $m \times p$. Thus, we denoted by $A^{(j)}$ the $G \times p$ matrix given by

$$A^{(j)} = \begin{pmatrix} (A_1)_{j.} \\ \vdots \\ (A_G)_{j.} \end{pmatrix}. \tag{1.8}$$

That is, to form $A^{(j)}$ where we stack the jth rows of the submatrices under each other.

Notice if C is a $r \times G$ matrix and D is a $s \times m$ matrix, then from Equation 1.6

$$C \otimes D = \begin{pmatrix} c^{1'} \otimes d^{1'} \\ \vdots \\ c^{1'} \otimes d^{s'} \\ \vdots \\ c^{r'} \otimes d^{1'} \\ \vdots \\ c^{r'} \otimes d^{s'} \end{pmatrix}$$

so

$$[(C \otimes D)A]^{(j)} = \begin{pmatrix} c^{1'} \otimes d^{j'} \\ \vdots \\ c^{r'} \otimes d^{j'} \end{pmatrix} A = (C \otimes d^{j'})A. \qquad (1.9)$$

A special case of interest to us is when D is an identity matrix, in which case

$$[(C \otimes I_m)A]^{(j)} = (C \otimes e_j^{m'})A = C(I_G \otimes e_j^{m'})A = CA^{(j)}. \quad (1.10)$$

Using this notation, we have the following theorem, which demonstrates that we can write $A\tau_{Gmn}B$ in terms of a vector of τ_{G1n} cross-products.

Theorem 1.6 *For A and B as previously specified,*

$$A\,\tau_{Gmn}B = \begin{pmatrix} A^{(1)} & \tau_{G1n} & B \\ \vdots & \vdots & \vdots \\ A^{(m)} & \tau_{G1n} & B \end{pmatrix}.$$

Proof: Using the properties of Kronecker products we write,

$$A\tau_{Gmn}B = A_1 \otimes B_1 + \cdots + A_G \otimes B_G$$
$$= \begin{pmatrix} (A_1)_{1\cdot} \otimes B_1 + \cdots + (A_G)_{1\cdot} \otimes B_G \\ \vdots \qquad\qquad \vdots \\ (A_1)_{m\cdot} \otimes B_1 + \cdots + (A_G)_{m\cdot} \otimes B_G \end{pmatrix} = \begin{pmatrix} A^{(1)} & \tau_{G1n} & B \\ \vdots & \vdots & \vdots \\ A^{(m)} & \tau_{G1n} & B \end{pmatrix}. \quad \blacksquare$$

Theorem 1.7 *Let a be an $n \times 1$ vector. Then,*

$$a\tau_{n1G}B = (a' \otimes I_G)B.$$

Proof: Clearly,

$$a\tau_{n1G}B = a_1 \otimes B_1 + \cdots + a_n \otimes B_n$$

where now we partition B as $B = (B_1' \ldots B_n')'$ each of the submatrices being $G \times q$.

But,

$$a_1 \otimes B_1 = a_1 B_1$$

so

$$a\,\tau_{n1G}B = a_1 B_1 + \cdots + a_n B_n = (a' \otimes I_G)B. \qquad \blacksquare$$

A special case of this theorem is when $G = 1$ so B is $n \times q$. Then,

$$a\tau_{n11}B = a'B = B\tau_{n11}a.$$

Theorem 1.8 *Let A, B, and C be $m \times p$, $mG \times q$, and $r \times G$ matrices, respectively. Then,*

$$C(A\tau_{m1G}B) = A\tau_{m1r}(I_m \otimes C)B.$$

Proof: If we partition B as

$$B = \begin{pmatrix} B_1 \\ \vdots \\ B_m \end{pmatrix}$$

where each submatrix in this partitioning is $G \times q$ then

$$\begin{aligned} C(A\tau_{m1G}B) &= C(A_1. \otimes B_1 + \cdots + A_m. \otimes B_m) \\ &= A_1. \otimes CB_1 + \cdots + A_m. \otimes CB_m = A\tau_{m1r}(I_m \otimes C)B. \qquad \blacksquare \end{aligned}$$

The cross-product operator, like the Kronecker product, is intimately connected with the vec operator. In the next section, we look at the vec operator that works with columns of a given matrix, stacking them underneath each other. The rvec operator works with rows of a matrix, stacking them alongside each other. The generalized vec and rvec operators are generalization of the basic operators, which are particularly useful when we are deal-ing with partitioned matrices. Theorems involving these operators and the cross-product operator are presented in the following sections.

1.4 Vecs, Rvecs, Generalized Vecs, and Rvecs

1.4.1 Basic Operators

Let A be an $m \times n$ matrix with a_i its ith column and $a^{j'}$ its jth row. Then, **vec** A is the $mn \times 1$ vector given by

$$\text{vec } A = \begin{pmatrix} a_1 \\ \vdots \\ a_n \end{pmatrix}.$$

That is, the vec operator transforms A into an $mn \times 1$ column vector by stacking the columns of A one underneath the other. Similarly, **rvec** A is the $1 \times mn$ row vector:

$$\text{rvec } A = (a^{1'} \ldots a^{m'}).$$

That is, the rvec operator transforms A into a $1 \times mn$ row vector by stacking the rows of A alongside each other.

Both operators are intimately connected as

$$(\text{vec } A)' = (a'_1 \ldots a'_n) = \text{rvec } A'$$

and

$$\text{vec } A' = \begin{pmatrix} a^1 \\ \vdots \\ a^m \end{pmatrix} = (\text{rvec } A)'.$$

These basic relationships mean that results for one of the operators can be readily obtained from results for the other operator.

Both operators are connected with the Kronecker product operator. From

$$ab' = b' \otimes a = a \otimes b',$$

a property noted in Section 1.2, it is clear that the jth column of ab' is $b_j a$ and the ith row of ab' is $a_i b'$, so

$$\text{vec } ab' = \text{vec}(b' \otimes a) = b \otimes a \tag{1.11}$$

and

$$\text{rvec } ab' = \text{rvec}(a \otimes b') = a' \otimes b'.$$

More generally, if A, B, and C are three matrices such that the product ABC is defined, then

$$\text{vec } ABC = (C' \otimes A)\text{vec } B$$

and

$$\text{rvec } ABC = \text{rvec } B(A' \otimes C).$$

Often, we will have occasion to take the vec of a partitioned matrix. Let A be a $m \times np$ matrix and partition A so that $A = (A_1 \ldots A_p)$, where each submatrix is $m \times n$. Then, it is clear that

$$\text{vec } A = \begin{pmatrix} \text{vec } A_1 \\ \vdots \\ \text{vec } A_p \end{pmatrix}.$$

An application of this result follows. Suppose B is any $n \times q$ matrix and consider

$$A(I_p \times B) = (A_1 B \ldots A_p B).$$

Then,

$$\text{vec } A(I_p \otimes B) = \begin{pmatrix} \text{vec } A_1 B \\ \vdots \\ \text{vec } A_p B \end{pmatrix} = \begin{pmatrix} I_q \otimes A_1 \\ \vdots \\ I_q \otimes A_p \end{pmatrix} \text{vec } B.$$

If A is a $m \times n$ matrix and x is any vector, then

$$\text{vec}(A \otimes x) = \text{vec}(a_1 \otimes x \ldots a_n \otimes x) = \begin{pmatrix} a_1 \otimes x \\ \vdots \\ a_n \otimes x \end{pmatrix} = \text{vec } A \otimes x$$

$$\text{vec}(x' \otimes A) = \text{vec}(x_1 A \ldots x_n A) = x \otimes \text{vec } A. \tag{1.12}$$

and

$$\text{vec}(A \otimes x') = \text{vec}(a_1 \otimes x' \ldots a_n \otimes x')$$

$$= \begin{pmatrix} \text{vec}(a_1 \otimes x') \\ \vdots \\ \text{vec}(a_n \otimes x') \end{pmatrix} = \begin{pmatrix} x \otimes a_1 \\ \vdots \\ x \otimes a_n \end{pmatrix} = \text{vec}(x \otimes a_1 \ldots x \otimes a_n)$$

$$= \text{vec}(x \otimes (a_1 \ldots a_n)) = \text{vec}(x \otimes A), \tag{1.13}$$

where in our analysis we have used Equations 1.11 and 1.5. Using Equations 1.12 and 1.13, we have that if x and y are any vectors

$$\text{vec}(y' \otimes x') = \text{vec}(x \otimes y') = \text{vec}(y' \otimes x) = y \otimes x.$$

Finally, if A is $n \times n$ and x is $n \times 1$, then

$$\text{vec} x' A = \text{vec}(x' a_1 \ldots x' a_n) = \begin{pmatrix} a_1' x \\ \vdots \\ a_n' x \end{pmatrix} = A' x.$$

By taking transposes and using the fact that rvec $A' = (\text{vec } A)'$, we get the corresponding results for the rvec operator.

1.4.2 Vecs, Rvecs, and the Cross-Product Operator

Just as Kronecker products are intimately connected with vecs and rvecs, so are cross-products. The following theorem gives this basic connection.

Theorem 1.9 *Let A be $n \times p$ and B be $nG \times q$. Then,*

$$A \tau_{n1G} B = ((\text{vec } A)' \otimes I_G)(I_p \otimes B).$$

Proof: Write $A = (a_1 \ldots a_p)$ where a_j is the jth column of A. Then,

$$((\text{vec } A)' \otimes I_G)(I_p \otimes B) = (a_1' \otimes I_G \ldots a_p' \otimes I_G) \begin{pmatrix} B & & O \\ & \ddots & \\ O & & B \end{pmatrix}$$

$$= (a_1' \otimes I_G) B \ldots (a_p' \otimes I_G) B.$$

Partition B such that

$$B = \begin{pmatrix} B_1 \\ \vdots \\ B_n \end{pmatrix}$$

where each submatrix in this partition is $G \times q$.
   Then,

$$(a_j' \otimes I_G) B = (a_{1j} I_G \ldots a_{nj} I_G) \begin{pmatrix} B_1 \\ \vdots \\ B_n \end{pmatrix} = a_{1j} B_1 + \cdots + a_{nj} B_n,$$

so

$$(\text{vec } A' \otimes I_G)(I_p \otimes B) = a_{11}B_1 + \cdots + a_{n1}B_n \ldots a_{1p}B_1 + \cdots + a_{np}B_n$$
$$= (a_{11}B_1 \ldots a_{1p}B_1) + \cdots + (a_{n1}B_n \ldots a_{np}B_n)$$
$$= a^{1'} \otimes B_1 + \cdots + a^{n'} \otimes B_n = A\tau_{n1G}B. \qquad \blacksquare$$

A special case of this theorem is when B is $n \times q$ so $G = 1$. We have then that

$$A\tau_{n11}B = (\text{vec } A)'(I_p \otimes B) = ((I_p \otimes B')\text{vec } A)'$$
$$= (\text{vec } B'A)' = (\text{rvec } I_n)(A \otimes B).$$

In a similar vein, if C is $r \times m$ and D is $s \times m$, then

$$\text{vec } C \, \tau_{mrs}\text{vec } D = \text{vec } DC' = (C \otimes D)\text{vec } I_m.$$

Another theorem involving cross-products and rvecs that will be useful in our future work is the following:

Theorem 1.10   *Let A and B be $m \times n$ and $p \times q$ matrices, respectively. Then,*

$$I_m\tau_{m1p}(A \otimes B) = \text{rvec } A \otimes B.$$

Proof: From our definition of cross-products given in Section 1.3,

$$I_m\tau_{m1p}(A \otimes B) = e_1^{m'} \otimes (a^{1'} \otimes B) + \cdots + e_m^{m'} \otimes (a^{m'} \otimes B)$$
$$= (a^{1'} \otimes B \, O \ldots O) + \cdots + (O \ldots O \, a^{m'} \otimes B)$$
$$= (a^{1'} \otimes B \ldots a^{m'} \otimes B) = (a^{1'} \ldots a^{m'}) \otimes B = \text{rvec } A \otimes B.$$
$$\blacksquare$$

Cross-products come into their own when we are dealing with partitioned matrices. Often with a partitioned matrix, we want to stack submatrices in the partition underneath each other or alongside each other. Operators that do this are called generalized vec or generalized rvec operators. Section 1.4.4 looks at these operators in detail and later we see that there are several theorems linking cross-products with those generalized operators.

To finish this section, we briefly look at expressing traces in term of our vec and rvec operators. It is easily shown that

$$\text{tr}AB = (\text{vec } A')'\text{vec } B = \text{rvec } A \text{ vec } B.$$

When it comes to the trace of a product of three matrices, we can write

$$\text{tr}ABC = \text{rvec } A \text{ vec } BC = \text{rvec } A(I \otimes B)\text{vec } C$$

for an appropriate identity matrix I. Other expressions for trABC in terms of vecs and rvecs can be similarly achieved using the fact that

$$\text{tr}ABC = \text{tr}CAB = \text{tr}BCA.$$

1.4.3 Related Operators: Vech and $\bar{\text{v}}$

In taking the vec of a square matrix A, we form a column vector by using all the elements of A. The vech and the $\bar{\text{v}}$ operators form column vectors from select elements of A.

Let A be the $n \times n$ matrix:

$$A = \begin{pmatrix} a_{11} & \cdots & a_{1n} \\ \vdots & & \vdots \\ a_{n1} & \cdots & a_{nn} \end{pmatrix}.$$

Then, **vech A** is the $\frac{1}{2}n(n+1) \times 1$ vector

$$\text{vech}A = \begin{pmatrix} a_{11} \\ \vdots \\ a_{n1} \\ a_{22} \\ \vdots \\ a_{n2} \\ \vdots \\ a_{nn} \end{pmatrix},$$

that is, we form vech$A$ by stacking the elements of A on and below the main diagonal, one underneath the other.

The vector $\bar{\text{v}}(A)$ is the $\frac{1}{2}n(n-1) \times 1$ vector given by

$$\bar{\text{v}}(A) = \begin{pmatrix} a_{21} \\ \vdots \\ a_{n1} \\ a_{32} \\ \vdots \\ a_{n2} \\ \vdots \\ a_{n\,n-1} \end{pmatrix},$$

that is, we form $\bar{\text{v}}(A)$ by stacking the elements of A below the main diagonal, one underneath the other.

If A is symmetric, that is, $A' = A$, then $a_{ij} = a_{ji}$ and the elements of A, below the main diagonal are duplicated by the elements above the main diagonal. Often, we wish to form a vector from A that consists of the essential elements of A without duplication. Clearly, the vech operator allows us to do this.

An obvious example is in statistics where A is the covariance matrix. The unknown parameters associated with the covariance matrix are given by vech$A$. If we wished to form a vector consisting of only the covariances of the covariance matrix, but not the variances, then we take $\bar{v}(A)$.

Before we leave this section, note that for a square matrix A, not necessarily symmetric, vec$A$ contains all the elements in vech$A$ and in $\bar{v}(A)$, and more.

It follows that we can obtain vech$A$ and $\bar{v}(A)$ by premultiplying vec$A$ by matrices whose elements are zeros or ones strategically placed. Likewise, $\bar{v}(A)$ can be obtained from vech$A$ by premultiplying vech$A$ by such a matrix. These matrices are examples of zero-one matrices called elimination matrices.

If A is symmetric then, as previously noted, vech$A$ contains all the essential elements of A. It follows that there exists a matrix, whose elements are all zeros or ones such that when we premultiply vech$A$ by this matrix we obtain vec$A$. In a similar manner, if A is strictly lower triangular, then $\bar{v}(A)$ contains the essential elements of A apart from zeros, so we must be able to obtain vec$A$ by premultiplying $\bar{v}(A)$ by a matrix whose elements are zeros or ones suitably placed. Such matrices are called duplication matrices.

Chapter 3 studies elimination matrices and duplication matrices, perhaps in a new way.

1.4.4 Generalized Vecs and Generalized Rvecs

When dealing with a matrix that has been partitioned into its columns, we often have occasion to stack the columns of the matrix underneath each other. If A is a large matrix, we often partition A into a number of submatrices. For example, if A is $m \times np$, we may write

$$A = (A_1 \ldots A_p)$$

where each submatrix in this partition is $m \times n$. Often, we want to stack these submatrices underneath each other to form the $mp \times n$ matrix.

$$\begin{pmatrix} A_1 \\ \vdots \\ A_p \end{pmatrix}.$$

The operator that does this for us is called the **generalized vec of order n**, denoted by **vec_n**. To form $\text{vec}_n A$, we stack columns of A underneath each other taking n at a time. Clearly, this operator is only performable on A if the number of columns of A is a multiple of n. Under this notation,

$$\text{vec } A = \text{vec}_1 A.$$

In a similar fashion, if A is partitioned into its rows we know that the rvec operator forms a row vector out of the elements of A by stacking the rows of A alongside each other. If A has a large number of rows, say, A is $mp \times n$ we often have occasion to partition A into p $m \times n$ matrices, so we write

$$A = \begin{pmatrix} A_1 \\ \vdots \\ A_p \end{pmatrix}$$

where each submatrix is $m \times n$ matrix. Again we may want to stack these submatrices alongside each other instead of underneath each other, to form the $m \times np$ matrix

$$(A_1 \ldots A_p).$$

The operator that does this for us is called the **generalized rvec of order m** denoted by **rvec_m**. To form **$\text{rvec}_m A$**, we stack rows of A alongside each other taking m at a time, so this operator is only performable on A if the number of rows of A is a multiple of m. Under this notation,

$$\text{rvec } A = \text{rvec}_1 A.$$

For a given matrix A, which is $m \times n$, the number of generalized vecs (rvecs) that can be performed on A clearly depends on the number of columns n(rows m) of A. If $n(m)$ is a prime number, then only two generalized vec (rvec) operators can be performed on A, $\text{vec}_1 A = \text{vec } A$ and $\text{vec}_n A = A$, $\text{rvec}_1 A = \text{rvec } A$, and $\text{rvec}_m A = A$.

For $n(m)$ any other number, the number of generalized vec (rvec) operators that can be performed on A is the number of positive integers that divide into $n(m)$.

As with the vec and rvec operators, the vec_n and rvec_n operators are intimately connected. Let A be a $m \times np$ matrix and, as before, write

$$A = (A_1 \ldots A_p)$$

where each submatrix A_i is $m \times n$. Then,

$$\text{vec}_n A = \begin{pmatrix} A_1 \\ \vdots \\ A_p \end{pmatrix}$$

so

$$(\text{vec}_n A)' = (A_1' \ldots A_p') = \text{rvec}_n A'. \tag{1.14}$$

Similarly, if B is $mp \times n$ and we partition B as

$$B = \begin{pmatrix} B_1 \\ \vdots \\ B_p \end{pmatrix}$$

where each submatrix B_j is $m \times n$ then

$$\text{vec}_m B' = \begin{pmatrix} B_1' \\ \vdots \\ B_p' \end{pmatrix} = (\text{rvec}_m B)'. \tag{1.15}$$

As before, we need only derive theorems for one of these operators. Then, using Equations 1.14 or 1.15, we can readily obtain the corresponding results for the other operator.

Clearly, we can take generalized vecs of matrices, which are Kronecker products. Let A and B be $m \times n$ and $p \times q$ matrices, respectively, and write $A = (a_1 \ldots a_n)$, where a_j is the jth column of A. Then, we can write

$$A \otimes B = (a_1 \otimes B \ldots a_n \otimes B)$$

so

$$\text{vec}_q(A \otimes B) = \begin{pmatrix} a_1 \otimes B \\ \vdots \\ a_n \otimes B \end{pmatrix} = \text{vec } A \otimes B. \tag{1.16}$$

As a special case, $\text{vec}_q(a' \otimes B) = a \otimes B$.

Now write $A = (a^1 \ldots a^m)'$, where $a^{i'}$ is the ith row of A. Then,

$$A \otimes B = \begin{pmatrix} a^{1'} \otimes B \\ \vdots \\ a^{m'} \otimes B \end{pmatrix}$$

so

$$\mathrm{rvec}_p(A \otimes B) = (a^{1'} \otimes B \dots a^{m'} \otimes B) = \mathrm{rvec}\, A \otimes B, \qquad (1.17)$$

and as a special case $\mathrm{rvec}_p(a \otimes B) = a' \otimes B$.

The generalized vec of a matrix can be undone by taking the appropriate generalized rvec of the vec. This property induced the author to originally call generalized rvecs, generalized devecs (see Turkington (2005)). If A is $m \times n$, for example, then clearly

$$\mathrm{rvec}_m(\mathrm{vec}\, A) = A.$$

In fact, if $\mathrm{vec}_j A$ refers to a generalized vec operator that is performable on A, then the following relationships exist between the two operators

$$\mathrm{rvec}(\mathrm{vec}\, A) = (\mathrm{vec}\, A)' = \mathrm{rvec}\, A',$$

$$\mathrm{rvec}_m(\mathrm{vec}_j A) = A$$

$$\mathrm{rvec}(\mathrm{vec}_j A) = 1 \times mn \text{ vectors where elements are obtained}$$

$$\text{from a permutation of those of } (\mathrm{vec}\, A)'.$$

In a similar fashion, the generalized vec operator can be viewed as undoing the rvec of a matrix.

If $\mathrm{rvec}_i A$ refers to a generalized rvec operator that is performable on A, then we have

$$\mathrm{vec}(\mathrm{rvec}\, A) = \mathrm{vec}\, A' = (\mathrm{rvec}\, A)'$$

$$\mathrm{vec}_n(\mathrm{rvec}_i A) = A$$

$$\mathrm{vec}(\mathrm{rvec}_i A) = mn \times 1 \text{ vectors whose elements are obtained}$$

$$\text{from a permutation of those of } \mathrm{vec}\, A'.$$

There are some similarities between the behavior of vecs on the one hand and that of generalized vecs on the other. For example, if A is an $m \times n$ matrix, then as

$$A = A I_n I_n$$

we have

$$\mathrm{vec}\, A = (I_n \otimes A)\mathrm{vec}\, I_n.$$

If A be an $m \times nG$ matrix, we have the following theorem:

Theorem 1.11 *For A a $m \times nG$ matrix*

$$\mathrm{vec}_G A = (I_n \otimes A)(\mathrm{vec}_G I_{nG}).$$

Proof: Partition A is $A = (a_1 \ldots a_n)$ so

$$\text{vec}_G A = \begin{pmatrix} A_1 \\ \vdots \\ A_n \end{pmatrix},$$

where each submatrix A_i is $m \times G$.

Now

$$A_i = (A_1 \ldots A_n) \begin{pmatrix} O \\ \vdots \\ I_G \\ \vdots \\ O \end{pmatrix} = A\left(e_i^n \otimes I_G\right)$$

so

$$\text{vec}_G A = \begin{pmatrix} A\left(e_i^n \otimes I_G\right) \\ \vdots \\ A\left(e_n^n \otimes I_G\right) \end{pmatrix} = (I_n \otimes A) \begin{pmatrix} e_1^n \otimes I_G \\ \vdots \\ e_n^n \otimes I_G \end{pmatrix}$$
$$= (I_n \otimes A)(\text{vec} I_n \otimes I_G) = (I_n \otimes A)\text{vec}_G I_{nG},$$

by Equation 1.16. ∎

Also, for A $m \times n$ and B $n \times p$ then as $AB = ABI_p$, we have

$$\text{vec } AB = (I_p \otimes A)\text{vec } B.$$

For A a $m \times n$ matrix and B a $n \times Gp$ matrix, we have the following theorem.

Theorem 1.12 *If A and B are $m \times n$ and $n \times Gp$ matrices, respectively, then*

$$\text{vec}_G AB = (I_p \otimes A)\text{vec}_G B.$$

Proof: Partition B as $B = (B_1 \ldots B_p)$ where each submatrix B_j is $n \times G$. Then,

$$AB = (AB_1 \ldots AB_p)$$

so

$$\text{vec}_G\, AB = \begin{pmatrix} AB_1 \\ \vdots \\ AB_p \end{pmatrix} = (I_p \otimes A)\text{vec}_G B.$$ ■

However, the similarities end here. There appears to be no equivalent theorems for generalized vecs that correspond to

$$\text{vec}\, AB = (B' \otimes I_m)\text{vec}\, A$$

or

$$\text{vec}\, ABC = (C' \otimes A)\text{vec}\, B.$$

Notice in Theorem 1.12 if B itself was a Kronecker product, say $B = C \otimes D$ where C and D are $r \times p$ and $s \times G$ matrices, respectively, so $n = rs$, then we are using Equation 1.16

$$\text{vec}_G[\,A(C \otimes D)] = (I_p \otimes A)\,\text{vec}_G(C \otimes D) = (I_p \otimes A)(\text{vec}C \otimes D).$$

$$(1.18)$$

We can write this generalized vec another way as shown by the following theorem.

Theorem 1.13   *Let A, C and D be $m \times rs$, $r \times p$, and $s \times G$ matrices respectively. Then,*

$$\text{vec}_G[A(C \otimes D)] = (C' \otimes I_m)(\text{vec}_s A)D.$$

Proof: Partition A as $A = (A_1 \dots A_r)$ where each submatrix is $m \times s$. Then,

$$\text{vec}_G[A(C \otimes D)] = \text{vec}_G[(A_1 \dots A_r)] \begin{pmatrix} c^{1'} \otimes D \\ \vdots \\ c^{r'} \otimes D \end{pmatrix}$$

$$= \text{vec}_G[A_1(c^{1'} \otimes D) + \cdots + A_r(c^{r'} \otimes D)]$$

$$= \text{vec}_G[(c^{1'} \otimes A_1 D) + \cdots + (c^{r'} \otimes A_r D)]$$

$$= \begin{pmatrix} c_{11} A_1 D \\ \vdots \\ c_{1p} A_1 D \end{pmatrix} + \cdots + \begin{pmatrix} c_{r1} A_r D \\ \vdots \\ c_{rp} A_r D \end{pmatrix}$$

where $C = \{c_{ij}\}$. Consider the first submatrix

$$c_{11}A_1D + \cdots + c_{r1}A_rD = (c_1' \otimes I_m)\begin{pmatrix} A_1 \\ \vdots \\ A_r \end{pmatrix}D$$

$$= (c_1' \otimes I_m)(\text{vec}_sA)D.$$

The result follows.   ∎

The equivalent results for generalized rvecs are listed as:

If A is a $mG \times n$ matrix, then

$$\text{rvec}_GA = (\text{rvec}I_m \otimes I_G)(I_m \otimes A) = (\text{rvec}_mI_{mG})(I_m \otimes A).$$

If B is a $n \times p$ matrix, then

$$\text{rvec}_G AB = \text{rvec}_GA(I_m \otimes B). \tag{1.19}$$

If C and D are $m \times r$ and $G \times s$, respectively, and $n = rs$,

$$\text{rvec}_G(C \otimes D)B = (\text{rvec}C \otimes D)(I_m \otimes B) = D(\text{rvec}_sB)(C' \otimes I_p).$$

If C and D are $m \times r$ and $G \times G$, respectively, so $n = rG$, then

$$\text{rvec}_G[(C \otimes D)B] = \text{rvec}_G[(I_r \otimes D)B](C \otimes I_p).$$

This section finishes with a result that is useful in dealing with a partitioned vector.

Theorem 1.14   *Let x be a $mp \times 1$ vector and y be a $m \times 1$ vector. Then,*

$$x'(y \otimes I_p) = y'\text{vec}_px'.$$

Proof: Partition x is $x = (x_1' \ldots x_m')'$ where each subvector is $p \times 1$. Then,

$$x'(y \otimes I_p) = (x_1' \ldots x_m')\begin{pmatrix} y_1I_p \\ \vdots \\ y_mI_p \end{pmatrix} = y_1x_1' + \cdots + y_mx_m' = y'\text{vec}_px'.$$ ∎

Note from Theorem 1.7, we have that

$$y\tau_{m11}\text{vec}_px' = x'(y \otimes I_p).$$

For further theorems, on generalized vecs and rvecs see Turkington (2005).

1.4.5 Generalized Vec Operators and the Cross-Product Operator

Generalized vec operators like the cross-product operator really come into their own when we are dealing with large partitioned matrices. In this section, we present theorems that link the operators.

First, if we take the transpose of a cross-product, we get a cross-product of generalized vecs as the following theorem shows.

Theorem 1.15 *Let A be $mG \times p$ and B be $nG \times q$, partitioned as in Equation 1.7 of Section 1.3. Then,*

$$(A\tau_{Gmn}B)' = \text{vec}_m(A')\tau_{Gpq}\text{vec}_n(B').$$

Proof:

$$(A\tau_{Gmn}B)' = (A_1 \otimes B_1 + \cdots + A_G \otimes B_G)'$$
$$= A_1' \otimes B_1' + \cdots + A_G' \otimes B_G'.$$

Now $A' = (A_1' \ldots A_G')$ where each A_i' is $p \times m$ so

$$\text{vec}_m A' = \begin{pmatrix} A_1' \\ \vdots \\ A_G' \end{pmatrix}.$$

Similarly,

$$\text{vec}_n B' = \begin{pmatrix} B_1' \\ \vdots \\ B_G' \end{pmatrix}$$

where each submatrix B_j' is $q \times n$ so the result holds. ∎

A generalized vec or rvec can be written as a cross-product as the following theorem shows.

Theorem 1.16 *Let A be a $mG \times p$ matrix. Then,*

$$\text{rvec}_m A = I_G\tau_{G1m}A.$$

Proof: Partitioning A as in Equation 1.7, we have

$$\text{rvec}_m A = (A_1 \ldots A_G).$$

But $I_G = (e_1^G \ldots e_G^G)'$ where e_j^G refers to the jth column of I_G.

So

$$I_G \tau_{G1m} A = e_1^{G'} \otimes A_1 + \cdots + e_G^{G'} \otimes A_G = (A_1 \ldots A_G).$$ ■

A consequence of this theorem is that some cross-products can be written as a generalized rvecs.

When we take the generalized vec of a cross-product, we get another cross-product that involves a vec of a generalized rvec, as the following theorem shows.

Theorem 1.17 *Let A and B be mG × p and nG × q matrices, respectively, and partition A and B as in Equation 1.7. Then,*

$$\text{vec}_q(A\tau_{Gmn}B) = \text{vec}(\text{rvec}_m A)\tau_{G,mp,n}B.$$

Proof: As $A\tau_{Gmn}B = A_1 \otimes B_1 + \cdots + A_G \otimes B_G$, we have, using Equation 1.16,

$$\begin{aligned}
\text{vec}_q(A\tau_{Gmn}B) &= \text{vec}_q(A_1 \otimes B_1) + \cdots + \text{vec}_q(A_G \otimes B_G) \\
&= \text{vec}\, A_1 \otimes B_1 + \cdots + \text{vec}\, A_G \otimes B_G \\
&= \begin{pmatrix} \text{vec}\, A_1 \\ \vdots \\ \text{vec}\, A_G \end{pmatrix} \tau_{G,mp,n}B.
\end{aligned}$$

But

$$\begin{pmatrix} \text{vec}\, A_1 \\ \vdots \\ \text{vec}\, A_G \end{pmatrix} = \text{vec}(A_1 \ldots A_G) = \text{vec}(\text{rvec}_m A).$$ ■

One final theorem involving cross-products and generalized vecs:

Theorem 1.18 *Let A, B, C be p × mG, G × q, and m × r matrices, respectively. Then,*

$$A(B \otimes C) = B\tau_{G1p}(\text{vec}_m A)C.$$

Proof: Write

$$A(B \otimes C) = A(B \otimes I_m)(I_q \otimes C)$$

and partition A as $A = (A_1 \ldots A_G)$ where each submatrix in this partitioning is p × m.

Then,

$$
A(B \otimes I_m) = (A_1 \ldots A_G) \begin{pmatrix} b^{1'} \otimes I_m \\ \vdots \\ b^{G'} \otimes I_m \end{pmatrix}
$$
$$
= A_1 \big(b^{1'} \otimes I_m \big) + \cdots + A_G \big(b^{G'} \otimes I_m \big)
$$
$$
= b^{1'} \otimes A_1 + \cdots + b^{G'} \otimes A_G = B\tau_{G1p}\mathrm{vec}_m A,
$$

so,

$$
A(B \otimes C) = (B\tau_{G1p}\mathrm{vec}_m A)(I_q \otimes C) = B\tau_{G1p}(\mathrm{vec}_m A)C,
$$

by Theorem 1.5. ∎

TWO

Zero-One Matrices

2.1 Introduction

A matrix whose elements are all either one or zero is, naturally enough, called a zero-one matrix. Such matrices have had a long association with statistics and econometrics, although their prominence has really come to the fore with the advent of matrix calculus. In this chapter, the intent is not to give a list of all known zero-one matrices plus their properties. The reader is referred to Magnus (1988), Magnus and Neudecker (1999), Lutkepohl (1996), and Turkington (2005) for such material. Instead, what is presented are zero-one matrices that may be new to the reader, but which I have found useful in the evaluation of certain matrix calculus results. Having said that, I do talk about some known zero-one matrices and their properties in order for the reader to have a full understanding of the new matrices. The later sections of this chapter are reserved for theorems linking the zero-one matrices with the mathematical operators we looked at in Chapter 1.

2.2 Selection Matrices and Permutation Matrices

Probably the first zero-one matrix to appear in statistics and econometrics was a selection matrix. A selection matrix is a matrix whose (rows) columns are a selection of the (rows) columns of an identity matrix. Consider A, an $m \times n$ matrix, and write $A = (a_1 \ldots a_n)$ where a_i is the ith column of A. Suppose from A we wish to form a new matrix, B, whose columns consist of the first, fourth, and fifth columns of A. Let S be the selection matrix given by $S = (e_1^n \ e_4^n \ e_5^n)$, where e_j^n is the jth column of the $n \times n$ identity matrix I_n. Then,

$$AS = (a_1 \ a_4 \ a_5) = B.$$

Selection matrices have an obvious application in econometrics. The matrix A, for example, may represent the observations on all the endogenous variables in an econometric model, and the matrix B may represent the observations on the endogenous variables that appear on the right-hand side of a particular equation in the model. Often, it is mathematically convenient to use selection matrices and write $B = AS$.

Similarly, if we premultiply a matrix A by a selection matrix made up of rows of the identity matrix, we get a new matrix consisting of a selection of the rows of A.

Selection matrices can be used to select the (i, j)th element of a matrix. Let A be $m \times n$ matrix, then as $e_i^{m'} A$ selects the ith row of A and $(e_i^{m'} A)e_j^n$ selects the jth column of this vector, it follows that

$$a_{ij} = e_i^{m'} A e_j^n.$$

When it comes to selecting the (i, j)th element from a Kronecker product, we have to specify exactly where the ith row and jth column are located in the matrix. Let A be an $m \times n$ matrix and B be an $p \times q$ matrix. Then,

$$A \otimes B = \begin{pmatrix} a^{1'} \otimes B \\ \vdots \\ a^{m'} \otimes B \end{pmatrix},$$

so if i takes a value between 1 and p the ith row is $a^{1'} \otimes b^{i'}$, if i takes a value between $p + 1$ and $2p$ the ith row is $a^{2'} \otimes b^{i'}$, and so on until the last possibility where i takes a value between $(m - 1)p$ and pm in which case the ith row is $a^{m'} \otimes b^{i'}$. To cater for all of these possibilities, we write

$$i = (c - 1)p + \bar{i},$$

where c is some value between 1 and m and $\bar{i}$ is some value between 1 and p. By setting $c = 1$ and letting $\bar{i}$ range from 1 to p, then setting $c = 2$ and letting $\bar{i}$ take the same values and so on until we set $c = m$ and let $\bar{i}$ take values between 1 and p, we generate all possible values for i, namely $i = 1, 2, \ldots mp$.

If we do this, set $i = (c - 1)p + \bar{i}$, then the ith row of $A \otimes B$ is $a^{c'} \otimes b^{\bar{i}'}$. But $a^{c'} = e_c^{m'} A$ and $b^{\bar{i}'} = e_{\bar{i}}^{p'} B$ so the ith row of $A \otimes B$ is

$$\left(e_c^{m'} \otimes e_{\bar{i}}^{p'} \right)(A \otimes B).$$

A similar analysis can be carried out for the columns of $A \otimes B$. As

$$A \otimes B = (a_1 \otimes B \ldots a_n \otimes B)$$

when talking about the jth column of this matrix, we must specify the exact location of this column. We do this by writing

$$j = (d-1)q + \bar{j},$$

for suitable d between 1 and n, and suitable $\bar{j}$ between 1 and q. If we set $d = 1$, let $\bar{j}$ range from 1 to q, set $d = 2$ and let $\bar{j}$ range over the same values, then continue in this manner until we set $d = n$ and let $\bar{j}$ take the values 1 to q, we generate all possible values for j, namely $j = 1, 2, \ldots, nq$. Writing j in this manner, the jth column of $A \otimes B$ is $a_d \otimes b_{\bar{j}}$. But $a_d = A e_d^n$ and $b_{\bar{j}} = B e_{\bar{j}}^q$ so the jth column of $A \otimes B$ is

$$(A \otimes B)\left(e_d^n \otimes e_{\bar{j}}^q\right).$$

We can put our analysis together in the following theorem.

Theorem 2.1 *Let A be an $m \times n$ matrix and B be an $p \times q$ matrix. In selecting the (i, j)th element of $A \otimes B$ write*

$$i = (c-1)p + \bar{i}$$
$$j = (d-1)q + \bar{j}$$

for suitable c between 1 and m, suitable $\bar{i}$ between 1 and p, suitable d between 1 and n, and suitable $\bar{j}$ between 1 and q. Then,

$$(A \otimes B)_{ij} = a_{cd} b_{\bar{i}\bar{j}}.$$

Proof: The ith row of $A \otimes B$ is given by

$$(A \otimes B)_{i\cdot} = \left(e_c^{m'} \otimes e_{\bar{i}}^{p'}\right)(A \otimes B),$$

and the jth column of $A \otimes B$ is given by

$$(A \otimes B)_{\cdot j} = (A \otimes B)\left(e_d^n \otimes e_{\bar{j}}^q\right).$$

Putting these two results together gives

$$(A \otimes B)_{ij} = \left(e_c^{m'} \otimes e_{\bar{i}}^{p'}\right)(A \otimes B)\left(e_d^n \otimes e_{\bar{j}}^q\right)$$
$$= e_c^{m'} A e_d^n \otimes e_{\bar{i}}^{p'} B e_{\bar{j}}^q$$
$$= a_{cd} b_{\bar{i}\bar{j}}. \qquad \blacksquare$$

To illustrate the use of this theorem, suppose A is 2×3 and B is 4×5. If we want to find $(A \otimes B)_{79}$, we would write

$$7 = 1 \times 4 + 3$$

so $c = 2$ and $\bar{i} = 3$ and we would write

$$9 = 1 \times 5 + 4$$

so $d = 2$ and $\bar{j} = 4$. According to the theorem,

$$(A \otimes B)_{79} = a_{22}\, b_{34}.$$

An important application of this analysis comes about when we are dealing with large identity matrices, I_{mn} say. Write

$$I_{mn} = \left(e_1^{mn} \dots e_{mn}^{mn} \right)$$

where, as per usual, e_j^{mn} refers to the jth column of this matrix. The question is, can we get an expression for e_j^{mn} in terms of columns of smaller identity matrices? Writing I_{mn} as a Kronecker product, we have

$$I_{mn} = I_m \otimes I_n$$

so our expression for e_j^{mn} depends on the exact location of this jth column. If we write,

$$j = (d-1)n + \bar{j}$$

for suitable d between 1 and m and suitable $\bar{j}$ between 1 and n, then

$$e_j^{mn} = (I_m \otimes I_n)\left(e_d^m \otimes e_{\bar{j}}^n \right) = e_d^m \otimes e_{\bar{j}}^n.$$

For example, consider I_6 and suppose we write

$$I_6 = I_3 \otimes I_2.$$

If we are interested in the 5th column of I_6, we write

$$5 = 2 \times 2 + 1,$$

so $d = 3$ and $\bar{j} = 1$, and we can write

$$e_5^6 = e_3^3 \otimes e_1^2.$$

Sometimes, we wish to retrieve the element a_{ij} from the vec A or from the rvec A. This is a far simpler operation, as shown by Theorem 2.2.

Theorem 2.2 *Let A be an* $m \times n$ *matrix. Then,*

$$a_{ij} = \left(e_j^{n'} \otimes e_i^{m'}\right)\operatorname{vec} A = (\operatorname{rvec} A)\left(e_i^m \otimes e_j^n\right).$$

Proof: We have

$$a_{ij} = e_i^{m'} A e_j^n.$$

But $a_{ij} = \operatorname{vec} a_{ij} = \left(e_j^{n'} \otimes e_i^{m'}\right)\operatorname{vec} A$. Also, $a_{ij} = \operatorname{rvec} a_{ij} = (\operatorname{rvec} A)$ $\left(e_i^m \otimes e_j^n\right)$. ∎

The concept of a selection matrix can be generalized to handle the case where our matrices are partitioned matrices. Suppose A is an $m \times nG$ matrix and we partition A as

$$A = (A_1 \ldots A_n) \tag{2.1}$$

where each submatrix is $m \times G$. To select the submatrix A_i from A, we post multiply A by $e_i^n \otimes I_G$ where e_i^n is the ith column of I_n. That is,

$$A_i = A\left(e_i^n \otimes I_G\right).$$

Suppose now we want to form the matrix $B = (A_1 \ A_4 \ A_5)$ from A. Then,

$$B = A(S \otimes I_G)$$

where $S = (e_1^n \ e_4^n \ e_5^n)$.

In like manner, consider C an $mG \times n$ matrix partitioned as

$$C = \begin{pmatrix} C_1 \\ \vdots \\ C_G \end{pmatrix} \tag{2.2}$$

where each submatrix is $m \times n$. If from C we wish to select C_j, we pre-multiply C by $e_j^{G'} \otimes I_m$.

That is,

$$C_j = \left(e_j^{G'} \otimes I_m\right) C.$$

If we wish to form

$$D = \begin{pmatrix} C_2 \\ C_3 \\ C_7 \end{pmatrix}$$

we premultiply C by the selection matrix $S \otimes I_m$ where $S = \begin{pmatrix} e_2^{G'} \\ e_3^{G'} \\ e_7^{G'} \end{pmatrix}$.

Finally, staying with the same partition of C notice that

$$\left(I_G \otimes e_j^{m'} \right) C = \begin{pmatrix} e_j^{m'} C_1 \\ \vdots \\ e_j^{m'} C_G \end{pmatrix} = \begin{pmatrix} (C_1)_{j\cdot} \\ \vdots \\ (C_G)_{j\cdot} \end{pmatrix} = C^{(j)},$$

where we use the notation introduced by Equation 1.8 in Chapter 1. That is, $\left(I_G \otimes e_j^{m'} \right)$ is the selection matrix that selects $C^{(j)}$ from C.

Sometimes instead of selecting rows or columns from a matrix A, we want to rearrange the rows or columns of A. The zero-one matrix that does this for us is called a permutation matrix. A **permutation matrix** P is obtained from a permutation of the rows or columns of an identity matrix. The result is a matrix in which each row and each column of the matrix contains a single element, one, and all the remaining elements are zeros. As the columns or rows of an identity matrix form an orthonormal set of vectors, it is quite clear that every permutation matrix is orthogonal, that is, $P' = P^{-1}$. Where a given matrix A is premultiplied (postmultiplied) by a permutation matrix, formed from the rows (columns) of an identity matrix, the result is a matrix whose rows (columns) are obtained from a permutation of the rows (columns) of A.

As with selection matrices, the concept of permutation matrices can be generalized to handle partitioned matrices. If A is $m \times nG$ and we partition A as in Equation 2.1, and we want to rearrange the submatrices in this partitioning, we can do this by post multiplying A by

$$P \otimes I_G$$

where P is the appropriate permutation matrix formed from the columns of the identity matrix I_n.

Similarly, if we want to rearrange the submatrices in C given by Equation 2.2, we premultiply C by

$$P \otimes I_m$$

where P is the appropriate permutation matrix formed from the rows of the identity matrix I_G.

2.3 The Elementary Matrix E_{ij}^{mn}

Sometimes, it is convenient to express an $m \times n$ matrix A as a sum involving its elements. A zero-one matrix that allows us to do this is the elementary matrix, (not to be confused with elementary matrices that give rise to elementary row or column operations). The **elementary matrix** E_{ij}^{mn} is the $m \times n$ matrix whose elements are all zeros except the (i, j)th element, which is 1. That is, E_{ij}^{mn} is defined by

$$E_{ij}^{mn} = e_i^m \, e_j^{n'}.$$

Clearly if $A = \{a_{ij}\}$ is an $m \times n$ matrix then

$$A = \sum_{i=1}^{m} \sum_{j=1}^{n} a_{ij} \, E_{ij}^{mn}.$$

Also,

$$\left(E_{ij}^{mn}\right)' = e_j^n \, e_i^{m'} = E_{ji}^{nm}.$$

Notice that if A is an $m \times n$ matrix and B is an $p \times q$ matrix, then

$$A E_{ij}^{np} B = a_i b_j'.$$

The ith row and the jth column of a Kronecker product can be written in terms of elementary matrices. Note that

$$\mathrm{vec}_q(a' \otimes b') = a \otimes b' = ab'$$

where b is $q \times 1$. Returning to the ith row of $A \otimes B$, which we wrote as

$$(A \otimes B)_{i.} = a^{c'} \otimes b^{\bar{i}'}$$

where $b^{\bar{i}}$ is $q \times 1$, it follows that

$$\mathrm{vec}_q(A \otimes B)_{i.} = a^c b^{\bar{i}'} = A' e_c^m e_{\bar{i}}^{p'} B = A' E_{c\bar{i}}^{mp} B. \tag{2.3}$$

If we undo the vec_q by taking the rvec of both sides, we have

$$(A \otimes B)_{i.} = \mathrm{rvec}\, A' E_{c\bar{i}}^{mp} B. \tag{2.4}$$

Similarly,

$$\mathrm{rvec}_p(a \otimes b) = a' \otimes b = ba'$$

where b is now $p \times 1$. Returning to the jth column of $A \otimes B$, which we wrote as

$$(A \otimes B)._j = a_d \otimes b_{\bar{j}}$$

where $b_{\bar{j}}$ is $p \times 1$, it follows that

$$\mathrm{rvec}_p (A \otimes B)._j = b_{\bar{j}} a_d' = Be_{\bar{j}}^q e_d^{n'} A' = BE_{\bar{j}d}^{qn} A'. \tag{2.5}$$

Undoing the rvec_p by taking the vec of both sides, gives

$$(A \otimes B)._j = \mathrm{vec}\, BE_{\bar{j}d}^{qn} A'. \tag{2.6}$$

These results will be important for us in our work in Chapter 4 where we look at different concepts of matrix derivatives.

Elementary matrices will be important for us as certain concepts of matrix differentiation make use of these matrices.

2.4 The Commutation Matrix

One of the most useful permutation matrices for statistics, econometrics, and matrix calculus is the commutation matrix. Consider an $m \times n$ matrix A, which using our notation for columns and rows, we write as

$$A = (a_1 \ldots a_n) = \begin{pmatrix} a^{1'} \\ \vdots \\ a^{m'} \end{pmatrix},$$

where a_j is the jth column of A and $a^{i'}$ is the ith row of A. Then,

$$\mathrm{vec}\, A = \begin{pmatrix} a_1 \\ \vdots \\ a_n \end{pmatrix}$$

whereas

$$\mathrm{vec}\, A' = \begin{pmatrix} a^1 \\ \vdots \\ a^m \end{pmatrix}.$$

Clearly, both $\mathrm{vec}\, A$ and $\mathrm{vec}\, A'$ contain all the elements of A, although arranged in different orders. It follows that there exists a $mn \times mn$

permutation matrix K_{mn} that has the property

$$K_{mn}\text{vec } A = \text{vec } A'. \tag{2.7}$$

This matrix is called the **commutation matrix**. The order of the subscripts is important. The notation is that K_{mn} is the commutation matrix associated with an $m \times n$ matrix A and takes vec A to vec A'. On the other hand, K_{nm} is the commutation matrix associated with an $n \times m$ matrix and as A' is such a matrix it follows that

$$K_{nm}\text{vec } A' = \text{vec } (A')' = \text{vec } A.$$

Using Equation 2.7, it follows that the two commutation matrices are linked by

$$K_{nm}K_{mn}\text{vec } A = \text{vec } A$$

so it follows that $K_{nm} = K_{mn}^{-1} = K_{mn}'$, where the last equality comes about because K_{mn}, like all permutation matrices, is orthogonal.

If the matrix A is a vector a, so $m = 1$, we have that

$$\text{vec } a = \text{vec } a'$$

so

$$K_{1n} = K_{n1} = I_n.$$

The commutation matrix can also be used to take us from a rvec to a vec. For A as previously, we have

$$(\text{rvec } A)K_{mn} = (\text{vec } A')'K_{mn} = (K_{mn}\text{vec } A)'K_{mn}$$
$$= (\text{vec } A)'K_{nm}K_{mn} = (\text{vec} A)'.$$

There are several explicit expressions for the commutation matrix. Two of the most useful, particularly when working with partitioned matrices are these:

$$K_{mn} = \begin{bmatrix} I_n \otimes e_1^{m'} \\ \vdots \\ I_n \otimes e_m^{m'} \end{bmatrix} = \begin{bmatrix} I_m \otimes e_1^n \ldots I_m \otimes e_n^n \end{bmatrix}, \tag{2.8}$$

where, as always in this book, e_j^m is the jth column of the $m \times m$ identity matrix I_m. For example,

$$K_{32} = \begin{bmatrix} I_2 \otimes e_1^{3'} \\ I_2 \otimes e_2^{3'} \\ I_2 \otimes e_3^{3'} \end{bmatrix} = \begin{bmatrix} I_3 \otimes e_1^2 & I_3 \otimes e_2^2 \end{bmatrix}$$

$$= \begin{bmatrix} 1 & 0 & 0 & 0 & 0 & 0 \\ 0 & 0 & 0 & 1 & 0 & 0 \\ 0 & 1 & 0 & 0 & 0 & 0 \\ 0 & 0 & 0 & 0 & 1 & 0 \\ 0 & 0 & 1 & 0 & 0 & 0 \\ 0 & 0 & 0 & 0 & 0 & 1 \end{bmatrix}.$$

The commutation matrix K_{mn} can be written in terms of elementary matrices. Write

$$K_{mn} = \begin{bmatrix} I_n \otimes e_1^{m'} \\ \vdots \\ I_n \otimes e_m^{m'} \end{bmatrix} = \begin{bmatrix} e_1^n \otimes e_1^{m'} & \cdots & e_n^n \otimes e_1^{m'} \\ \vdots & & \vdots \\ e_1^n \otimes e_m^{m'} & \cdots & e_n^n \otimes e_m^{m'} \end{bmatrix}.$$

From Equation 1.2 of Section 1.2 in Chapter 1 for vectors a and b, $a' \otimes b = b \otimes a' = ba'$, so

$$K_{mn} = \begin{bmatrix} e_1^n e_1^{m'} & \cdots & e_n^n e_1^{m'} \\ \vdots & & \vdots \\ e_1^n e_m^{m'} & \cdots & e_n^n e_m^{m'} \end{bmatrix} = \begin{bmatrix} E_{11}^{nm} & \cdots & E_{n1}^{nm} \\ \vdots & & \vdots \\ E_{1m}^{nm} & \cdots & E_{nm}^{nm} \end{bmatrix}.$$

We have occasion to use this expression for K_{mn} throughout this book. Notice that K_{nn} is symmetric and is its own inverse. That is, $K_{nn}' = K_{nn}$ and $K_{nn}K_{nn} = I_{n^2}$, so K_{nn} is a symmetric idempotent matrix.

For other expressions, see Magnus (1988), Graham (1981), and Henderson and Searle (1979).

Large commutation matrices can be written in terms of smaller commutation matrices as the following result shows. (See Magnus (1988), Chapter 3).

$$K_{st,n} = (I_s \otimes K_{tn})(K_{sn} \otimes I_t) = (I_t \otimes K_{sn})(K_{tn} \otimes I_s). \qquad (2.9)$$

Moreover,

$$K_{st,n} = K_{s,tn}K_{t,ns} = K_{t,ns}K_{s,tn}. \qquad (2.10)$$

2.4.1 Commutation Matrices, Kronecker Products, and Vecs

Some of the most interesting properties of commutation matrices are concerned with how they interact with Kronecker products. Using commutation matrices, we can interchange matrices in a Kronecker product as the following well-known results illustrate (see Neudecker and Magnus (1988), p.47 and Magnus (1988), Chapter 3).

Let A be an $m \times n$ matrix, B be an $p \times q$ matrix, and b be an $p \times 1$ vector. Then,

$$K_{pm}(A \otimes B) = (B \otimes A)K_{qn} \qquad (2.11)$$

$$K_{pm}(A \otimes B)K_{nq} = B \otimes A \qquad (2.12)$$

$$K_{pm}(A \otimes b) = b \otimes A \qquad (2.13)$$

$$K_{mp}(b \otimes A) = A \otimes b. \qquad (2.14)$$

If B is $m \times n$, then

$$\mathrm{tr}(K_{mn}(A' \otimes B)) = \mathrm{tr}A'B.$$

Note if c is a $q \times 1$ vector, then as $bc' = c' \otimes b = b \otimes c'$, we have using Equations 2.13 and 2.14 that

$$K_{pm}(A \otimes bc') = b \otimes A \otimes c'$$

$$K_{mp}(bc' \otimes A) = c' \otimes A \otimes b.$$

Secondly, interesting properties of commutation matrices with respect to Kronecker products, perhaps not so well known, can be achieved by writing the commutation matrix as we did in Equation 2.8 and calling on the work we did on selection matrices in Section 2.2. Consider A and B as previously shown and partition B into its rows:

$$B = \begin{pmatrix} b^{1\prime} \\ \vdots \\ b^{p\prime} \end{pmatrix}.$$

Then, we know that in general

$$A \otimes B = A \otimes \begin{pmatrix} b^{1\prime} \\ \vdots \\ b^{p\prime} \end{pmatrix} \neq \begin{pmatrix} A \otimes b^{1\prime} \\ \vdots \\ A \otimes b^{p\prime} \end{pmatrix}. \qquad (2.15)$$

However, the last matrix in Equation 2.15 can be achieved from $A \otimes B$ using a commutation matrix as the following theorem shows.

Theorem 2.3 *If A and B are $m \times n$ and $p \times q$ matrices respectfully, then*

$$K_{pm}(A \otimes B) = \begin{pmatrix} A \otimes b^{1'} \\ \vdots \\ A \otimes b^{p'} \end{pmatrix}.$$

Proof: Using Equation 2.8

$$K_{pm}(A \otimes B) = \begin{pmatrix} I_m \otimes e_1^{p'} \\ \vdots \\ I_m \otimes e_p^{p'} \end{pmatrix} (A \otimes B) = \begin{pmatrix} A \otimes e_1^{p'} B \\ \vdots \\ A \otimes e_p^{p'} B \end{pmatrix} = \begin{pmatrix} A \otimes b^{1'} \\ \vdots \\ A \otimes b^{p'} \end{pmatrix}. \blacksquare$$

Similarly, if we partition B into its columns so $B = (b_1 \ldots b_q)$ then

$$A \otimes B = A \otimes (b_1 \ldots b_q) \neq (A \otimes b_1 \ldots A \otimes b_q). \tag{2.16}$$

However, the last matrix of Equation (2.16) can be achieved from $A \otimes B$ using the commutation matrix.

Theorem 2.4 *If A and B are $m \times n$ and $p \times q$ matrices, respectively, then*

$$(A \otimes B)K_{nq} = (A \otimes b_1 \ldots A \otimes b_q).$$

Proof: Using Equation 2.8, we write

$$(A \otimes B)K_{nq} = (A \otimes B)\left(I_n \otimes e_1^q \ldots I_n \otimes e_q^q \right) = \left(A \otimes Be_1^q \ldots A \otimes Be_q^q \right)$$
$$= (A \otimes b_1 \ldots A \otimes b_q). \blacksquare$$

An interesting implication of Theorems 2.3 and 2.4 is that

$$\begin{pmatrix} A \otimes b^{1'} \\ \vdots \\ A \otimes b^{p'} \end{pmatrix} = (B \otimes a_1 \ldots B \otimes a_n).$$

This result follows as $K_{pm}(A \otimes B) = (B \otimes A)K_{qn}.$

Notice that

$$
K_{pm}(A \otimes B) = \begin{pmatrix} a^{1'} \otimes b^{1'} \\ \vdots \\ a^{m'} \otimes b^{1'} \\ \vdots \\ a^{1'} \otimes b^{p'} \\ \vdots \\ a^{m'} \otimes b^{p'} \end{pmatrix}
$$

so using the operator introduced in Section 1.3 of Chapter 1, we have

$$
(K_{pm}(A \otimes B))^{(j)} = \begin{pmatrix} a^{j'} \otimes b^{1'} \\ \vdots \\ a^{j'} \otimes b^{p'} \end{pmatrix} = \begin{pmatrix} b^{1'}(a^{j'} \otimes I_q) \\ \vdots \\ b^{p'}(a^{j'} \otimes I_q) \end{pmatrix} = B(a^{j'} \otimes I_q).
$$

$$(2.17)$$

This result will be useful to us in Chapter 5.

In our work in Chapter 4, we have occasion to consider the ith row of $K_{pm}(A \otimes B)$. From Theorem 2.3, it is clear that in obtaining this row we must specify exactly where the ith row is located in this matrix. If i is between 1 and m, the ith row is $a^{i'} \otimes b^{1'}$, if between $m+1$ and $2m$ it is $a^{i'} \otimes b^{2'}$ and so on, until i is between $(p-1)m$ and pm, in which case the ith row is $a^{i'} \otimes b^{p'}$. To cater for all possibilities, we use the device introduced in Section 2.2 of this chapter. We write

$$
i = (c-1)m + \bar{i}
$$

for c some value between 1 and p and $\bar{i}$ some value between 1 and m. Then,

$$
[K_{pm}(A \otimes B)]_{i\cdot} = a^{\bar{i}'} \otimes b^{c'} \tag{2.18}
$$

where b^c is $q \times 1$. Taking the vec_q of both sides of Equation 2.18, we have

$$
\mathrm{vec}_q [K_{pm}(A \otimes B)]_{i\cdot} = a^{\bar{i}} b^{c'} = A' e_{\bar{i}}^m e_c^{p'} B = A' E_{\bar{i}c}^{mp} B. \tag{2.19}
$$

In comparing Equation 2.19 with Equation 2.3, we note that the difference in taking the vec_q of $[K_{pm}(A \otimes B)]_{i\cdot}$ as compared to taking the vec_q of $(A \times B)_{i\cdot}$ is that the subscripts of the elementary matrix are interchanged.

Undoing the vec_q by taking the rvec of each side, we get another way of writing $[K_{pm}(A \otimes B)]_{i\cdot}$ namely

$$
[K_{pm}(A \otimes B)]_{i\cdot} = \mathrm{rvec}\, A' E_{\bar{i}c}^{np} B. \tag{2.20}
$$

We will also have occasion to consider the jth column of $[(A \otimes B)K_{nq}]$. Referring to Theorem 2.4 again, we have to specify exactly where the jth column is in the matrix. Conducting a similar analysis leads us to write

$$j = (d-1)n + \bar{j}$$

where d takes a suitable value between 1 and q and $\bar{j}$ takes a suitable value between 1 and n. Then,

$$[(A \otimes B)K_{nq}]_{\cdot j} = a_{\bar{j}} \otimes b_d \qquad (2.21)$$

where b_d is $p \times 1$. Taking the rvec$_p$ of both sides of Equation 2.21, gives

$$\mathrm{rvec}_p\left[(A \otimes B)K_{nq}\right]_{\cdot j} = b_d a_{\bar{j}}' = Be_d^q e_{\bar{j}}^{n'} A' = BE_{d\bar{j}}^{qn} A'. \qquad (2.22)$$

Again, comparing Equation 2.22 with Equation 2.5, we see that the subscripts of the elementary matrix are interchanged. Undoing the rvec$_p$ by taking the vec, we get another way of writing $[(A \otimes B)K_{nq}]_{\cdot j}$, namely

$$[(A \otimes B)K_{nq}]_{\cdot j} = \mathrm{vec}\, BE_{d\bar{j}}^{qn} A'.$$

In Section 2.2, we saw that when it comes to partitioned matrices, selection matrices of the form $e_i^{G'} \otimes I_m$ or $e_j^G \otimes I_n$ are useful in selecting submatrices. Using these matrices, we can generalize Theorems 2.3 and 2.4 to the case where B is a large partitioned matrix.

Theorem 2.5   *Let A be an $m \times n$ matrix and B be an $pG \times q$ matrix and partition B as follows:*

$$B = \begin{pmatrix} B_1 \\ \vdots \\ B_G \end{pmatrix},$$

where each submatrix B_i is $p \times q$. Then,

$$(K_{Gm} \otimes I_p)(A \otimes B) = \begin{pmatrix} A \otimes B_1 \\ \vdots \\ A \otimes B_G \end{pmatrix}.$$

Proof: Using Equation 2.8, we write

$$(K_{Gm} \otimes I_p)(A \otimes B) = \begin{pmatrix} I_m \otimes \left(e_1^{G'} \otimes I_p \right) \\ \vdots \\ I_m \otimes \left(e_G^{G'} \otimes I_p \right) \end{pmatrix} (A \otimes B)$$

$$= \begin{pmatrix} A \otimes \left(e_1^{G'} \otimes I_p \right) B \\ \vdots \\ A \otimes \left(e_G^{G'} \otimes I_p \right) B \end{pmatrix} = \begin{pmatrix} A \otimes B_1 \\ \vdots \\ A \otimes B_G \end{pmatrix}. \qquad \blacksquare$$

The following corollary of this theorem is important for us:

Corollary 2.1 *Let A be an $m \times n$ matrix and B be $p \times q$. Then,*

$$(K_{qm} \otimes I_p)(A \otimes \mathrm{vec}\, B) = \begin{pmatrix} A \otimes b_1 \\ \vdots \\ A \otimes b_q \end{pmatrix}$$

where b_j is the jth column of B. $\qquad \blacksquare$

Note that

$$(I_q \otimes K_{mp})(\mathrm{vec}\, B \otimes A) = \begin{pmatrix} K_{mp} & & O \\ & \ddots & \\ O & & K_{mp} \end{pmatrix} \begin{pmatrix} b_1 \otimes A \\ \vdots \\ b_q \otimes A \end{pmatrix}$$

$$= \begin{pmatrix} K_{mp}(b_1 \otimes A) \\ \vdots \\ K_{mp}(b_q \otimes A) \end{pmatrix} = \begin{pmatrix} A \otimes b_1 \\ \vdots \\ A \otimes b_q \end{pmatrix},$$

so we have

$$(K_{qm} \otimes I_p)(A \otimes \mathrm{vec}\, B) = \begin{pmatrix} A \otimes b_1 \\ \vdots \\ A \otimes b_q \end{pmatrix} = (I_p \otimes K_{mp})(\mathrm{vec}\, B \otimes A). \qquad (2.23)$$

A consequence of Theorems 2.3 and 2.5, which is useful for our work throughout many chapters, is the following result.

Theorem 2.6 *Let A and B be matrices as specified in Theorem 2.5. Then,*

$$K_{pG,m}(A \otimes B) = \begin{pmatrix} A \otimes (B_1)_{1.} \\ \vdots \\ A \otimes (B_1)_{p.} \\ \vdots \\ A \otimes (B_G)_{1.} \\ \vdots \\ A \otimes (B_G)_{p.} \end{pmatrix}.$$

Proof: Using Equation 2.9, we can write

$$K_{pG,m}(A \otimes B) = (I_G \otimes K_{pm})(K_{Gm} \otimes I_p)(A \otimes B)$$

$$= \begin{pmatrix} K_{pm} & & O \\ & \ddots & \\ O & & K_{pm} \end{pmatrix} \begin{pmatrix} A \otimes B_1 \\ \vdots \\ A \otimes B_G \end{pmatrix}$$

by Theorem 2.5. Thus, we have

$$K_{pG,m}(A \otimes B) = \begin{pmatrix} K_{pm}(A \otimes B_1) \\ \vdots \\ K_{pm}(A \otimes B_G) \end{pmatrix} = \begin{pmatrix} A \otimes (B_1)_{1.} \\ \vdots \\ A \otimes (B_1)_{p.} \\ \vdots \\ A \otimes (B_G)_{1.} \\ \vdots \\ A \otimes (B_G)_{p.} \end{pmatrix}$$

by Theorem 2.3. ∎

The generalization of Theorem 2.4 to the case where B is a $p \times qG$ matrix is as follows:

Theorem 2.7 *Let A be an $m \times n$ matrix and B be an $p \times qG$ matrix partitioned as follows:*

$$B = (B_1 \dots B_G)$$

where each submatrix B_j is $p \times q$.

Then,

$$(A \otimes B)(K_{nG} \otimes I_q) = (A \otimes B_1 \dots A \otimes B_G).$$

Proof: Using Equation 2.8, we write

$$
\begin{aligned}
(A \otimes B)(K_{nG} \otimes I_q) &= (A \otimes B)\left[\left(I_n \otimes e_1^G \dots I_n \times e_G^G\right) \otimes I_q\right] \\
&= (A \otimes B)\left[I_n \otimes \left(e_1^G \otimes I_q\right) \dots I_n \otimes \left(e_G^G \otimes I_q\right)\right] \\
&= A \otimes B\left(e_1^G \otimes I_q\right) \dots A \otimes B\left(e_G^G \otimes I_q\right) \\
&= (A \otimes B_1 \dots A \otimes B_G).
\end{aligned}
$$
∎

A corollary of this theorem is as follows:

Corollary 2.2 *Let A be $m \times n$ and B be $p \times q$. Then,*

$$(A \otimes \operatorname{rvec} B)(K_{np} \otimes I_q) = (A \otimes b^{1'} \dots A \otimes b^{p'})$$

Note that

$$
(\operatorname{rvec} B \otimes A)(I_p \otimes K_{qn})
$$

$$
= (b^{1'} \otimes A \dots b^{p'} \otimes A)
\begin{pmatrix}
K_{qn} & & O \\
 & \ddots & \\
O & & K_{qn}
\end{pmatrix}
$$

$$
= (b^{1'} \otimes A)K_{qn} \dots (b^{p'} \otimes A)K_{qn} = A \otimes b^{1'} \dots A \otimes b^{p'},
$$

so we have

$$
\begin{aligned}
(A \otimes \operatorname{rvec} B)&(K_{np} \otimes I_q) \\
&= A \otimes b^{1'} \dots A \otimes b^{p'} = (\operatorname{rvec} B \otimes A)(I_p \otimes K_{qn}).
\end{aligned} \tag{2.24}
$$

The result corresponding to Theorem 2.6 is that for A and B specified as in Theorem 2.7, then

$$
\begin{aligned}
(A \otimes B)&K_{n,Gq} \\
&= (A \otimes (B_1)_{.1} \dots A \otimes (B_1)_{.q} \dots A \otimes (B_G)_{.1} \dots A \otimes (B_G)_{.q}).
\end{aligned} \tag{2.25}
$$

The basic properties of commutation matrices with respect to Kronecker products as presented by Equations 2.11 to 2.14 can be generalized in a similar fashion.

Corollary 2.1 and Equation 2.23 allow us to come up with the zero-one matrix that converts the vec of a Kronecker product into the Kronecker product of vecs and vice versa. Partitioning both A and B into their columns, we have:

$$A = (a_1 \ldots a_n), \quad B = (b_1 \ldots b_q).$$

We saw in Section 1.2 of Chapter 1, that we can write

$$A \otimes B = (a_1 \otimes b_1 \ldots a_1 \otimes b_q \ldots a_n \otimes b_1 \ldots a_n \otimes b_q),$$

so

$$\text{vec}(A \otimes B) = \begin{pmatrix} a_1 \otimes b_1 \\ \vdots \\ a_1 \otimes b_q \\ \vdots \\ a_n \otimes b_1 \\ \vdots \\ a_n \otimes b_q \end{pmatrix},$$

whereas

$$\text{vec } A \otimes \text{vec } B = \begin{pmatrix} a_1 \otimes \begin{pmatrix} b_1 \\ \vdots \\ b_q \end{pmatrix} \\ \vdots \\ a_n \otimes \begin{pmatrix} b_1 \\ \vdots \\ b_q \end{pmatrix} \end{pmatrix}.$$

Clearly, both vectors have the same elements, although these elements are rearranged in moving from one vector to another. Each vector must then be able to be obtained by premultiplying the other by a suitable zero-one matrix.

An application of Corollary 2.1 gives the following theorem:

Theorem 2.8

$$\text{vec}(A \otimes B) = (I_n \otimes K_{qm} \otimes I_p)(\text{vec } A \otimes \text{vec } B)$$
$$(I_n \otimes K_{mq} \otimes I_p)\text{vec}(A \otimes B) = \text{vec } A \otimes \text{vec } B.$$

Proof: We write

$$(I_n \otimes K_{qm} \otimes I_p)(\text{vec}\,A \otimes \text{vec}\,B)$$

$$= \begin{pmatrix} K_{qm} \otimes I_p & & O \\ & \ddots & \\ O & & K_{qm} \otimes I_p \end{pmatrix} \begin{pmatrix} a_1 \otimes \begin{pmatrix} b_1 \\ \vdots \\ b_q \end{pmatrix} \\ \vdots \\ a_n \otimes \begin{pmatrix} b_1 \\ \vdots \\ b_q \end{pmatrix} \end{pmatrix}$$

$$= \begin{pmatrix} (K_{qm} \otimes I_p) \left(a_1 \otimes \begin{pmatrix} b_1 \\ \vdots \\ b_q \end{pmatrix} \right) \\ \vdots \\ (K_{qm} \otimes I_p) \left(a_n \otimes \begin{pmatrix} b_1 \\ \vdots \\ b_q \end{pmatrix} \right) \end{pmatrix} = \text{vec}\,(A \otimes B),$$

using Corollary 2.1. As $K_{mq} = K_{qm}^{-1}$ the inverse of $(I_n \otimes K_{qm} \otimes I_p)$ is $(I_n \otimes K_{mq} \otimes I_p)$, which gives the second result. ∎

Theorem 2.8 and Equation 2.23 can also be used to show that $\text{vec}(A \otimes B)$ can be written in terms of either $\text{vec}\,A$ or $\text{vec}\,B$:

Theorem 2.9

$$\text{vec}(A \otimes B) = \left[I_n \otimes \begin{pmatrix} I_m \otimes b_1 \\ \vdots \\ I_m \otimes b_q \end{pmatrix} \right] \text{vec}\,A,$$

and

$$\text{vec}(A \otimes B) = \left[\begin{pmatrix} I_q \otimes a_1 \\ \vdots \\ I_q \otimes a_n \end{pmatrix} \otimes I_p \right] \text{vec}\,B.$$

Proof: By Theorem 2.8

$$\text{vec}(A \otimes B) = (I_n \otimes K_{qm} \otimes I_p)(\text{vec } A \otimes \text{vec } B)$$
$$= (I_n \otimes K_{qm} \otimes I_p)\text{vec}[\text{vec } B(\text{vec } A)'],$$

by Equation 1.11 from Chapter 1.

But,

$$\text{vec}[\text{vec } B(\text{vec } A)'] = [I_n \otimes (I_m \otimes \text{vec } B)]\text{vec } A = [\text{vec } A \otimes I_q \otimes I_p]\text{vec } B,$$

so

$$\text{vec}(A \otimes B) = \{I_n \otimes [(K_{qm} \otimes I_p)(I_m \otimes \text{vec } B)]\}\text{vec } A$$
$$= \{[(I_n \otimes K_{qm})(\text{vec } A \otimes I_q)] \otimes I_p\}\text{vec } B$$

Applying Equation 2.23 gives the result. ∎

Notice from Theorem 2.4 that

$$(I_m \otimes B)K_{mq} = (I_m \otimes b_1 \dots I_m \otimes b_q)$$

and each of the submatrices $I_m \otimes b_j$ are $mp \times m$.

It follows that

$$\text{vec}_m\left[(I_m \otimes B)K_{mq}\right] = \begin{pmatrix} I_m \otimes b_1 \\ \vdots \\ I_m \otimes b_q \end{pmatrix}$$

so from Theorem 2.9, we can write

$$\text{vec}(A \otimes B) = \{I_n \otimes \text{vec}_m[(I_m \otimes B)K_{mq}]\}\text{vec } A.$$

But all vecs can be undone by applying a suitable rvec, in this case, rvec_{mp}, so we have

$$A \otimes B = \text{rvec}_{mp}\{I_n \otimes \text{vec}_m[(I_m \otimes B)K_{mq}]\}\text{vec } A.$$

In like manner,

$$\text{vec}(A \otimes B) = [\text{vec}_q[(I_q \otimes A)K_{qn}] \otimes I_p]\text{vec } B \qquad (2.26)$$

and

$$A \otimes B = \text{rvec}_{mp}\{\text{vec}_q[(I_q \otimes A)K_{qn}] \otimes I_p\}\text{vec } B. \qquad (2.27)$$

By taking transposes we can get equivalent results in terms of vec_{mp}, rvec_q, and rvec_p, but the details are left to the reader.

A final property for the commutation matrix that is important for us concentrates on the fact that the commutation matrix is a permutation matrix. In Section 2.2, we noted that when a matrix A is premultiplied by a permutation matrix, the result is a matrix whose rows are obtained from a permutation of the rows of A. It is of interest to us then to see what permutation of the rows of A that results from A being premultiplied by the commutation matrix K_{mn}. The answer is provided by the following theorem, which calls on the notation introduced in Equation 1.8 of Section 1.3.

Theorem 2.10   *Let A be an $mn \times p$ matrix and partition A as*

$$A = \begin{pmatrix} A_1 \\ \vdots \\ A_n \end{pmatrix} \tag{2.28}$$

where each submatrix is $m \times p$. Then,

$$K_{mn}A = \begin{pmatrix} (A_1)_{1\cdot} \\ \vdots \\ (A_n)_{1\cdot} \\ \vdots \\ (A_1)_{m\cdot} \\ \vdots \\ (A_n)_{m\cdot} \end{pmatrix} = \begin{pmatrix} A^{(1)} \\ \vdots \\ A^{(m)} \end{pmatrix}.$$

Proof: Using Equation 2.8, we have

$$K_{mn}A = \begin{pmatrix} I_n \otimes e_1^{m'} \\ \vdots \\ I_n \otimes e_m^{m'} \end{pmatrix} A = \begin{pmatrix} \left(I_n \otimes e_1^{m'} \right) A \\ \vdots \\ \left(I_n \otimes e_m^{m'} \right) A \end{pmatrix}.$$

But,

$$\left(I_n \otimes e_j^{m'} \right) A = \begin{pmatrix} e_j^{m'} & & O \\ & \ddots & \\ O & & e_j^{m'} \end{pmatrix} \begin{pmatrix} A_1 \\ \vdots \\ A_n \end{pmatrix} = \begin{pmatrix} e_j^{m'} A_1 \\ \vdots \\ e_j^{m'} A_n \end{pmatrix} = \begin{pmatrix} (A_1)_{j\cdot} \\ \vdots \\ (A_n)_{j\cdot} \end{pmatrix}. \blacksquare$$

Notice that when we use this property of K_{mn}, the second subscript of the commutation matrix refers to the number of submatrices in the partition of A whereas the first subscript refers to the number of rows in each of the submatrices of the partition of A. Thus,

$$K_{nm}A = \begin{pmatrix} A^{(1)} \\ \vdots \\ A^{(n)} \end{pmatrix}$$

where the stacking of the rows refer to a different partitioning of A namely

$$A = \begin{pmatrix} A_1 \\ \vdots \\ A_m \end{pmatrix}$$

and now each submatrix in this partitioning is $n \times p$.

A similar discussion can be made from the case where we postmultiply an $p \times mn$ matrix B by K_{mn}.

Consider the case where A is a Kronecker product, say $A = B \otimes C$ where B is an $n \times r$ matrix and C is an $m \times s$ matrix. Then,

$$B \otimes C = \begin{pmatrix} b^{1'} \otimes C \\ \vdots \\ b^{n'} \otimes C \end{pmatrix}$$

where each submatrix $b^{i'} \otimes C$ is $m \times rs$, for $i = 1, \ldots, n$. In Section 1.2 of Chapter 1, we saw that the jth row of $b^{i'} \otimes C$ is $b^{i'} \otimes c^{j'}$, so

$$K_{mn}(B \otimes C) = \begin{pmatrix} B \otimes c^{1'} \\ \vdots \\ B \otimes c^{m'} \end{pmatrix}$$

which we already knew from Theorem 2.3.

Notice also that as $K_{nm}K_{mn} = I_{mn}$, we have

$$K_{nm}K_{mn}A = K_{nm}\begin{pmatrix} A^{(1)} \\ \vdots \\ A^{(m)} \end{pmatrix} = \begin{pmatrix} A_1 \\ \vdots \\ A_n \end{pmatrix}.$$

That is, premultiplying $K_{mn}A$ as given in Theorem 2.10 by K_{nm} takes us back to the original partitioning.

More will be made of this property of the commutation matrix in Section 2.7 of this chapter where we discuss a new zero-one matrix called a twining matrix.

2.4.2 Commutation Matrices and Cross-Products

The basic properties of commutation matrices with respect to Kronecker products, as presented in Equations 2.11 to 2.14, can be used to illustrate how commutation matrices interact with cross-products:

Theorem 2.11 *Let A be a $mG \times p$ matrix and B be a $nG \times q$ matrix. Let C be $r \times G$ matrix. Then,*

$$K_{nm}(A \tau_{Gmn} B) = (B \tau_{Gnm} A) K_{qp}$$

$$K_{nm}(A \tau_{Gmn} B) K_{pq} = B \tau_{Gnm} A$$

$$K_{rm}(A \tau_{Gmr} \text{vec } C) = \text{vec } C \tau_{Grm} A$$

$$K_{mr}(\text{vec } C \tau_{Grm} A) = A \tau_{Gmr} \text{vec } C$$

Proof: Partition A and B as in Equation 1.7 of Section 1.3. Then,

$$K_{nm}(A \tau_{Gmn} B) = K_{nm}(A_1 \otimes B_1 + \cdots + A_G \otimes B_G)$$

$$= K_{nm}(A_1 \otimes B_1) + \cdots + K_{nm}(A_G \otimes B_G)$$

$$= (B_1 \otimes A_1) K_{qp} + \cdots + (B_G \otimes A_G) K_{qp} = (B \tau_{Gnm} A) K_{qp}.$$

The second result is proved in a similar manner.

Now, partition C into its columns:

$$C = (c_1 \ldots c_G).$$

Then,

$$K_{rm}(A \tau_{Gmr} \text{vec } C) = K_{rm}(A_1 \otimes c_1 + \cdots + A_G \otimes c_G)$$

$$= c_1 \otimes A_1 + \cdots + c_G \otimes A_G = \text{vec } C \tau_{Grm} A.$$

The final result is proved similarly. ∎

Recall that Theorem 1.6 of Section 1.3 in Chapter 1 demonstrated that for A a $mG \times p$ matrix and B a $nG \times q$ matrix, we can write $A \tau_{Gmn} B$ in terms of a vector of τ_{G1n} cross-products, namely

$$A \tau_{Gmn} B = \begin{pmatrix} A^{(1)} \tau_{G1n} B \\ \vdots \\ A^{(m)} \tau_{G1n} B \end{pmatrix}.$$

Contrast this with the following theorem:

Theorem 2.12 *Let A be a mG × p matrix and B be a nG × q partitioned as in Equation 1.7 of Section 1.3. Then,*

$$K_{nm}(A \tau_{Gmn} B) = \begin{pmatrix} A \tau_{Gm1} B^{(1)} \\ \vdots \\ A \tau_{Gm1} B^{(n)} \end{pmatrix}.$$

Proof: We have

$$A \tau_{Gmn} B = A_1 \otimes B_1 + \cdots + A_G \otimes B_G$$

and from Theorem 2.3

$$K_{nm}(A_i \otimes B_i) = \begin{pmatrix} A_i \otimes (B_i)_{1.} \\ \vdots \\ A_i \otimes (B_i)_{n.} \end{pmatrix}$$

for $i = 1, \ldots, G$. It follows that

$$K_{nm}(A \tau_{Gmn} B)$$
$$= \begin{pmatrix} A_1 \otimes (B_1)_{1.} + \cdots + A_G \otimes (B_G)_{1.} \\ \vdots \\ A_1 \otimes (B_1)_{n.} + \cdots + A_G \otimes (B_G)_{n.} \end{pmatrix} = \begin{pmatrix} A \tau_{Gm1} B^{(1)} \\ \vdots \\ A \tau_{Gm1} B^{(n)} \end{pmatrix}. \blacksquare$$

The following theorems tell us what happens when the commutation matrix appears in the cross-product.

Theorem 2.13 *Let A and B be mG × p and nm × q matrices, respectively. Partition A as*

$$A = \begin{pmatrix} A_1 \\ \vdots \\ A_G \end{pmatrix}$$

where each submatrix in this partitioning is m × p. Then,

$$K_{mG} A \tau_{mGn} B = \begin{pmatrix} A_1 \tau_{m1n} B \\ \vdots \\ A_G \tau_{m1n} B \end{pmatrix}.$$

Proof: Given our partitioning of A, we have from Theorem 2.10 that

$$K_{mG}A = \begin{pmatrix} A^{(1)} \\ \vdots \\ A^{(m)} \end{pmatrix}$$

where each submatrix $A^{(j)}$ is $G \times p$, so if we partition B as

$$B = \begin{pmatrix} B_1 \\ \vdots \\ B_m \end{pmatrix}$$

and each submatrix in this partitioning is $n \times q$, then

$$K_{mG}A\,\tau_{mGn}B = A^{(1)} \otimes B_1 + \cdots + A^{(m)} \otimes B_m$$
$$= \begin{pmatrix} (A_1)_{1\cdot} \otimes B_1 + \cdots + (A_1)_{m\cdot} \otimes B_m \\ \vdots \\ (A_G)_{1\cdot} \otimes B_1 + \cdots + (A_G)_{m\cdot} \otimes B_m \end{pmatrix} = \begin{pmatrix} A_1\tau_{m1n}B \\ \vdots \\ A_G\tau_{m1n}B \end{pmatrix}. \blacksquare$$

Theorem 2.14 *Let A and B be $nm \times p$ and $nG \times q$ matrices, respectively, and partition B as*

$$B = \begin{pmatrix} B_1 \\ \vdots \\ B_G \end{pmatrix}$$

where each submatrix is $n \times q$. Then,

$$K_{Gm}(A\,\tau_{nmG}K_{nG}B) = \begin{pmatrix} A\,\tau_{nm1}B_1 \\ \vdots \\ A\,\tau_{nm1}B_G \end{pmatrix}.$$

Proof: From Theorem 2.10 given our partitioning of B

$$K_{nG}B = \begin{pmatrix} B^{(1)} \\ \vdots \\ B^{(n)} \end{pmatrix}$$

where each submatrix $B^{(j)}$ is $G \times q$. Applying Theorem 2.12 gives the result. $\blacksquare$

Notice that if A is $n \times p$ in Theorem 2.14, so $m = 1$ and $K_{G1} = I_G$, we have

$$A \tau_{n1G} K_{nG} B = \begin{pmatrix} A \tau_{n11} B_1 \\ \vdots \\ A \tau_{n11} B_G \end{pmatrix},$$

a result that will be useful to us in our future work.

The following theorem demonstrates that a vec of a product matrix can be written as a cross-product of vectors involving the commutation matrix:

Theorem 2.15 *Let A be an $G \times m$ matrix and B be an $G \times n$ matrix. Then,*

$$K_{Gn} \text{vec } B \tau_{Gnm} K_{Gm} \text{vec } A = \text{vec } A'B.$$

Proof: Partitioning A and B into their columns, we have $A = (a_1 \ldots a_m)$ and $B = (b_1 \ldots b_n)$, so

$$K_{Gn} \text{vec } B = \begin{pmatrix} b^{(1)} \\ \vdots \\ b^{(G)} \end{pmatrix} \quad \text{and} \quad K_{Gm} \text{vec } A = \begin{pmatrix} a^{(1)} \\ \vdots \\ a^{(G)} \end{pmatrix}$$

and

$$K_{Gn} \text{vec } B \tau_{Gnm} K_{Gm} \text{vec } A = b^{(1)} \otimes a^{(1)} + \cdots + b^{(G)} \otimes a^{(G)}. \quad (2.29)$$

Consider the first block of the right-hand side of Equation 2.29:

$$(b_1)_1 \otimes a^{(1)} + \cdots + (b_1)_G \otimes a^{(G)} = (b_1)_1 a^{(1)} + \cdots + (b_1)_G a^{(G)}$$

$$= (b_1' \otimes I_m) \begin{pmatrix} a^{(1)} \\ \vdots \\ a^{(G)} \end{pmatrix}$$

$$= (b_1' \otimes I_m) K_{Gm} \text{vec } A$$

$$= (I_m \otimes b_1') \text{vec } A = \text{vec } b_1' A.$$

It follows that the left-hand side of Equation 2.29 can be written as:

$$\begin{pmatrix} \text{vec} b_1' A \\ \vdots \\ \text{vec} b_n' A \end{pmatrix} = \text{vec } (b_1' A \ldots b_n' A) = \text{vec } \left[(b_1' \ldots b_n')(I_n \otimes A) \right]$$

$$= \text{vec } \left[(\text{vec } B)'(I_n \otimes A) \right] = (I_n \otimes A') \text{vec } B = \text{vec } A'B. \quad \blacksquare$$

The following theorem demonstrates what happens if the commutation matrix itself is part of a cross-product.

Theorem 2.16 *Let A be an $mn \times p$ matrix. Then,*

$$K_{mG}\tau_{mGn}A = I_G \otimes \text{rvec}_n A$$
$$A\tau_{mnG}K_{mG} = (\text{rvec}_n A \otimes I_G)K_{m,Gp}.$$

Proof: Recall that

$$K_{mG} = \begin{pmatrix} I_G \otimes e_1^{m'} \\ \vdots \\ I_G \otimes e_m^{m'} \end{pmatrix}$$

so if we partition A as

$$A = \begin{pmatrix} A_1 \\ \vdots \\ A_m \end{pmatrix}$$

where each submatrix is $n \times p$, we have

$$K_{mG}\tau_{mGn}A = \left(I_G \otimes e_1^{m'} \otimes A_1\right) + \cdots + \left(I_G \otimes e_m^{m'} \otimes A_m\right)$$

$$= \begin{pmatrix} e_1^{m'} \otimes A_1 & & O \\ & \ddots & \\ O & & e_1^{m'} \otimes A_1 \end{pmatrix} + \cdots + \begin{pmatrix} e_m^{m'} \otimes A_m & & O \\ & \ddots & \\ O & & e_m^{m'} \otimes A_m \end{pmatrix}$$

$$= \begin{pmatrix} (A_1 O \ldots O) & & O \\ & \ddots & \\ O & & (A_1 O \ldots O) \end{pmatrix} + \cdots$$

$$+ \begin{pmatrix} (O \ldots O A_m) & & O \\ & \ddots & \\ O & & (O \ldots O A_m) \end{pmatrix}$$

$$= \begin{pmatrix} (A_1 \ldots A_m) & & O \\ & \ddots & \\ O & & (A_1 \ldots A_m) \end{pmatrix} = I_G \otimes \text{rvec}_n A.$$

Now, by Theorems 2.11 and 2.16

$$A\tau_{mnG}K_{mG} = K_{nG}(K_{mG}\tau_{mGn}A)K_{mG,p} = K_{nG}(I_G \otimes \text{rvec}_n A)K_{mG,p}.$$

But $K_{mG,p} = K_{G,mp}K_{m,Gp}$ by Equation 2.10, so we can write

$$A\tau_{mnG}K_{mG} = K_{nG}(I_G \otimes \text{rvec}_n A)K_{G,mp}K_{m,Gp} = (\text{rvec}_n A \otimes I_G)K_{m,Gp}.$$ ■

Notice in Theorem 2.16, if we let $A = K_{mn}$, then we have

$$K_{mG}\tau_{mGn}K_{mn} = I_G \otimes \text{rvec}_n K_{mn}$$

and

$$K_{mn}\tau_{mnG}K_{mG} = (\text{rvec}_n K_{mn} \otimes I_G)K_{m,Gmn}.$$

Interchanging the n and G in the second of these equations gives the result that

$$K_{mG}\tau_{mGn}K_{mn} = I_G \otimes \text{rvec}_n K_{mn} = (\text{rvec}_G K_{mG} \otimes I_n)K_{m,nmG}.$$

Cross-products can be written as an expression involving Kronecker products, one of which involves the commutation matrix, as the following two theorems show.

Theorem 2.17 *Let A be an* $mG \times p$ *matrix and B be an* $nG \times q$ *matrix partitioned as in Equation 1.7 of Section 1.3.*
Then,

$$A\tau_{Gmn}B = [(\text{rvec}_m A)K_{Gp} \otimes I_n](I_p \otimes B).$$

Proof: Write

$$A\tau_{Gmn}B = A_1 \otimes B_1 + \cdots + A_G \otimes B_G$$
$$= (A_1 \otimes I_n)(I_p \otimes B_1) + \cdots + (A_G \otimes I_n)(I_p \otimes B_G)$$
$$= (A_1 \otimes I_n \ldots A_G \otimes I_n)\begin{pmatrix} I_p \otimes B_1 \\ \vdots \\ I_p \otimes B_G \end{pmatrix}$$
$$= ((A_1 \ldots A_G) \otimes I_n)(K_{Gp} \otimes I_n)(I_p \otimes B),$$

by Theorem 2.5. It follows that $A\tau_{Gmn}B = ((\text{rvec}_m A)(K_{Gp} \otimes I_n)(I_p \otimes B)$.

■

Theorem 2.18 *If A is an* $p \times mG$ *matrix and B is an* $n \times q$ *matrix, then*

$$\text{vec}_m A\tau_{Gpn}(I_G \otimes B) = (A \otimes B)(K_{Gm} \otimes I_q).$$

Proof: Partition A as $A = (A_1 \ldots A_G)$ where each submatrix is $p \times m$, so

$$\mathrm{vec}_m A = \begin{pmatrix} A_1 \\ \vdots \\ A_G \end{pmatrix}.$$

It follows that

$$\mathrm{vec}_m A \tau_{Gpn}(I_G \otimes B) = A_1 \otimes e_1^{G'} \otimes B + \cdots + A_G \otimes e_G^{G'} \otimes B.$$

But from the definition of the commutation matrix given in Equation 2.8,

$$(A \otimes B)(K_{Gm} \otimes I_q) = (A_1 \otimes B \ldots A_G \otimes B) \begin{pmatrix} I_m \otimes e_1^{G'} \otimes I_q \\ \vdots \\ I_m \otimes e_G^{G'} \otimes I_q \end{pmatrix}$$

$$= A_1 \left(I_m \otimes e_1^{G'} \right) \otimes B + \cdots + A_G \left(I_m \otimes e_G^{G'} \right) \otimes B$$

$$= A_1 \otimes e_1^{G'} \otimes B + \cdots + A_G \otimes e_G^{G'} \otimes B. \qquad \blacksquare$$

One final theorem involving cross-products and commutation matrices:

Theorem 2.19 *Let A, B, C and D be $m \times n$, $p \times q$, $mr \times s$, and $pr \times t$ matrices respectively. Then,*

$$C\tau_{mrp}(A \otimes B)K_{nq} = (C \otimes B)\tau_{m,pr,1}A$$

and

$$K_{pm}(A \otimes B)\tau_{pmr}D = A \otimes (B\tau_{p1r}D).$$

Proof: From the property of the commutation matrices given by Equation 2.11 and Theorem 2.3, we have

$$(A \otimes B)K_{nq} = K_{mp}(B \otimes A) = \begin{pmatrix} B \otimes a^{1'} \\ \vdots \\ B \otimes a^{m'} \end{pmatrix}.$$

Partitioning C as

$$C = \begin{pmatrix} C_1 \\ \vdots \\ C_m \end{pmatrix}$$

where each submatrix in this partitioning is $r \times s$, enables us to write

$$C\tau_{mrp}(A \otimes B)K_{nq} = C_1 \otimes B \otimes a^{1'} + \cdots + C_m \otimes B \otimes a^{m'}$$
$$= (C \otimes B)\tau_{m,pr,1}A$$

as $C_j \otimes B$ is $pr \times sq$ for $j = 1, \ldots, m$. Using Theorem 2.3 again, we write

$$K_{pm}(A \otimes B) = \begin{pmatrix} A \otimes b^{1'} \\ \vdots \\ A \otimes b^{p'} \end{pmatrix}$$

whereas we partition D as follows:

$$D = \begin{pmatrix} D_1 \\ \vdots \\ D_p \end{pmatrix}$$

where each submatrix in this partitioning is $r \times t$. It follows that

$$K_{pm}(A \otimes B)\tau_{pmr}D = (A \otimes b^{1'}) \otimes D_1 + \cdots + (A \otimes b^{p'}) \otimes D_p$$
$$= A \otimes (b^{1'} \otimes D_1) + \cdots + A \otimes (b^{p'} \otimes D_p)$$
$$= A \otimes (b^{1'} \otimes D_1 + \cdots + b^{p'} \otimes D_p) = A \otimes (B\tau_{p1r}D).$$

∎

2.5 Generalized Vecs and Rvecs of the Commutation Matrix

At the start of Section 2.3, we saw that we can write the commutation matrix K_{mn} as

$$K_{mn} = \begin{bmatrix} I_n \otimes e_1^{m'} \\ \vdots \\ I_n \otimes e_m^{m'} \end{bmatrix} = \begin{bmatrix} I_m \otimes e_1^n \ldots I_m \otimes e_n^n \end{bmatrix},$$

where e_j^n is the jth column of the $n \times n$ identity matrix I_n. It follows that $\mathrm{rvec}_n K_{mn}$ is the $n \times nm^2$ matrix given by

$$\mathrm{rvec}_n K_{mn} = \begin{bmatrix} I_n \otimes e_1^{m'} \ldots I_n \otimes e_m^{m'} \end{bmatrix} \tag{2.30}$$

and $\text{vec}_m K_{mn}$ is the $mn^2 \times m$ matrix given by

$$\text{vec}_m K_{mn} = \begin{bmatrix} I_m \otimes e_1^n \\ \vdots \\ I_m \otimes e_n^n \end{bmatrix}. \tag{2.31}$$

For example,

$$\text{rvec}_2 K_{32} = \begin{bmatrix} 100000010000001000 \\ 000100000010000001 \end{bmatrix},$$

and

$$\text{vec}_3 K_{32} = \begin{bmatrix} 100 \\ 000 \\ 010 \\ 000 \\ 001 \\ 000 \\ 000 \\ 100 \\ 000 \\ 010 \\ 000 \\ 001 \end{bmatrix}.$$

These matrices will be important for us in matrix calculus in deriving derivatives of expressions involving $\text{vec}(A \otimes I_G)$ or $\text{vec}(I_G \otimes A)$.

From Theorem 2.9, we see that for an $m \times n$ matrix A

$$\text{vec}(A \otimes I_G) = \begin{bmatrix} I_n \otimes \begin{pmatrix} I_m \otimes e_1^G \\ \vdots \\ I_m \otimes e_G^G \end{pmatrix} \end{bmatrix} \text{vec } A.$$

Using Equation 2.31, we can now write

$$\text{vec}(A \otimes I_G) = (I_n \otimes \text{vec }_m K_{mG}) \text{vec } A. \tag{2.32}$$

Note for the special case in which A is an $m \times 1$ vector a, we have

$$\text{vec}(a \otimes I_G) = (\text{vec}_m K_{mG}) a. \tag{2.33}$$

In a similar fashion, we can write

$$
\operatorname{vec}(I_G \otimes A) = \left[\begin{pmatrix} I_n \otimes e_1^G \\ \vdots \\ I_n \otimes e_G^G \end{pmatrix} \otimes I_m \right] \operatorname{vec} A
$$
$$
= (\operatorname{vec}_n K_{nG} \otimes I_m) \operatorname{vec} A, \tag{2.34}
$$

and for the special case where a is $m \times 1$, we have

$$
\operatorname{vec}(I_G \otimes a) = (\operatorname{vec} I_G \otimes I_m)a. \tag{2.35}
$$

In Chapter 4, we have occasion to take the vec of a generalized vec of a commutation matrix. The following theorem tells us what happens when we do this.

Theorem 2.20

$$
\operatorname{vec}(\operatorname{vec}_m K_{mn}) = \operatorname{vec} I_{mn} = \operatorname{vec}\,(\operatorname{vec}_m K_{mn})' = \operatorname{vec} I_{nm}.
$$

Proof: Write

$$
\operatorname{vec}_m K_{mn} = \begin{pmatrix} I_m \otimes e_1^n \\ \vdots \\ I_m \otimes e_n^n \end{pmatrix} = \begin{pmatrix} e_1^m \otimes e_1^n & \cdots & e_m^m \otimes e_1^n \\ \vdots & & \vdots \\ e_1^m \otimes e_n^n & \cdots & e_m^m \otimes e_n^n \end{pmatrix},
$$

so

$$
\operatorname{vec}(\operatorname{vec}_m K_{mn}) = \begin{pmatrix} e_1^m \otimes e_1^n \\ \vdots \\ e_1^m \otimes e_n^n \\ \vdots \\ e_m^m \otimes e_1^n \\ \vdots \\ e_m^m \otimes e_n^n \end{pmatrix}
$$
$$
= \operatorname{vec}\left(e_1^m \otimes e_1^n \ldots e_1^m \otimes e_n^n \ldots e_m^m \otimes e_1^n \ldots e_m^m \otimes e_n^n \right)
$$
$$
= \operatorname{vec}\left(e_1^m \otimes \left(e_1^n \ldots e_n^n \right) \ldots e_m^m \otimes \left(e_1^n \ldots e_n^n \right) \right)
$$
$$
= \operatorname{vec}\left(e_1^m \otimes I_n \ldots e_m^m \otimes I_n \right) = \operatorname{vec}\,(I_m \otimes I_n) = \operatorname{vec} I_{mn},
$$

where in our working we have used Equation 1.4 of Chapter 1.

Now,

$$vec(vec_m K_{mn})' = vec\left(I_m \otimes e_1^{n'} \ldots I_m \otimes e_n^{n'}\right)$$

$$= \begin{pmatrix} vec\left(I_m \otimes e_1^{n'}\right) \\ \vdots \\ vec\left(I_m \otimes e_n^{n'}\right) \end{pmatrix} = \begin{pmatrix} vec\left(e_1^n \otimes I_m\right) \\ \vdots \\ vec\left(e_n^n \otimes I_m\right) \end{pmatrix}$$

$$= vec\left(e_1^n \otimes I_m \ldots e_n^n \otimes I_m\right) = vec\, I_{nm},$$

where in our working we have used Equation 1.13 of Chapter 1.   ∎

2.5.1 Deriving Results for Generalized Vecs and Rvecs of the Commutation Matrix

Recall that for A a $m \times n$ matrix and B an $n \times Gp$ matrix

$$vec_G AB = (I_p \otimes A)vec_G B.$$

We can use this property to derive results for generalized vecs of commutation matrices from known results about commutation matrices. For example, as

$$K_{Gn} K_{nG} = I_{nG}$$

we have taking the vec_n of both sides that

$$(I_G \otimes K_{Gn})vec_n K_{nG} = vec_n I_{nG} = (vec\, I_G \otimes I_n),$$

using Equation 1.16 of Section 1.4.1 in Chapter 1, so we can now write $vec_n K_{nG}$ in terms of the commutation matrix K_{nG} as follows

$$vec_n K_{nG} = (I_G \otimes K_{nG})(vec\, I_G \otimes I_n). \tag{2.36}$$

An alternative expression in terms of the commutation matrix K_{Gn} can be obtained by noting that

$$vec\, I_G \otimes I_n = K_{G^2 n}(I_n \otimes vec\, I_G)$$

so using Equation 2.9 of Section 2.3, we have

$$vec_n K_{nG} = (I_G \otimes K_{nG})(I_G \otimes K_{Gn})(K_{Gn} \otimes I_G)(I_n \otimes vec\, I_G)$$
$$= (K_{Gn} \otimes I_G)(I_n \otimes vec\, I_G). \tag{2.37}$$

Recall also that for A an $m \times np$ matrix

$$rvec_n A' = (vec_n A)' \tag{2.38}$$

so the equivalent results for $\text{rvec}_n K_{Gn}$ are found by taking the transposes of Equations 2.37 and 2.36. They are

$$\text{rvec}_n K_{Gn} = [I_n \otimes \text{rvec}\, I_G](K_{nG} \otimes I_G) = [\text{rvec}\, I_G \otimes I_n](I_G \otimes K_{Gn}).$$
(2.39)

Other results for $\text{vec}_n K_{nG}$ and $\text{rvec}_G K_{nG}$ can be obtained in a similar manner. For example, if A is an $m \times n$ matrix and B is an $p \times q$ matrix, we know that

$$K_{pm}(A \otimes B) = (B \otimes A)K_{qn}.$$

Then, taking the vec_q of both sides, using Theorem 1.12 of Section 1.4.3 in Chapter 1, we have

$$(I_n \otimes K_{pm})\text{vec}_q(A \otimes B) = (I_n \otimes B \otimes A)\text{vec}_q K_{qn}.$$

That is,

$$(I_n \otimes B \otimes A)\text{vec}_q K_{qn} = (I_n \otimes K_{pm})(\text{vec}\, A \otimes B)$$
$$= \begin{pmatrix} B \otimes a_1 \\ \vdots \\ B \otimes a_n \end{pmatrix},$$

by Equation 2.23.

If b is an $p \times 1$ vector, we know that

$$K_{pm}(A \otimes b) = b \otimes A$$
$$K_{mp}(b \otimes A) = A \otimes b.$$

Taking the generalized rvecs of both sides of these equations, we have using Equations 1.18 and 1.19 of Section 1.4.4 in Chapter 1, that

$$(\text{rvec}_m K_{pm})(I_p \otimes A \otimes b) = b' \otimes A$$
(2.40)

$$(\text{rvec}_p K_{mp})(I_m \otimes b \otimes A) = \text{rvec}\, A \otimes b.$$
(2.41)

Further results about generalized vecs and rvecs can be obtained by applying the following theorem:

Theorem 2.21

$$(\text{rvec}_G K_{nG})(K_{nG} \otimes I_n)K_{nG,n} = (\text{rvec}_G K_{nG})(I_n \otimes K_{Gn})K_{n,nG} = \text{rvec}_G K_{nG}$$
$$K_{n,nG}(K_{Gn} \otimes I_n)\text{vec}_G K_{Gn} = K_{nG,n}(I_n \otimes K_{nG})\text{vec}_G K_{Gn} = \text{vec}\,_G K_{Gn}.$$

Proof: Using Equation 2.39 and Equation 2.9

$$(\text{rvec}_G K_{nG})(K_{nG} \otimes I_n)K_{nG,n} = [I_G \otimes (\text{vec } I_n)'](K_{Gn} \otimes I_n)(K_{nG} \otimes I_n)K_{nG,n}$$
$$= [I_G \otimes (\text{vec } I_n')](I_G \otimes K_{nn})(K_{Gn} \otimes I_n)$$
$$= [I_G \otimes (\text{vec } I_n)'K_{nn}](K_{Gn} \otimes I_n)$$
$$= [I_G \otimes (\text{vec } I_n)'](K_{Gn} \otimes I_n) = \text{rvec}_G K_{nG}.$$

The second result for $\text{rvec}_G K_{nG}$ can be achieved in a similar manner provided we note that $K_{n,nG} = (K_{nG,n})'$.

The equivalent results for $\text{vec}_G K_{Gn}$ can then be obtained by taking transposes. ∎

To illustrate the use of Theorem 2.21, write the left-hand side of Equation 2.40 as:

$$\text{rvec}_m K_{pm}[I_p \otimes K_{mp}(b \otimes A)]$$
$$= \text{rvec}_m K_{pm}(I_p \otimes K_{mp})[I_p \otimes (b \otimes A)]$$
$$= \text{rvec}_m K_{pm}(I_p \otimes K_{mp})K_{p,mp}((b \otimes A) \otimes I_p)K_{np}$$
$$= \text{rvec}_m K_{pm}(b \otimes A \otimes I_p)K_{np},$$

so from Equation 2.40, we have that

$$(\text{rvec}_m K_{pm})(b \otimes A \otimes I_p) = (b' \otimes A)K_{pn} = A \otimes b'.$$

In a similar fashion, using Equation 2.41, we get

$$(\text{rvec}_p K_{mp})(A \otimes b \otimes I_m) = b \otimes (\text{vec } A)'.$$

Similar results can be achieved by taking the appropriate generalized vec of both sides of Equation 2.40 and 2.41, but the details are left to the reader.

For a final example of the use of this technique, consider A an $m \times n$ matrix and consider the basic definition of the commutation matrix K_{mn}, namely

$$K_{mn} \text{vec } A = \text{vec } A'.$$

Taking the rvec_n of both sides of this equation, we have

$$(\text{rvec}_n K_{mn})(I_m \otimes \text{vec } A) = \text{rvec}_n \text{vec } A' = A'$$

but

$$(\text{rvec}_n K_{mn})(I_m \otimes \text{vec } A) = (\text{rvec}_n K_{mn})(I_m \otimes K_{nm} \text{vec } A')$$
$$= (\text{rvec}_n K_{mn})(I_m \otimes K_{nm})K_{m,mn}(\text{vec } A' \otimes I_m)$$
$$= \text{rvec}_n K_{mn}(\text{vec } A' \otimes I_m)$$

so

$$\operatorname{rvec}_n K_{mn}(\operatorname{vec} A' \otimes I_m) = A'$$

as well.

Another theorem linking the generalized rvec of a commutation matrix with other commutation matrices is as follows:

Theorem 2.22

$$(I_G \otimes \operatorname{rvec}_m K_{qm})(K_{G,qm} \otimes I_q) = K_{Gm}\operatorname{rvec}_{mG}K_{q,mG} \qquad (2.42)$$

Proof: Using the definition of the commutation matrix given by Equation 2.8, we can write the left-hand side of Equation 2.42 as

$$\begin{pmatrix} \operatorname{rvec}_m K_{qm} & & O \\ & \ddots & \\ O & & \operatorname{rvec}_m K_{qm} \end{pmatrix} \begin{pmatrix} I_{qm} \otimes e_1^{G'} \otimes I_q \\ \vdots \\ I_{qm} \otimes e_G^{G'} \otimes I_q \end{pmatrix}$$

$$= \begin{pmatrix} \operatorname{rvec}_m K_{qm}\left(I_{qm} \otimes e_1^{G'} \otimes I_q \right) \\ \vdots \\ \operatorname{rvec}_m K_{qm}\left(I_{qm} \otimes e_G^{G'} \otimes I_q \right) \end{pmatrix}.$$

Consider the first block in this matrix, which using the definition of the generalized rvec of the commutation matrix given by Equation 2.30 can be written as

$$\left(I_m \otimes e_1^{q'} \ldots I_m \otimes e_q^{q'} \right) \begin{pmatrix} I_m \otimes e_1^{G'} \otimes I_q & & O \\ & \ddots & \\ O & & I_m \otimes e_1^{G'} \otimes I_q \end{pmatrix}$$

$$= I_m \otimes e_1^{q'}\left(e_1^{G'} \otimes I_q \right) \ldots I_m \otimes e_q^{q'}\left(e_1^{G'} \otimes I_q \right)$$

$$= I_m \otimes e_1^{G'} \otimes e_1^{q'} \ldots I_m \otimes e_1^{G'} \otimes e_q^{q'}$$

$$= \left(e_1^{q'} \otimes I_m \otimes e_1^{G'} \right) K_{q,mG} \ldots \left(e_q^{q'} \otimes I_m \otimes e_1^{G'} \right) K_{q,mG}$$

$$= \left(e_1^{q'} \otimes I_m \otimes e_1^{G'} \ldots e_q^{q'} \otimes I_m \otimes e_1^{G'} \right) (I_q \otimes K_{q,mG})$$

$$= \left(\operatorname{rvec} I_q \otimes \left(I_m \otimes e_1^{G'} \right) \right) (I_q \otimes K_{q,mG}).$$

It follows this that the left-hand side of Equation 2.42 can be written as

$$\begin{pmatrix} \operatorname{rvec} I_q \otimes I_m \otimes e_1^{G'} \\ \vdots \\ \operatorname{rvec} I_q \otimes I_m \otimes e_G^{G'} \end{pmatrix} (I_q \otimes K_{q,mG})$$

$$= \begin{pmatrix} I_m \otimes e_1^{G'} \otimes \operatorname{rvec} I_q \\ \vdots \\ I_m \otimes e_G^{G'} \otimes \operatorname{rvec} I_q \end{pmatrix} K_{mG,q^2}(I_q \otimes I_{q,mG})$$

$$= (K_{Gm} \otimes \operatorname{rvec} I_q)(K_{mG,q} \otimes I_q)$$

$$= K_{mG}(I_{mG} \otimes \operatorname{rvec} I_q)(K_{mG,q} \otimes I_q)$$

$$= K_{mG}\operatorname{rvec}_{mG}K_{mG,q}$$

where in the working we have used Equations 2.9 and 2.39. ∎

Other theorems stand on their own:

Theorem 2.23 *Let b be an $n \times 1$ vector and let A be an $Gn \times p$ matrix. Then,*

$$(\operatorname{rvec}_G K_{nG})(b \otimes A) = (I_G \otimes b')A.$$

Proof: Write $(\operatorname{rvec}_G K_{nG})(b \otimes A) = (\operatorname{rvec}_G K_{nG})(b \otimes I_{nG})A.$
Now,

$$\operatorname{rvec}_G K_{nG}(b \otimes I_{nG}) = \left(I_G \otimes e_1^{n'} \ldots I_G \otimes e_n^{n'}\right) \begin{pmatrix} b_1 I_{nG} \\ \vdots \\ b_n I_{nG} \end{pmatrix}$$

$$= b_1\left(I_G \otimes e_1^{n'}\right) + \cdots + b_n\left(I_G \otimes e_n^{n'}\right) = I_G \otimes b'. \quad ∎$$

Theorem 2.24 *Let A and B be $mG \times p$ and $nG \times q$ matrices, respectively, and let C and D be $G \times r$ and $G \times s$ matrices respectively.*
  Then,

$$(\operatorname{rvec}_m K_{Gm})(A \otimes C) = (\operatorname{rvec}_m A)K_{Gp}(I_p \otimes C)$$

$$(\operatorname{rvec}_n K_{Gn})(D \otimes B) = (\operatorname{rvec}_n K_{Gn}B)(D \otimes I_q).$$

Proof: Partition A as in Equation 1.7 of Section 1.3 in Chapter 1. Then,

$$(\text{rvec}_m K_{Gm})(A \otimes I_G) = \left(I_m \otimes e_1^{G'} \ldots I_m \otimes e_G^{G'} \right) \begin{pmatrix} A_1 \otimes I_G \\ \vdots \\ A_G \otimes I_G \end{pmatrix}$$

$$= A_1 \otimes e_1^{G'} + \cdots + A_G \otimes e_G^{G'}$$

$$= (A_1 \ldots A_G) \begin{pmatrix} I_p \otimes e_1^{G'} \\ \vdots \\ I_p \otimes e_G^{G'} \end{pmatrix} = (\text{rvec}_m A) K_{Gp}.$$

The first result follows.
  Write

$$(\text{rvec}_n K_{Gn})(D \otimes B) = \text{rvec}_n K_{Gn}(I_G \otimes B)(D \otimes I_q) = (\text{rvec}_n K_{Gn} B)(D \otimes I_q).$$

∎

The equivalent results for generalized vecs are

$$(b' \otimes A')\text{vec}_G K_{Gn} = A'(I_G \otimes b).$$

$$(A' \otimes C')\text{vec}_m K_{mG} = (I_p \otimes C')K_{pG}\text{vec}_m A'$$

$$(D' \otimes B')\text{vec}_n K_{nG} = (D' \otimes I_q)\text{vec}_n B' K_{nG}.$$

Suppose now A is an $p \times G$ matrix. Then, by Equation 1.19 of Section 1.3 in Chapter 1,

$$\text{rvec}_m \left[K_{Gm}(I_m \otimes A') \right] = (\text{rvec}_m K_{Gm})(I_{Gm} \otimes A').$$

The following theorem shows there are several ways of writing this matrix.

Theorem 2.25 *Let A be an $p \times G$ matrix. Then,*

$$(\text{rvec}_m K_{Gm})(I_{Gm} \otimes A') = (\text{rvec}_m K_{pm})(A \otimes I_{pm}) = I_m \otimes a_1' \ldots I_m \otimes a_G'$$
$$= (\text{rvec } A' \otimes I_m)(I_G \otimes K_{pm}),$$

where a_j is the jth column of A.

Proof: Using Equation 2.30, we write

$$(\text{rvec}_m K_{Gm})(I_{Gm} \otimes A')$$

$$= \left(I_m \otimes e_1^{G'} \dots I_m \otimes e_G^{G'} \right) \begin{pmatrix} I_m \otimes A' & & O \\ & \ddots & \\ O & & I_m \otimes A' \end{pmatrix}$$

$$= I_m \otimes e_1^{G'} A' \dots I_m \otimes e_G^{G'} A' = I_m \otimes a_1' \dots I_m \otimes a_G'$$

where a_j is the jth column of A. Again using the Equation 2.30, we write

$$(\text{rvec}_m K_{pm})(A \otimes I_{pm}) = \left(I_m \otimes e_1^{p'} \dots I_m \otimes e_p^{p'} \right) \begin{pmatrix} a_{11} I_{mp} & \cdots & a_{1G} I_{mp} \\ \vdots & & \vdots \\ a_{p1} I_{mp} & \cdots & a_{pG} I_{mp} \end{pmatrix}.$$

Consider the jth block of this expression, which is

$$a_{1j} \left(I_m \otimes e_1^{p'} \right) + \cdots + a_{pj} \left(I_m \otimes e_p^{p'} \right)$$

$$= I_m \otimes \left(a_{ij} e_1^{p'} + \cdots + a_{pj} e_p^{p'} \right) = I_m \otimes a_j'$$

so the result follows.

Finally,

$$I_m \otimes a_1' \dots I_m \otimes a_G' = (a_1' \otimes I_m) K_{pm} \dots (a_G' \otimes I_m) K_{pm}$$

$$= \left[(a_1' \dots a_G') \otimes I_m \right] (I_G \otimes K_{pm})$$

$$= (\text{rvec } A' \otimes I_m)(I_G \otimes K_{pm}). \qquad \blacksquare$$

Theorem 2.26 *Let A be an mG × p matrix. Then,*

$$(\text{rvec}_{qG} K_{m,qG})(I_{qm} \otimes A) = I_q \otimes A^{(1)} \dots I_q \otimes A^{(m)}.$$

Proof: From the definition of the generalized rvec of the commutation matrix given by Equation 2.30, we can write

$$(\text{rvec}_{qG} K_{m,qG})(I_{qm} \otimes A)$$

$$= \left(I_{qG} \otimes e_1^{m'} \dots I_{qG} \otimes e_m^{m'} \right) \begin{pmatrix} I_q \otimes A & & O \\ & \ddots & \\ O & & I_q \otimes A \end{pmatrix}$$

$$= I_q \otimes \left(I_G \otimes e_1^{m'} \right) A \dots I_q \otimes \left(I_G \otimes e_m^{m'} \right) A = I_q \otimes A^{(1)} \dots I_q \otimes A^{(m)},$$

as in Section 2.2, we saw that

$$\left(I_G \otimes e_j^{m'}\right) A = A^{(j)}.$$ ∎

From Theorem 2.4, if A is $m \times n$ and B is $p \times q$, then

$$(A \otimes B)K_{nq} = (A \otimes b_1 \ldots A \otimes b_q),$$

where each submatrix $A \otimes b_j$ is $mp \times n$.

It follows that

$$\text{vec}_n\left[(A \otimes B)K_{nq}\right] = \begin{pmatrix} A \otimes b_1 \\ \vdots \\ A \otimes b_q \end{pmatrix}.$$

But the following theorem shows there are several ways of writing this matrix, two involving a generalized vec of the commutation matrix.

Theorem 2.27 *Let A and B be $m \times n$ and $p \times q$ matrices, respectively. Then,*

$$\text{vec}_n[(A \otimes B)K_{nq}] = (I_q \otimes A \otimes B)\text{vec}_n K_{nq} = (I_q \otimes K_{mp})(\text{vec } B \otimes A)$$
$$= (K_{qm} \otimes I_p)(A \otimes \text{vec } B) = (B' \otimes I_{mp})(\text{vec}_m K_{mp})A.$$

Proof: From the properties of generalized vec operators, we have

$$\text{vec}_n[(A \otimes B)K_{nq}] = (I_q \otimes A \otimes B)\text{vec}_n K_{nq}.$$

Now,

$$\text{vec}_n[(A \otimes B)K_{nq}] = \text{vec }_n[K_{mp}(B \otimes A)] = (I_q \otimes K_{mp})\text{vec}_n(B \otimes A)$$
$$= (I_q \otimes K_{mp})(\text{vec } B \otimes A).$$

But

$$(I_q \otimes K_{mp})(\text{vec } B \otimes A) = (I_q \otimes K_{mp})K_{pq,m}(A \otimes \text{vec } B)$$
$$= (K_{qm} \otimes I_p)(A \otimes \text{vec } B),$$

where we have used Equation 2.9 of Section 2.3. Finally, using Theorem 1.13 of Section 1.4.4 in Chapter 1, we have

$$\text{vec}_n[K_{mp}(B \otimes A)] = (B' \otimes I_{mp})(\text{vec}_m K_{mp})A.$$ ∎

The equivalent results for generalized rvec operators are found by taking transposes. If C is a $n \times m$ matrix and D is a $q \times p$ matrix, then

$$\text{rvec}_n[K_{qn}(C \otimes D)] = [(\text{rvec}_n K_{qn})(I_q \otimes C \otimes D)]$$
$$= (\text{rvec } D \otimes C)(I_q \otimes K_{pm}) = (C \otimes \text{rvec } D)(K_{mq} \otimes I_p)$$
$$= C(\text{rvec}_m K_{pm})(D' \otimes I_{mp}) = (C \otimes d^{1'} \dots C \otimes d^{q'}).$$

For further such theorems on generalized vecs and rvecs of the commutation, see Turkington (2005).

2.5.2 Generalized Vecs and Rvecs of the Commutation Matrix and Cross-Products

In this section, we demonstrate that there are intimate connections between the cross-product $A\tau_{Gmn}B$, the Kronecker product $A \otimes B$, and the generalized rvec of the commutation matrix.

The next two theorems clearly bring out the relationships that exist between these concepts.

Theorem 2.28 *Let A be an $mG \times p$ matrix and B be an $nG \times q$ matrix. Then,*

$$A\tau_{Gmn}B = (\text{rvec}_m K_{Gm} \otimes I_n)(A \otimes B)$$

$$K_{Gm}A\tau_{Gmn}K_{Gn}B = (I_m \otimes \text{rvec}_n K_{Gn})(A \otimes B).$$

Proof: Using Equation 2.30 of Section 2.5 and partitioning A and B as in Equation 1.7 of Section 1.3 in Chapter 1, we write

$$(\text{rvec}_m K_{Gm} \otimes I_n)(A \otimes B)$$

$$= \left(I_m \otimes e_1^{G'} \otimes I_n \dots I_m \otimes e_G^{G'} \otimes I_n\right) \begin{pmatrix} A_1 \otimes B \\ \vdots \\ A_G \otimes B \end{pmatrix}$$

$$= A_1 \otimes \left(e_1^{G'} \otimes I_n\right) B + \dots + A_G \otimes \left(e_G^{G'} \otimes I_n\right) B$$

$$= A_1 \otimes B_1 + \dots + A_G \otimes B_G = A\tau_{Gmn}B.$$

Now,

$$K_{Gm}A\tau_{Gmn}K_{Gn}B = (K_{Gm}\tau_{Gmn}K_{Gn})(A \otimes B) = (I_m \otimes \text{rvec}_n K_{Gn})(A \otimes B)$$

by Theorem 2.16.   ∎

Notice that Theorem 2.28 is easily reconciled with Theorem 2.17 using Theorem 2.24.

Theorem 2.29 *Suppose A be an $Gm \times p$ matrix and B be an $G \times q$ matrix. Then,*

$$(\text{rvec}_m K_{Gm})(A \otimes B) = A\tau_{Gm1} B.$$

Proof: Partition A as follows

$$A = \begin{pmatrix} A_1 \\ \vdots \\ A_G \end{pmatrix}$$

where each submatrix is $m \times p$, so

$$A \otimes B = \begin{pmatrix} A_1 \otimes B \\ \vdots \\ A_G \otimes B \end{pmatrix},$$

and

$$(\text{rvec}_m K_{Gm})(A \otimes B) = \left(I_m \otimes e_1^{G'} \cdots I_m \otimes e_G^{G'} \right) \begin{pmatrix} A_1 \otimes B \\ \vdots \\ A_G \otimes B \end{pmatrix}$$

$$= A_1 \otimes b^{1'} + \cdots + A_G \otimes b^{G'} = A\tau_{Gm1} B. \quad \blacksquare$$

We finish this section with a theorem that gives yet another way of writing the cross-product of $A\tau_{Gmn}B$ involving this time $\text{rvec}_G K_{mG}A$.

Theorem 2.30 *Let A be $mG \times p$ and B be $nG \times q$. Then,*

$$A\tau_{Gmn}B = \text{vec}_{pq}\left[(\text{rvec}_G K_{mG}A)\tau_{G1n}B \right].$$

Proof: From Theorem 1.6 of Section 1.3 in Chapter 1

$$A\tau_{Gmn}B = \begin{pmatrix} A^{(1)}\tau_{G1n}B \\ \vdots \\ A^{(m)}\tau_{G1n}B \end{pmatrix}.$$

But, we saw in Theorem 2.10 that $K_{mG}A = \begin{pmatrix} A^{(1)} \\ \vdots \\ A^{(m)} \end{pmatrix}$ so $\mathrm{rvec}_G K_{mG}A =$

$(A^{(1)} \ldots A^{(m)})$ and $\mathrm{rvec}\, K_{mG}A\tau_{G1n}B = (A^{(1)} \ldots A^{(m)})\tau_{G1n}B = (A^{(1)}\tau_{G1n}$ $B \ldots A^{(m)}\tau_{G1n}B)$, by Theorem 1.3 of Section 1.3 in Chapter 1. As each of the submatrices $A^{(i)}\tau_{G1n}B$ is $1 \times pq$ for $i = 1, \ldots, m$ it follows that $\mathrm{vec}_{pq}[(\mathrm{rvec}_G K_{mG}A)\tau G_{1n}B] = A\tau_{Gmn}B$ by Theorem 1.6 of Chapter 1. ■

2.5.3 $K_{nG,G}$ versus $\mathrm{Rvec}_n K_{Gn}$

Both $K_{nG,G}$ and $\mathrm{rvec}_n K_{Gn}$ have nG^2 columns so it is of some interest to contrast what happens to a Kronecker product with nG^2 rows when it is premultiplied by these matrices. Let D be $G \times r$ and B be $nG \times q$, then $D \otimes B$ is such a matrix. From Theorem 2.3 of Section 2.4.1,

$$K_{nG,G}(D \otimes B) = \begin{pmatrix} D \otimes b^{1'} \\ \vdots \\ D \otimes b^{nG'} \end{pmatrix}.$$

The result for $\mathrm{rvec}_n K_{Gn}$ is given by the following theorem.

Theorem 2.31 *Let D be an $G \times r$ matrix and B be an $nG \times p$ matrix. Then,*

$$(\mathrm{rvec}_n K_{Gn})(D \otimes B) = \left[(I_n \otimes d_1')B \ldots (I_n \otimes d_r')B\right]$$

where d_j is the jth column of D.

Proof: Write

$$(\mathrm{rvec}_n K_{Gn})(D \otimes B) = (\mathrm{rvec}_n K_{nG})(D \otimes I_{nG})(I_r \otimes B),$$

where

$$(\mathrm{rvec}_n K_{nG})(D \otimes I_{nG}) = (\mathrm{rvec}_n K_{nG})(d_1 \otimes I_{nG} \ldots d_r \otimes I_{nG}).$$

But,

$$\mathrm{rvec}_n K_{nG}(d_1 \otimes I_{nG}) = I_n \otimes d_1'$$

by Theorem 2.23. ■

From Theorem 2.29, we have that

$$(\mathrm{rvec}_n K_{Gn})(B \otimes D) = B\tau_{Gn1}D.$$

The result for $K_{nG,G}(B \otimes D)$ is given by the following theorem.

Theorem 2.32 *Let D and B be $G \times r$ and $nG \times p$ matrices, respectively. Then,*

$$K_{nG,G}(B \otimes D) = \begin{pmatrix} B^{(1)} \otimes d^{1'} \\ \vdots \\ B^{(1)} \otimes d^{G'} \\ \vdots \\ B^{(n)} \otimes d^{1'} \\ \vdots \\ B^{(n)} \otimes d^{G'} \end{pmatrix}.$$

Proof: Write

$$K_{nG,G}(B \otimes D) = \begin{pmatrix} I_G \otimes e_1^{nG'} \\ \vdots \\ I_G \otimes e_{nG}^{nG'} \end{pmatrix} (B \otimes D).$$

Consider the first submatrix

$$\left(I_G \otimes e_1^{nG'} \right) (B \otimes D) = \left(I_G \otimes e_1^{n'} \otimes e_1^{G'} \right) (B \otimes D) = \left(I_G \otimes e_1^{n'} \right) B \otimes e_1^{G'} D.$$

But from our work in selection matrices in Section 2.2, $(I_G \otimes e_1^{n'})B = B^{(1)}$ and $e_1^{G'} D = d^{1'}$. The other submatrices are analysed in a similar fashion and the result follows. ∎

2.5.4 The Matrix N_n

Associated with the commutation matrix K_{nn} is the $n^2 \times n^2$ matrix N_n, which is defined by

$$N_n = \frac{1}{2}(I_{n^2} + K_{nn}).$$

From Equation 2.8, it is clear that we can write

$$N_n = \frac{1}{2} \begin{pmatrix} e_1^{n'} \otimes I_n + I_n \otimes e_1^{n'} \\ \vdots \\ e_n^{n'} \otimes I_n + I_n \otimes e_n^{n'} \end{pmatrix} \tag{2.43}$$

$$= \frac{1}{2} \left(e_1^n \otimes I_n + I_n \otimes e_1^n \dots e_n^n \otimes I_n + I_n \otimes e_n^n \right). \tag{2.44}$$

For example,

$$N_3 = \frac{1}{2} \begin{pmatrix} e_1^{3\prime} \otimes I_3 + I_3 \otimes e_1^{3\prime} \\ e_2^{3\prime} \otimes I_3 + I_3 \otimes e_2^{3\prime} \\ e_3^{3\prime} \otimes I_3 + I_3 \otimes e_3^{3\prime} \end{pmatrix}.$$

$$= \frac{1}{2} \begin{pmatrix} 200 & 000 & 000 \\ 010 & 100 & 000 \\ 001 & 000 & 100 \\ 010 & 100 & 000 \\ 000 & 020 & 000 \\ 000 & 001 & 010 \\ 001 & 000 & 100 \\ 000 & 001 & 010 \\ 000 & 000 & 002 \end{pmatrix}.$$

Clearly, N_n is not a zero-one matrix. It is an important matrix for us as

$$N_n \text{vec} \, A = \text{vec} \, \frac{1}{2}(A + A') \tag{2.45}$$

and if A is symmetric

$$N_n \text{vec} \, A = \text{vec} \, A. \tag{2.46}$$

Suppose A is an $n^2 \times p$ matrix and we partition A as

$$A = \begin{pmatrix} A_1 \\ \vdots \\ A_n \end{pmatrix}$$

where each submatrix in this partitioning is $n \times p$. Then, using Theorem 2.10 of the previous section, we have that

$$N_n A = \frac{1}{2}(I_{n^2} + K_{nn})A = \frac{1}{2}\begin{pmatrix} A_1 \\ \vdots \\ A_n \end{pmatrix} + \frac{1}{2}\begin{pmatrix} A^{(1)} \\ \vdots \\ A^{(n)} \end{pmatrix} = \frac{1}{2}\begin{pmatrix} A_1 + A^{(1)} \\ \vdots \\ A_n + A^{(n)} \end{pmatrix}$$

$$\tag{2.47}$$

That is, the jth submatrix of $N_n A$ is formed by adding onto A_j the matrix consisting of the jth rows of the submatrices of A.

Notice also that as K_{nn} is symmetric and its own inverse

$$N_n K_{nn} = N_n = K_{nn} N_n.$$

and

$$N_n' = \frac{1}{2}(I_{n^2} + K_{nn})' = \frac{1}{2}(I_{n^2} + K_{nn}) = N_n$$

$$N_n N_n = \frac{1}{4}\left(I_{n^2} + K_{nn} + K_{nn} + K_{nn}^2\right) = N_n,$$

so N_n is symmetric idempotent.

Other properties for N_n can be derived from the corresponding properties for K_{nn}. If A and B are $n \times p$ and $n \times q$ matrices, respectively, then

$$N_n(A \otimes B) = \frac{1}{2}\left[(A \otimes B) + K_{nn}(A \otimes B)\right] = \frac{1}{2}\begin{pmatrix} a^{1'} \otimes B + A \otimes b^{1'} \\ \vdots \\ a^{n'} \otimes B + A \otimes b^{n'} \end{pmatrix},$$

(2.48)

where we have used Theorem 2.3. Similarly, if C and D are $p \times n$ and $q \times n$ matrices, respectively,

then

$$(C \otimes D)N_n = \frac{1}{2}(c_1 \otimes D + C \otimes d_1 \dots c_n \otimes D + C \otimes d_n) \quad (2.49)$$

where we have used Theorem 2.4.

If A and B are both $n \times n$ matrices, then

$$N_n(A \otimes B)N_n = \frac{1}{2}\begin{pmatrix} a^{1'} \otimes B + A \otimes b^{1'} \\ \vdots \\ a^{n'} \otimes B + A \otimes b^{n'} \end{pmatrix} N_n$$

$$= \frac{1}{4}\begin{pmatrix} a^{1'} \otimes B + A \otimes b^{1'} + B \otimes a^{1'} + b^{1'} \otimes A \\ \vdots \\ a^{n'} \otimes B + A \otimes b^{n'} + B \otimes a^{n'} + b^{n'} \otimes A \end{pmatrix}. \quad (2.50)$$

From these properties of N_n, it is clear that if A and B are $n \times n$ matrices and b is a $n \times 1$ vector, then

$$N_n(A \otimes B)N_n = N_n(B \otimes A)N_n$$

$$N_n(A \otimes A)N_n = N_n(A \otimes A) = (A \otimes A)N_n$$

$$N_n(A \otimes b) = N_n(b \otimes A) = \frac{1}{2}(A \otimes b + b \otimes A).$$

Additional properties of N_n can be found in Magnus (1988).

2.6 The Matrix U_{mn}

In Section 2.4, we wrote the commutation matrix K_{mn} in terms of elementary matrices as

$$K_{mn} = \begin{bmatrix} E_{11}^{nm} & \cdots & E_{n1}^{nm} \\ \vdots & & \vdots \\ E_{1m}^{nm} & \cdots & E_{nm}^{nm} \end{bmatrix}.$$

As each of these elementary matrices is $n \times m$, the commutation matrix, as we know, is $mn \times mn$. But in the commutation matrix, the subscripts of these elementary matrices appear out of natural order. For example, in the first block row we have $E_{11}^{nm} \ldots E_{n1}^{nm}$, whilst in the last block row we have $E_{1m}^{nm} \ldots E_{nm}^{nm}$. Moreover, the superscripts of the elementary matrices appear out of natural order as nm instead of mn.

A matrix that appears often in our work in Chapter 4 is made up of elementary matrices whose subscripts and superscripts appear in natural order. For want of a better symbol, the author denotes this matrix by U_{mn}. That is, U_{mn} is the $m^2 \times n^2$ matrix given by

$$U_{mn} = \begin{pmatrix} E_{11}^{mn} & \cdots & E_{1n}^{mn} \\ \vdots & & \vdots \\ E_{m1}^{mn} & \cdots & E_{mn}^{mn} \end{pmatrix}. \tag{2.51}$$

For example,

$$U_{32} = \begin{pmatrix} 1 & 0 & 0 & 1 \\ 0 & 0 & 0 & 0 \\ 0 & 0 & 0 & 0 \\ 0 & 0 & 0 & 0 \\ 1 & 0 & 0 & 1 \\ 0 & 0 & 0 & 0 \\ 0 & 0 & 0 & 0 \\ 0 & 0 & 0 & 0 \\ 1 & 0 & 0 & 1 \end{pmatrix}.$$

There are several ways we can write this matrix. Substituting $E_{ij}^{mn} = e_i^m e_j^{n'}$ into the matrix, we have

$$U_{mn} = \begin{pmatrix} e_1^m e_1^{n'} & \cdots & e_1^m e_n^{n'} \\ \vdots & & \vdots \\ e_m^m e_1^{n'} & \cdots & e_m^m e_n^{n'} \end{pmatrix}.$$

But $e_i^m e_j^{n'} = e_j^{n'} \otimes e_i^m = e_i^m \otimes e_j^{n'}$, so

$$U_{mn} = \begin{pmatrix} e_1^{n'} \otimes e_1^m & \cdots & e_n^{n'} \otimes e_1^m \\ \vdots & & \vdots \\ e_1^{n'} \otimes e_m^m & \cdots & e_n^{n'} \otimes e_m^m \end{pmatrix} = \begin{pmatrix} \text{rvec } I_n \otimes e_1^m \\ \vdots \\ \text{rvec } I_n \otimes e_m^m \end{pmatrix} \quad (2.52)$$

or

$$U_{mn} = \begin{pmatrix} e_1^m \otimes e_1^{n'} & \cdots & e_1^m \otimes e_n^{n'} \\ \vdots & & \vdots \\ e_m^m \otimes e_1^{n'} & \cdots & e_m^m \otimes e_n^{n'} \end{pmatrix} = \left(\text{vec } I_m \otimes e_1^{n'} \ldots \text{vec } I_m \otimes e_n^{n'} \right). \quad (2.53)$$

Using the same property again, we can write Equation 2.52 as

$$U_{mn} = \text{vec } I_m \otimes \text{rvec } I_n,$$

whereas Equation 2.53 can be written as

$$U_{mn} = \text{rvec } I_n \otimes \text{vec } I_m.$$

One final application of this property renders

$$U_{mn} = \text{vec } I_m \otimes \text{rvec } I_n = \text{rvec } I_n \otimes \text{vec } I_m = (\text{vec } I_m)(\text{rvec } I_n). \quad (2.54)$$

Notice that as $(E_{ij}^{mn})' = E_{ji}^{nm}$, we have $U_{mn}' = U_{nm}$.

In our work in Chapter 4, we need to know how U_{mn} interacts with Kronecker products. The following theorem tells us how.

Theorem 2.33 *Let A be an $r \times m$ matrix and B be an $s \times m$ matrix whilst C and D are $n \times u$ and $n \times v$ matrices, respectively. Then,*

$$(A \otimes B)U_{mn}(C \otimes D) = (\text{vec } BA')(\text{rvec } C'D) = (\text{vec } A\tau_{mrs}\text{vec } B)(C\tau_{n11}D).$$

Proof: From Equation 2.54

$$(A \otimes B)U_{mn}(C \otimes D) = (A \otimes B)\text{vec } I_m\text{rvec } I_n(C \otimes D).$$

But $(A \otimes B)\text{vec} I_m = \text{vec } BA'$ and $\text{rvec } I_n(C \otimes D) = \text{rvec } C'D$. In Section 1.4.2 of Chapter 1, we saw that $\text{rvec } I_n(C \otimes D) = C\tau_{n11}D$ and that $(A \otimes B)\text{vec } I_m = \text{vec } A\tau_{mrs}\text{vec } B$. ∎

2.7 Twining Matrices

2.7.1 Introduction

Often, in statistics and econometrics, we work with matrices that are formed by intertwining the rows (columns) of a set of matrices.

To understand what I mean by intertwining rows of matrices, consider two $m \times n$ matrices $A = \{a_{ij}\}$ and $B = \{b_{ij}\}$. Suppose we want to form a new matrix C from A and B by intertwining single rows of A and B together, taking the first row of A as the first row of C. That is,

$$
C = \begin{pmatrix}
a_{11} & a_{12} & \cdots & a_{1n} \\
b_{11} & b_{12} & \cdots & b_{1n} \\
\vdots & \vdots & & \vdots \\
a_{m1} & a_{m2} & \cdots & a_{mn} \\
b_{m1} & b_{m2} & \cdots & b_{mn}
\end{pmatrix}.
$$

Suppose we form a new matrix D from A and B by intertwining rows of A and B, taking two rows at a time, assuming m is even so

$$
D = \begin{pmatrix}
a_{11} & a_{12} & \cdots & a_{1n} \\
a_{21} & a_{22} & \cdots & a_{2n} \\
b_{11} & b_{12} & \cdots & b_{1n} \\
b_{21} & b_{22} & \cdots & b_{2n} \\
\vdots & \vdots & & \vdots \\
a_{m-11} & a_{m-12} & \cdots & a_{m-1n} \\
a_{m1} & a_{m2} & \cdots & a_{mn} \\
b_{m-11} & b_{m-12} & \cdots & b_{m-1n} \\
b_{m1} & b_{m2} & \cdots & b_{mn}
\end{pmatrix}.
$$

Clearly, from A and B we can form a new matrix by intertwining any r rows at a time where r is a divisor of m.

Suppose, more generally now, A is $m \times n$ and B is $2m \times n$, and I want to form a new matrix E by intertwining rows of A and B, taking one row from A and two rows from B so

$$E = \begin{pmatrix} a_{11} & a_{12} & \cdots & a_{1n} \\ b_{11} & b_{12} & \cdots & b_{1n} \\ b_{21} & b_{22} & \cdots & b_{2n} \\ \vdots & \vdots & & \vdots \\ a_{m1} & a_{m2} & \cdots & a_{mn} \\ b_{2m-11} & b_{2m-12} & \cdots & b_{2m-1n} \\ b_{2m1} & b_{2m2} & \cdots & b_{2mn} \end{pmatrix}.$$

In this section, it is shown that such intertwining of any number of rows of A and B, where the number of rows from A may differ from those of B, can be achieved by premultiplying the matrix $(A'B')'$ by a permutation matrix which, as I say, I call a twining matrix.

2.7.2 Definition and Explicit Expressions for a Twining Matrix

Let A and B be two matrices and partition these matrices as follows:

$$A = \begin{pmatrix} A_1 \\ \vdots \\ A_G \end{pmatrix}, \quad B = \begin{pmatrix} B_1 \\ \vdots \\ B_G \end{pmatrix} \tag{2.55}$$

where each submatrix A_i is $m_i \times \ell$ for $i = 1, \ldots, G$, and each submatrix B_j is $p_j \times \ell$ for $j = 1, \ldots, G$. Then, T is a **twining matrix** if

$$T \begin{pmatrix} A \\ B \end{pmatrix} = \begin{pmatrix} A_1 \\ B_1 \\ \vdots \\ A_G \\ B_G \end{pmatrix}.$$

Clearly, T is the $(m + p) \times (m + p)$ permutation matrix, where $m = \sum_{i=1}^{G} m_i$ and $p = \sum_{j=1}^{G} p_j$ given by

$$T = \begin{pmatrix} I_{m_1} & O & \cdots & O & \cdot & O & O & \cdots & O \\ O & O & \cdots & O & \cdot & I_{p1} & O & \cdots & O \\ O & I_{m_2} & \cdots & O & \cdot & O & O & \cdots & O \\ O & O & \cdots & O & \cdot & O & I_{p_2} & \cdots & O \\ \vdots & \vdots & & \vdots & \cdot & \vdots & \vdots & & \vdots \\ O & O & \cdots & I_{m_G} & \cdot & O & O & \cdots & O \\ O & O & \cdots & O & \cdot & O & O & & I_{p_G} \end{pmatrix}.$$

A lot of the mathematics in this book concerns itself with the case where A is an $mG \times p$ matrix and B is an $nG \times q$ matrix, and each of those matrices are partitioned into G submatrices. For A, each submatrix is of order $m \times p$ and for B, each submatrix is of order $n \times q$. If $p = q = \ell$ say, then the twining matrix can be written as

$$T = \left(I_G \otimes \begin{pmatrix} I_m \\ O \\ {}_{n \times m} \end{pmatrix} : I_G \otimes \begin{pmatrix} O \\ {}^{m \times n} \\ I_n \end{pmatrix} \right) \tag{2.56}$$

We now introduce the following notation:

Notation: Denote the twining matrix given by Equation 2.56 as $T_{G,m,n}$.

In this notation, the first subscript refers to the common number of submatrices in the partitions of the two matrices, the second subscript refers to the number of rows in each submatrix of A and the third subscript refers to the number of rows in each of the submatrices of B.

An example is,

$$T_{2,1,3} = \begin{pmatrix} 1 & 0 & 0 & 0 & 0 & 0 & 0 & 0 \\ 0 & 0 & 1 & 0 & 0 & 0 & 0 & 0 \\ 0 & 0 & 0 & 1 & 0 & 0 & 0 & 0 \\ 0 & 0 & 0 & 0 & 1 & 0 & 0 & 0 \\ 0 & 1 & 0 & 0 & 0 & 0 & 0 & 0 \\ 0 & 0 & 0 & 0 & 0 & 1 & 0 & 0 \\ 0 & 0 & 0 & 0 & 0 & 0 & 1 & 0 \\ 0 & 0 & 0 & 0 & 0 & 0 & 0 & 1 \end{pmatrix}.$$

Like all other permutation matrices, the twining matrix is orthogonal, that is $T_{G,m,n}^{-1} = T'_{G,m,n}$. Note also that $T_{1,m,n} = \begin{pmatrix} I_m & O \\ O & I_n \end{pmatrix} = I_{m+n}$. It is also of some interest that $T_{G,m,p}$ is an intertwined matrix itself. As $T_{G,m,n} I_{G(m+n)} = T_{G,m,n}$, the twining matrix is formed by intertwining submatrices of $(I_{Gm}\ O)$ and $(O\ I_{Gn})$.

2.7.3 Twining Matrix $T_{G,m,n}$ and the Commutation Matrix

The special twining matrix $T_{G,m,n}$ is intimately connected with the commutation matrix as the following theorem demonstrates.

Theorem 2.34

$$T_{G,m,n} = K_{G,m+n}\begin{pmatrix} K_{mG} & O \\ O & K_{nG} \end{pmatrix}$$

Proof: Write

$$K_{G,m+n}\begin{pmatrix} K_{mG} & O \\ O & K_{nG} \end{pmatrix} = \begin{pmatrix} I_{m+n} \otimes e_1^{G'} \\ \vdots \\ I_{m+n} \otimes e_G^{G'} \end{pmatrix}\begin{pmatrix} K_{mG} & O \\ O & K_{nG} \end{pmatrix}$$

and consider

$$\left(I_{m+n} \otimes e_1^{G'}\right)\begin{pmatrix} K_{mG} \\ O \end{pmatrix} = \begin{pmatrix} I_m \otimes e_1^{G'} & O \\ O & I_n \otimes e_1^{G'} \end{pmatrix}\begin{pmatrix} K_{mG} \\ O \end{pmatrix}$$

$$= \begin{pmatrix} \left(I_m \otimes e_1^{G'}\right) K_{mG} \\ \left(I_m \otimes e_1^{G'}\right) O \end{pmatrix}.$$

But, we saw in Section 2.2 that $(I_m \otimes e_1^{G'})K_{mG} = K_{mG}^{(1)}$, so

$$\left(I_{m+n} \otimes e_1^{G'}\right)\begin{pmatrix} K_{mG} \\ O \end{pmatrix} = \begin{pmatrix} e_1^{G'} \otimes e_1^{m'} \\ \vdots \\ e_1^{G'} \otimes e_m^{m'} \\ e_1^{G'} \otimes 0' \\ \vdots \\ e_1^{G'} \otimes 0' \end{pmatrix} = e_1^{G'} \otimes \begin{pmatrix} I_m \\ O \end{pmatrix}$$

by Equation 1.6 of Section 1.2 in Chapter 1.

In a similar manner,

$$\left(I_{m+n} \otimes e_1^{G'}\right) \begin{pmatrix} O \\ K_{nG} \end{pmatrix} = e_1^{G'} \otimes \begin{pmatrix} O \\ I_n \end{pmatrix}.$$

The result follows. ∎

In fact, the commutation matrix itself can be considered as a twining matrix. In Theorem 2.10 of Section 2.4.1, we saw that for A a $mG \times p$ matrix partitioned as

$$A = \begin{pmatrix} A_1 \\ \vdots \\ A_G \end{pmatrix}$$

where each submatrix in this partitioning is $m \times p$, then

$$K_{mG}A = \begin{pmatrix} A^{(1)} \\ \vdots \\ A^{(m)} \end{pmatrix}. \tag{2.57}$$

Therefore, the commutation matrix K_{mG} can be regarded as a twining matrix, which intertwines not two matrices but G matrices. In this intertwining, a new matrix is formed by taking one row at a time from each of the G submatrices of A.

If we return to the case in hand, where we are intertwining two matrices only, we have

$$T_{G,1,1} = K_{G2} \begin{pmatrix} K_{1G} & O \\ O & K_{1G} \end{pmatrix} = K_{G2} \begin{pmatrix} I_G & O \\ O & I_G \end{pmatrix} = K_{G2}.$$

In Section 2.3, we saw that $K_{Gn}^{-1} = K_{Gn}' = K_{nG}$. Using this result, we have from Theorem 2.34 that

$$K_{G,m+n} = T_{G,m,n} \begin{pmatrix} K_{mG} & O \\ O & K_{nG} \end{pmatrix}^{-1} = T_{G,m,n} \begin{pmatrix} K_{Gm} & O \\ O & K_{Gn} \end{pmatrix}.$$

That is, $K_{G,m+n}$ is formed by an intertwining of $(K_{Gm} \, O)$ and $(O \, K_{Gn})$.

2.7.4 Properties of the Twining Matrix $T_{G,m,n}$.

Properties of the twining matrix $T_{G,m,n}$ are easily derived from the properties of the commutation matrix itself. We present these properties as a series of theorems.

Theorem 2.35 *The inverse of $T_{G,m,n}$ is given by*

$$T_{G,m,n}^{-1} = \begin{pmatrix} K_{Gm} & O \\ O & K_{Gn} \end{pmatrix} K_{m+n,G}.$$

Proof: As $T_{G,m,n}$ is a permutation matrix, it is orthogonal so

$$T_{G,m,n}^{-1} = T_{G,m,n}' = \begin{pmatrix} K_{mG}' & O \\ O & K_{nG}' \end{pmatrix} K_{G,m+n}' = \begin{pmatrix} K_{Gm} & O \\ O & K_{Gn} \end{pmatrix} K_{m+n,G}$$

as $K_{mG}' = K_{Gm}$. ∎

Theorem 2.36 *The trace of $T_{G,m,n}$ is given by* $\operatorname{tr} T_{G,m,p} = m + n$.

Proof: Consider the first submatrix of $T_{G,m,n}$, namely $I_G \otimes \left(\begin{smallmatrix} I_m \\ O_{n\times m} \end{smallmatrix} \right)$. As $n \geq 1$, it follows that the only nonzero elements on the main diagonal of $T_{G,m,n}$ arising from this submatrix are those of the main diagonal of I_m. Likewise, consider the second submatrix $I_G \otimes \left(\begin{smallmatrix} O_{m\times p} \\ I_n \end{smallmatrix} \right)$. Again, as $m \geq 1$, it follows that the only nonzero elements on the main diagonal of $T_{G,m,n}$ arising from this submatrix are those on the main diagonal of I_n. Thus, $\operatorname{tr} T_{G,m,n} = m + n$. ∎

An interesting observation can be made from Theorem 2.36. The trace of a commutation matrix is a complicated expression. (See, for example, Henderson and Searle (1979, 1981) and Magnus (1988)). It is

$$\operatorname{tr} K_{mn} = 1 + \gcd(m - 1, n - 1),$$

where $\gcd(m, n)$ is the greatest common divisor of m and n. However,

$$\operatorname{tr} K_{G,m+n} \begin{pmatrix} K_{mG} & O \\ O & K_{nG} \end{pmatrix} = m + n$$

is a very simple expression.

Theorem 2.37 *The determinant of $T_{G,m,n}$ is*

$$\left| T_{G,m,n} \right| = (-1)^{\frac{1}{2}G(G-1)[m(m-1)+n(n-1)+mn]}.$$

Proof: The proof uses the fact that $|K_{mn}| = (-1)^{\frac{1}{4}mn(m-1)(n-1)}$. (See Henderson and Searle (1981)).

From Theorem 2.34, we have

$$|T_{G,m,n}| = |K_{G,m+n}| \begin{vmatrix} K_{mG} & O \\ O & K_{nG} \end{vmatrix} = |K_{G,m+n}| \cdot |K_{mG}| \cdot |K_{nG}|$$

$$= (-1)^{\frac{1}{4}G(m+n)(G-1)(m+n-1)}(-1)^{\frac{1}{4}mG(m-1)(G-1)}(-1)^{\frac{1}{4}nG(n-1)(G-1)}$$

$$= (-1)^{\frac{1}{2}G(G-1)[m(m-1)+n(n-1)+mn]}.$$

∎

2.7.5 Some Special Cases

Consider the case where both A and B are block diagonal matrices given by

$$A = \begin{pmatrix} A_1 & & O \\ & \ddots & \\ O & & A_G \end{pmatrix} \text{ and } \begin{pmatrix} B_1 & & O \\ & \ddots & \\ O & & B_G \end{pmatrix}$$

where each A_i is $m \times \ell_i$ and each B_i is $n \times \ell_i$ for $i = 1, \ldots, G$. Then, $T_{G,m,n}\binom{A}{B}$ is the block diagonal matrix given by

$$T_{G,m,n}\begin{pmatrix} A \\ B \end{pmatrix} = \begin{pmatrix} \begin{pmatrix} A_1 \\ B_1 \end{pmatrix} & & O \\ & \ddots & \\ O & & \begin{pmatrix} A_G \\ B_G \end{pmatrix} \end{pmatrix}.$$

The next case of interest involves Kronecker products. Suppose A is a $G \times \ell$ matrix and c and d are $m \times 1$ and $n \times 1$ vectors respectively. Then, $A \otimes c$ is the $mG \times \ell$ matrix given by

$$A \otimes c = \begin{pmatrix} a_{11}c & \cdots & a_{1\ell}c \\ \vdots & & \vdots \\ a_{G1}c & \cdots & a_{G\ell}c \end{pmatrix}.$$

Likewise, $A \otimes d$ is the $nG \times \ell$ matrix given by

$$A \otimes d = \begin{pmatrix} a_{11}d & \cdots & a_{1\ell}d \\ \vdots & & \vdots \\ a_{a1}d & \cdots & a_{G\ell}d \end{pmatrix}.$$

It follows that

$$
T_{G,m,n}\begin{pmatrix} A \otimes c \\ A \otimes d \end{pmatrix} = \begin{pmatrix} a_{11}c & \cdots & a_{1\ell}c \\ a_{11}d & \cdots & a_{1\ell}d \\ \vdots & & \vdots \\ a_{G1}c & \cdots & a_{G\ell}c \\ a_{G1}d & \cdots & a_{G\ell}d \end{pmatrix}
$$

$$
= \begin{pmatrix} a_{11}\begin{pmatrix} c \\ d \end{pmatrix} & \cdots & a_{1\ell}\begin{pmatrix} c \\ d \end{pmatrix} \\ \vdots & & \\ a_{G1}\begin{pmatrix} c \\ d \end{pmatrix} & \cdots & a_{G\ell}\begin{pmatrix} c \\ d \end{pmatrix} \end{pmatrix} = A \otimes \begin{pmatrix} c \\ d \end{pmatrix}.
$$

This last result is a special case of a theorem on how twining matrices interact with Kronecker products, a topic that concerns us in the next section.

2.7.6 Kronecker Products and Twining Matrices

As to be expected, there are a number of results about twining matrices and Kronecker products when one of the matrices in the Kronecker product is a partitioned matrix.

Theorem 2.38 *Consider matrices A, E, and F whose orders are $G \times r$, $m \times \ell$, and $n \times \ell$, respectively. Then,*

$$
T_{G,m,n}\begin{pmatrix} A \otimes E \\ A \otimes F \end{pmatrix} = A \otimes \begin{pmatrix} E \\ F \end{pmatrix}. \tag{2.58}
$$

Proof:

$$
T_{G,m,n}\begin{pmatrix} A \otimes E \\ A \otimes F \end{pmatrix} = K_{G,m+n}\begin{pmatrix} K_{mG}(A \otimes E) \\ K_{nG}(A \otimes F) \end{pmatrix} = K_{G,m+n}\begin{pmatrix} (E \otimes A)K_{\ell r} \\ (F \otimes A)K_{\ell r} \end{pmatrix}
$$

$$
= K_{G,m+n}\left(\begin{pmatrix} E \\ F \end{pmatrix} \otimes A\right) K_{\ell r} = A \otimes \begin{pmatrix} E \\ F \end{pmatrix}. \tag{2.59}
$$

■

Theorem 2.39 *Consider B, C, and D where orders are $r \times G$, $s \times m$, and $s \times n$, respectively. Then,*

$$
(B \otimes (C\,D))\,T_{G,m,n} = (B \otimes C\,B \otimes D).
$$

Proof:

$(B \otimes (C\ D)) T_{G,m,n}$

$$= (B \otimes (C\ D)) K_{G,m+n} \begin{pmatrix} K_{mG} & O \\ O & K_{nG} \end{pmatrix} = K_{rs} (C \otimes B\ D \otimes B) \begin{pmatrix} K_{mG} & O \\ O & K_{nG} \end{pmatrix}$$

$$= K_{rs} ((C \otimes B) K_{mG}\ (D \otimes B) K_{nG}) = K_{rs} (K_{sr} (B \otimes C)\ K_{sr} (B \otimes D))$$

$$= (B \otimes C\ B \otimes D),$$

as $K_{rs}^{-1} = K_{sr}$. ∎

Notice that if we take the transposes of both sides of Equations 2.59 and 2.58, we have

$$T'_{G,m,n} \left(B' \otimes \begin{pmatrix} C' \\ D' \end{pmatrix} \right) = \begin{pmatrix} B' \otimes C' \\ B' \otimes D' \end{pmatrix}$$

and

$$(A' \otimes E'\ A' \otimes F') T'_{G,m,n} = A' \otimes (E'F').$$

That is, $T'_{G,m,n} = T^{-1}_{G,m,n}$ undoes the transformation brought about by $T_{G,m,n}$.

2.7.7 Generalizations

The results up to this point have to do largely with intertwining corresponding submatrices from two partitioned matrices. Moreover, we have concentrated on the case where the submatrices of each partitioned matrix all have the same order. If we stick to the latter qualification, our results easily generalize to the case where we intertwine corresponding submatrices from any number of partitioned matrices. All that happens is that the notation gets a little messy. Here, we content ourselves with generalizing the definition of a twining matrix and the two explicit expressions we derived for this matrix. The generalizations of the other results are obvious and are left to the reader.

A More General Definition of a Twining Matrix

Let $A^1, A^2, \ldots, A^r$ be $Gp_1 \times \ell, Gp_2 \times \ell, \ldots, Gp_r \times \ell$ matrices, respectively, and partition A^j as follows:

$$A^j = \begin{pmatrix} A_1^j \\ \vdots \\ A_G^j \end{pmatrix}, \quad j = 1, \ldots r,$$

where each submatrix A_i^j is $p_j \times \ell$ for $i = 1, \ldots, G$. The twining matrix, denoted by $T_{G,p_1,\ldots,p_r}$ is defined by

$$T_{G,p_1\cdots p_r}\begin{pmatrix} A^1 \\ \vdots \\ A^r \end{pmatrix} = \begin{pmatrix} A_1^1 \\ \vdots \\ A_1^r \\ \vdots \\ A_G^1 \\ \vdots \\ A_G^r \end{pmatrix} \qquad (2.60)$$

Two explicit expressions for $T_{G,p_1,\ldots,p_r}$

$$T_{G,p_1,\ldots,p_r} = \begin{pmatrix} I_G \otimes \begin{pmatrix} I_{p1} \\ O_{p_2 \times p_1} \\ \vdots \\ O_{p_r \times p_1} \end{pmatrix} & I_G \otimes \begin{pmatrix} O_{p_1 \times p_2} \\ I_{p_2} \\ \vdots \\ O_{p_r \times p_2} \end{pmatrix} & \cdots & I_G \otimes \begin{pmatrix} O_{p_1 \times p_r} \\ O_{p_2 \times p_r} \\ \vdots \\ I_{p_r} \end{pmatrix} \end{pmatrix}, \quad (2.61)$$

$$T_{G,p_1,\ldots,p_r} = K_{G,p_1+\cdots+p_r}\begin{pmatrix} K_{p_1 G} & & & O \\ & K_{p_2 G} & & \\ & & \ddots & \\ O & & & K_{p_r G} \end{pmatrix}. \qquad (2.62)$$

Consider the special case where $p_1 = \ldots = p_r = n$. Then,

$$T_{G,n,\ldots,n} = K_{G,nr}\begin{pmatrix} K_{nG} & & O \\ & \ddots & \\ O & & K_{nG} \end{pmatrix} = K_{G,nr}(I_r \otimes K_{nG}).$$

But from Equation 2.9 in Chapter 2,

$$K_{G,nr} = (K_{Gr} \otimes I_n)(I_r \otimes K_{Gn})$$

and as $K'_{nG} = K_{Gn} = K_{nG}^{-1}$, we have that

$$T_{G,n,\ldots,n} = (K_{Gr} \otimes I_n). \qquad (2.63)$$

2.7.8 Intertwining Columns of Matrices

Our discussion up to this point has focused on intertwining rows of matrices but, of course, a similar discussion would involve columns of matrices. Suppose A is $mG \times p$ and B is $nG \times q$, and partition these matrices as follows

$$A = \begin{pmatrix} A_1 \\ \vdots \\ A_G \end{pmatrix} \quad \text{and} \quad B = \begin{pmatrix} B_1 \\ \vdots \\ B_G \end{pmatrix}$$

where each submatrix of A is $m \times p$ and each submatrix of B is $n \times q$. Then, by definition

$$T_{G,m,n}\begin{pmatrix} A \\ B \end{pmatrix} = \begin{pmatrix} A_1 \\ B_1 \\ \vdots \\ A_G \\ B_G \end{pmatrix}. \tag{2.64}$$

Taking the transpose of this equation gives

$$(A'\, B')T'_{G,m,n} = \begin{pmatrix} A'_1 & B'_1 & \dots & A'_G & B'_G \end{pmatrix}. \tag{2.65}$$

Let C and D be the $p \times mG$ and $q \times nG$ matrices defined by

$$C = A' \quad D = B'.$$

Then,

$$C = (C_1 \dots C_G) = \begin{pmatrix} A'_1 \dots A'_G \end{pmatrix}.$$

and

$$D = (D_1 \dots D_G) = \begin{pmatrix} B'_1 \dots B'_G \end{pmatrix}$$

so Equation 2.61 yields

$$(C\, D)T'_{G,m,n} = (C_1\, D_1 \dots C_G\, D_G).$$

That is, when the matrix $(C\, D)$ is postmultiplied by $T'_{G,m,n}$, then columns of C and D are intertwined.

A special case that will be important for us in our future discussions is obtained by taking the transpose of both sides of Equation 2.57. We get

$$A'K_{Gm} = \begin{pmatrix} A^{(1)'} \dots A^{(m)'} \end{pmatrix}.$$

Again, letting $C = A'$, we have

$$CK_{Gm} = \left(C_{(1)} \ldots C_{(m)} \right) \qquad (2.66)$$

where our notation is

$$C_{(j)} = (C_1)_{.j} \ldots (C_G)_{.j}. \qquad (2.67)$$

That is, $C_{(j)}$ is formed by stacking the jth columns of the submatrices $C_1 \ldots C_G$ alongside each other. This notation is used in the proof of the following theorem.

Theorem 2.40 *Let C be an $p \times mG$ matrix. Then,*

$$\mathrm{vec}(\mathrm{vec}_m C) = \mathrm{vec}\, CK_{Gm}. \qquad (2.68)$$

Proof: Partition C as follows:

$$C = (C_1 \ldots C_G)$$

where each submatrix is $p \times m$. Then,

$$\mathrm{vec}_m C = \begin{pmatrix} C_1 \\ \vdots \\ C_G \end{pmatrix}$$

so

$$\mathrm{vec}(\mathrm{vec}_m C) = \begin{pmatrix} (C_1)_{.1} \\ \vdots \\ (C_G)_{.1} \\ \vdots \\ (C_1)_{.m} \\ \vdots \\ (C_G)_{.m} \end{pmatrix} = \begin{pmatrix} \mathrm{vec}C_{(1)} \\ \vdots \\ \mathrm{vec}C_{(m)} \end{pmatrix}$$

from Equation 2.67. But from Equation 2.66,

$$\mathrm{vec}\, CK_{Gm} = \begin{pmatrix} \mathrm{vec}C_{(1)} \\ \vdots \\ \mathrm{vec}C_{(m)} \end{pmatrix}. \qquad \blacksquare$$

The corresponding results for rvecs is found by taking the transpose of both sides of Equation 2.68 to obtain

$$\text{rvec}\left[(\text{vec}_m C)'\right] = \text{rvec}\left[(CK_{mG})'\right].$$

That is,

$$\text{rvec}\,(\text{rvec}_m A) = \text{rvec}\,K_{Gm}A$$

where A is a $mG \times p$ matrix.

A more general analysis also applies to intertwining columns of matrices. If we take the transpose of Equation 2.60, we have

$$(A^{1'} \ldots A^{r'})T'_{G,p_1,\ldots,p_r} = \left(A_1^{1'} \ldots A_1^{r'} \ldots A_G^{1'} \ldots A_G^{r'}\right),$$

then letting $C^j = A^{j'} = (A_1^{j'} \ldots A_G^{j'}) = (C_1^j \ldots C_G^j)$, for $j = 1,\ldots,r$, we have

$$(C^1 \ldots C^r)T'_{G,p_1,\ldots,p_r} = \left(C_1^1 \ldots C_1^r \ldots C_G^1 \ldots C_G^r\right),$$

where from Equation 2.62

$$T'_{G,p_1,\ldots,p_r} = \begin{pmatrix} K_{Gp_1} & & & O \\ & K_{Gp_2} & & \\ & & \ddots & \\ O & & & K_{Gp_r} \end{pmatrix} K_{p_1+\cdots+p_r,G}, \qquad (2.69)$$

and from Equation 2.63

$$T'_{G,n,\ldots,n} = (K_{Gr} \otimes I_n)' = K_{rG} \otimes I_n.$$

THREE

Elimination and Duplication Matrices

3.1 Introduction

A special group of selection matrices is associated with the vec, vech, and $\bar{v}(A)$ of a given square matrix A. These matrices are called **elimination matrices** and **duplication matrices**. They are extremely important in the application of matrix calculus to statistical models as we see in Chapter 6. The purpose of this chapter is not to list all the known results for these matrices. One can do no better than refer to Magnus (1988) for this. Rather, we seek to present these matrices in a new light and in such a way that facilitates the investigation as to how these matrices interact with other matrices, particularly Kronecker products. The mathematics involved in doing this entitles a new notation – well, at least it is new to me. But it is hoped that the use of this notation makes it clear how the otherwise complicated matrices behave.

3.2 Elimination Matrices

Consider A an $n \times n$ matrix. As noted in Section 1.4.3 of Chapter 1, $\mathrm{vec}\,A$ contains all the elements of A. It is the $n^2 \times 1$ vector formed by stacking the columns of A underneath each other. The $\mathrm{vech}\,A$ is the $\frac{1}{2}n(n+1) \times 1$ vector formed by stacking the elements on and beneath the main diagonal under each other. Finally, $\bar{v}(A)$ is the $\frac{1}{2}n(n-1) \times 1$ vector formed by stacking the elements beneath the main diagonal under each other. Clearly, $\mathrm{vec}\,A$ contains all the elements in $\mathrm{vech}\,A$ and $\bar{v}(A)$. It follows that there exists zero-one matrices L_n and $\bar{L}_n$ whose orders are $\frac{1}{2}n(n+1) \times n^2$ and $\frac{1}{2}n(n-1) \times n^2$, respectively, such that

$$L_n \mathrm{vec}\, A = \mathrm{vech}\, A$$

$$\bar{L}_n \mathrm{vec}\, A = \bar{v}(A).$$

Variations of these matrices are used in the case when A is a symmetric matrix.

Recall from Section 2.5.7 in Chapter 2 that

$$N_n \text{vec } A = \frac{1}{2}(\text{vec } A + \text{vec } A') = \text{vec } A,$$

if A is symmetric. It follows that when A is a symmetric matrix

$$L_n N_n \text{vec } A = L_n \text{vec } A = \text{vech } A$$

and

$$\bar{L}_n N_n \text{vec } A = \bar{L}_n \text{vec } A = \bar{\text{v}}(A).$$

Finally, note that as vech A contains all the elements in $\bar{\text{v}}(A)$ and more, there exists a $\frac{1}{2}n(n-1) \times \frac{1}{2}n(n+1)$ zero-one matrix L_n^* such that

$$L_n^* \text{ vech } A = \bar{\text{v}}(A).$$

All these matrices L_n, $L_n N_n$, $\bar{L}_n$, $\bar{L}_n N$ and L_n^* are called **elimination matrices** and in this section we study some of their properties in detail. We are particularly interested in how these matrices interact with Kronecker products.

The approach taken here differs from that taken by other authors such as Magnus (1988) and Magnus and Neudecker (1988). What we seek to do is to break these matrices down to smaller submatrices. Studying the properties of these submatrices facilitates achieving new results for the elimination matrices themselves.

3.2.1 The Elimination Matrix L_n

To begin, consider the following $n \times n$ matrix:

$$A = \begin{pmatrix} a_{11} & \cdots & a_{1n} \\ \vdots & \ddots & \vdots \\ a_{n1} & \cdots & a_{nn} \end{pmatrix}$$

Then,

$$
\text{vec } A = \begin{pmatrix} a_{11} \\ \vdots \\ a_{n1} \\ \vdots \\ a_{1n} \\ \vdots \\ a_{nn} \end{pmatrix}, \quad \text{vech } A = \begin{pmatrix} a_{11} \\ \vdots \\ a_{n1} \\ a_{22} \\ \vdots \\ a_{n2} \\ \vdots \\ a_{nn} \end{pmatrix}, \quad \bar{\text{v}}(A) = \begin{pmatrix} a_{21} \\ \vdots \\ a_{n1} \\ a_{32} \\ \vdots \\ a_{n2} \\ \vdots \\ a_{nn-1} \end{pmatrix},
$$

which are $n^2 \times 1$, $\frac{1}{2}n(n+1) \times 1$ and $\frac{1}{2}n(n-1) \times 1$ vectors, respectively. Comparing vech A with vec A, it is clear that L_n is the $\frac{1}{2}n(n+1) \times n^2$ block diagonal matrix given by

$$
L_n = \begin{pmatrix} I_n & & & O \\ & E_1 & & \\ & & \ddots & \\ O & & & E_{n-1} \end{pmatrix}, \tag{3.1}
$$

where E_j is the $n-j \times n$ matrix given by

$$
E_j = (\underset{n-j \times j}{O} \quad \underset{n-j \times n-j}{I_{n-j}}) \tag{3.2}
$$

for $j = 1, \ldots, n-1$.

Note, for convenience we only use one subscript j to identify E_j, the second parameter n being obvious from the content. For example, if we are dealing with L_3, then

$$
E_1 = (\underset{2\times1}{0} \quad \underset{2\times2}{I_2}) = \begin{pmatrix} 0 & 1 & 0 \\ 0 & 0 & 1 \end{pmatrix},
$$

$$
E_2 = (\underset{1\times2}{0} \quad I_1) = \begin{pmatrix} 0 & 0 & 1 \end{pmatrix}
$$

and

$$L_3 = \begin{pmatrix} I_3 & O & O \\ O & E_1 & O \\ O & O & E_2 \end{pmatrix}$$

$$= \begin{pmatrix} 1 & 0 & 0 & 0 & 0 & 0 & 0 & 0 & 0 \\ 0 & 1 & 0 & 0 & 0 & 0 & 0 & 0 & 0 \\ 0 & 0 & 1 & 0 & 0 & 0 & 0 & 0 & 0 \\ 0 & 0 & 0 & 0 & 1 & 0 & 0 & 0 & 0 \\ 0 & 0 & 0 & 0 & 0 & 1 & 0 & 0 & 0 \\ 0 & 0 & 0 & 0 & 0 & 0 & 0 & 0 & 1 \end{pmatrix}.$$

Also, for mathematical convenience, we take $E_0 = I_n$. Note that $E_{n-1} = e_n^{n'}$.

The matrix E_j itself can be regarded as an elimination matrix. If A and B are $n \times m$ and $p \times n$ matrices, respectively, then

$$E_j A = (A)_j, \quad j = 1, \ldots, n-1 \tag{3.3}$$

where $(A)_j$ is the $n - j \times m$ matrix formed from A by deleting the first j rows of A, and

$$B E_j' = (B)^j, \quad j = 1, \ldots, n-1 \tag{3.4}$$

where $(B)^j$ is the $p \times n - j$ matrix formed from B by deleting the first j column of B. For mathematical convenience, we said we would take $E_0 = I_n$, so this implies that we must also take

$$(A)_0 = A$$

and

$$(B)^0 = B.$$

Note that when we use this notation for $j = 1, \ldots, n-1$

$$(A)_j' = (A')^j$$

and

$$(B)^{j'} = (B')_j.$$

In particular, with A an $n \times m$ matrix

$$(\text{vec } A)_{nj}' = \begin{pmatrix} a_{j+1} \\ \vdots \\ a_m \end{pmatrix}' = (a_{j+1}' \quad \cdots \quad a_m') = ((\text{vec } A)')^{nj} = (\text{rvec } A')^{nj},$$

and

$$\left((\text{rvec } A)^{mj}\right)' = \left(a^{j+1'} \quad \cdots \quad a^{n'}\right)' = \begin{pmatrix} a^{j+1} \\ \vdots \\ a^n \end{pmatrix} = \left((\text{rvec } A)'\right)_{mj}$$

$$= (\text{vec } A')_{mj}.$$

When we apply this notation to Kronecker products, we have

$$(A \otimes x')_j = (A)_j \otimes x' \tag{3.5}$$

$$(x' \otimes A)_j = x' \otimes (A)_j \tag{3.6}$$

$$(B \otimes x)^j = (B)^j \otimes x$$

$$(x \otimes B)^j = x \otimes (B)^j.$$

When working with columns from identity matrices and indeed identity matrices themselves, we have

$$\left(e_j^n\right)_i = e_{j-i}^{n-i} \quad i < j$$
$$= 0 \qquad i \geq j \tag{3.7}$$

and

$$(I_n)_j = \begin{pmatrix} O & I_{n-j} \end{pmatrix} = E_j, \tag{3.8}$$

for $j = 1, \ldots, n-1$. Also,

$$(I_n)_j \otimes e_m^{p'} = \begin{pmatrix} O \\ {}_{n-j \times jp} \end{pmatrix} \quad I_{n-j} \otimes e_m^{p'} \end{pmatrix}$$

$$= \begin{pmatrix} O & O & e_1^{n-j} & O & \cdots & O & e_{n-j}^{n-j} & O \end{pmatrix} \tag{3.9}$$

by Theorem 1.1 of Chapter 1.

Returning to E_j, we have that for any vector x

$$E_j(x' \otimes A) = x' \otimes (A)_j \tag{3.10}$$

$$E_j(A \otimes x') = (A)_j \otimes x' \tag{3.11}$$

$$(x \otimes B)E_j' = x \otimes (B)^j$$

$$(B \otimes x)E_j' = (B)^j \otimes x$$

Using the properties of E_j, involving as they do our newly introduced notation, we can obtain properties for the elimination matrix L_n itself. Suppose A is $n^2 \times p$ and we partition it as

$$A = \begin{pmatrix} A_1 \\ \vdots \\ A_n \end{pmatrix} \tag{3.12}$$

where each submatrix in this partitioning is $n \times p$, then from Equation 3.1:

$$L_n A = \begin{pmatrix} A_1 \\ E_1 A_2 \\ \vdots \\ E_{n-1} A_n \end{pmatrix} = \begin{pmatrix} A_1 \\ (A_2)_1 \\ \vdots \\ (A_n)_{n-1} \end{pmatrix}.$$

Similarly, if B is an $q \times n^2$ matrix and we partition B as

$$B = (B_1 \quad \cdots \quad B_n) \tag{3.13}$$

where each submatrix in this partitioning is $q \times n$, then

$$BL'_n = \begin{pmatrix} B_1 & B_2 E'_1 & \cdots & B_n E_{n-1'} \end{pmatrix} = \begin{pmatrix} B_1 & (B_2)^1 & \cdots & (B_n)^{n-1} \end{pmatrix}.$$

If C is a $n^2 \times n^2$ matrix and initially partition C as

$$C = \begin{pmatrix} C_1 \\ \vdots \\ C_n \end{pmatrix}, \tag{3.14}$$

where each submatrix in this partitioning is $n \times n^2$, then

$$L_n C L'_n = \begin{pmatrix} C_1 \\ (C_2)_1 \\ \vdots \\ (C_n)_{n-1} \end{pmatrix} L'_n.$$

Now, if we partition C as

$$C = \begin{pmatrix} C_{11} & \cdots & C_{1n} \\ \vdots & & \vdots \\ C_{n1} & \cdots & C_{nn} \end{pmatrix} \tag{3.15}$$

where each submatrix C_{ij} in this partitioning is $n \times n$, then

$$L_n C L'_n = \begin{pmatrix} C_{11} & (C_{12})^1 & \cdots & (C_{1n})^{n-1} \\ (C_{21})_1 & ((C_{22})_1)^1 & \cdots & ((C_{2n})_1)^{n-1} \\ \vdots & & & \\ (C_{n1})_{n-1} & ((C_{n2})_{n-1})^1 & \cdots & ((C_{nn})_{n-1})^{n-1} \end{pmatrix}.$$

Of course, $n^2 \times p$, $q \times n^2$ and $n^2 \times n^2$ matrices often arise in Kronecker products. The following four theorems tell us how the elimination matrix interacts with Kronecker products.

Theorem 3.1 *Let A be an $n \times n$ matrix and b be an $n \times 1$ vector. Then,*

$$L_n(A \otimes b) = \begin{pmatrix} a^{1'} \otimes b \\ a^{2'} \otimes (b)_1 \\ \vdots \\ a^{n'} \otimes (b)_{n-1} \end{pmatrix}$$

$$L_n(b \otimes A) = \begin{pmatrix} b_1 A \\ b_2 (A)_1 \\ \vdots \\ b_n (A)_{n-1} \end{pmatrix}$$

$$(A \otimes b')L'_n = a_1 \otimes b' \ a_2 \otimes (b')^1 \ldots a_n \otimes (b')^{n-1}$$
$$(b' \otimes A)L'_n = b_1 A \ b_2 (A)^1 \ldots b_n (A)^{n-1}.$$

Proof: Using Equation 3.1

$$L_n(A \otimes b) = \begin{pmatrix} I_n & & & O \\ & E_1 & & \\ & & \ddots & \\ O & & & E_{n-1} \end{pmatrix} \begin{pmatrix} a'_1 \otimes b \\ \vdots \\ a^{n'} \otimes b \end{pmatrix}$$

$$= \begin{pmatrix} a^{1'} \otimes b \\ a^{2'} \otimes E_1 b \\ \vdots \\ a^{n'} \otimes E_{n-1} b \end{pmatrix} = \begin{pmatrix} a^{1'} \otimes b \\ a^{2'} \otimes (b)_1 \\ \vdots \\ a^{n'} \otimes (b)_{n-1} \end{pmatrix},$$

where we have used Equation 3.3.

Likewise,

$$L_n(b \otimes A) = \begin{pmatrix} I_n & & & O \\ & E_1 & & \\ & & \ddots & \\ O & & & E_{n-1} \end{pmatrix} \begin{pmatrix} b_1 A \\ \vdots \\ b_n A \end{pmatrix}$$

$$= \begin{pmatrix} b_1 A \\ b_2 E_1 A \\ \vdots \\ b_n E_{n-1} A \end{pmatrix} = \begin{pmatrix} b_1 A \\ b_2 (A)_1 \\ \vdots \\ b_n (A)_{n-1} \end{pmatrix},$$

from Equation 3.3.

Now,

$$(A \otimes b')L_n' = (a_1 \otimes b' \quad \cdots \quad a_n \otimes b') \begin{pmatrix} I_n & & & O \\ & E_1' & & \\ & & \ddots & \\ O & & & E_{n-1}' \end{pmatrix}$$

$$= a_1 \otimes b' \; a_2 \otimes b' E_1' \ldots a_n \otimes b' E_{n-1}$$

$$= a_1 \otimes b' \; a_2 \otimes (b')^1 \ldots a_n \otimes (b')^{n-1},$$

using Equation 3.4. Finally,

$$(b' \otimes A)L_n' = \begin{pmatrix} b_1 A & \cdots & b_n A \end{pmatrix} \begin{pmatrix} I_n & & & O \\ & E_1' & & \\ & & \ddots & \\ O & & & E_n' \end{pmatrix}$$

$$= b_1 A \; b_2 A E_1' \ldots b_n A E_{n-1}' = b_1 A \; b_2 (A)^1 \ldots b_n (A)^{n-1}. \quad \blacksquare$$

We are now in a position to represent $L_n(A \otimes B)$, $(A \otimes B)L_n'$, and $L_n(A \otimes B)L_n'$ in an informative way, where A and B are $n \times n$ matrices.

Theorem 3.2 *If A and B are both $n \times n$ matrices, then*

$$L_n(A \otimes B) = \begin{pmatrix} a^{1'} \otimes B \\ a^{2'} \otimes (B)_1 \\ \vdots \\ a^{n'} \otimes (B)_{n-1} \end{pmatrix}.$$

Proof: Using Equation 3.1, we write

$$L_n(A \otimes B) = \begin{pmatrix} I_n & & & O \\ & E_1 & & \\ & & \ddots & \\ O & & & E_{n-1} \end{pmatrix} \begin{pmatrix} a^{1'} \otimes B \\ a^{2'} \otimes B \\ \vdots \\ a^{n'} \otimes B \end{pmatrix}$$

$$= \begin{pmatrix} a^{1'} \otimes B \\ E_1(a^{2'} \otimes B) \\ \vdots \\ E_{n-1}(a^{n'} \otimes B) \end{pmatrix} = \begin{pmatrix} a^{1'} \otimes B \\ a^{2'} \otimes (B)_1 \\ \vdots \\ a^{n'} \otimes (B)_{n-1} \end{pmatrix},$$

where we have used Equation 3.10. ∎

Theorem 3.3 *If A and B are both $n \times n$ matrices, then*

$$(A \otimes B)L'_n = a_1 \otimes B \; a_2 \otimes (B)^1 \ldots a_n \otimes (B)^{n-1}.$$

Proof: Clearly,

$$(A \otimes B)L'_n = \begin{pmatrix} a^{1'} \otimes B \\ \vdots \\ a^{n'} \otimes B \end{pmatrix} L'_n = \begin{pmatrix} a_{11}B & a_{12}(B)^1 & \cdots & a_{1n}(B)^{n-1} \\ \vdots & \vdots & & \vdots \\ a_{n1}B & a_{n2}(B)^1 & \cdots & a_{nn}(B)^{n-1} \end{pmatrix}$$

$$= a_1 \otimes B \; a_2 \otimes (B)^1 \quad \ldots \quad a_n \otimes (B)^{n-1},$$

where we have used Theorem 3.1. ∎

Theorem 3.4 *If A and B are both $n \times n$ matrices, then*

$$L_n(A \otimes B)L'_n = \begin{pmatrix} a_{11}B & a_{12}(B)^1 & \cdots & a_{1n}(B)^{n-1} \\ a_{21}(B)_1 & a_{22}((B)_1)^1 & \cdots & a_{2n}((B)_1)^{n-1} \\ \vdots & \vdots & & \vdots \\ a_{n1}(B)_{n-1} & a_{n2}((B)_{n-1})^1 & \cdots & a_{nn}((B)_{n-1})^{n-1} \end{pmatrix}.$$

Proof: From Theorem 3.2

$$L_n(A \otimes B)L'_n = \begin{pmatrix} (a^{1'} \otimes B)L'_n \\ (a^{2'} \otimes (B)_1)L'_n \\ \vdots \\ (a^{n'} \otimes (B)_{n-1})L'_n \end{pmatrix}.$$

But from Theorem 3.1

$$\left(a^{j'} \otimes (B)_{j-1}\right) L'_n = a_{j1}(B)_{j-1} \; a_{j2}\left((B)_{j-1}\right)^1 \ldots a_{jn}\left((B)_{j-1}\right)^{n-1},$$

for $j = 2, \ldots, n$. ∎

3.2.2 The Elimination Matrix $L_n N_n$

Recall that $N_n = \frac{1}{2}(I_{n^2} + K_{nn})$ is the $n^2 \times n^2$ matrix with the property that for a square $n \times n$ matrix A

$$N_n \text{vec } A = \frac{1}{2} \text{vec} (A + A')$$

so if A is a symmetric matrix

$$N_n \text{vec } A = \text{vec } A.$$

It follows that for a symmetric matrix A

$$L_n \text{vec } A = L_n N_n \text{vec } A = \text{vech } A.$$

So, $L_n N_n$ itself can be regarded as an elimination matrix for symmetric matrices. The difference in the operating of L_n and $L_n N_n$ is this: for $i > j$, the elimination matrix L_n picks a_{ij} from vec$A$ directly. The matrix $L_n N_n$, however, recognises that A is symmetric and chooses a_{ij} for vech$A$ by picking a_{ij} and a_{ji} from vec$A$ and forming $a_{ij} + a_{ji}/2$. Because $L_n N_n$ recognises the symmetry in A, it is the elimination matrix that should be used in dealing with such symmetric matrices. We proceed in much the same way as we did for L_n. Our first task is to form explicit expressions for $L_n N_n$.

From Equation 2.44 in Chapter 2, we can write

$$L_n N_n = \frac{1}{2} L_n \left(I_n \otimes e_1^n + e_1^n \otimes I_n \ldots I_n \otimes e_n^n + e_n^n \otimes I_n\right).$$

Consider twice the jth submatrix in this matrix, which is

$$L_n \left(I_n \otimes e_j^n + e_j^n \otimes I_n\right).$$

Using Theorem 3.1, we can write the matrix as

$$L_n \left(I_n \otimes e_j^n + e_j^n \otimes I_n\right) = \begin{pmatrix} e_1^{n'} \otimes e_j^n \\ e_2^{n'} \otimes \left(e_j^n\right)_1 \\ \vdots \\ e_n^{n'} \otimes \left(e_j^n\right)_{n-1} \end{pmatrix} + \begin{pmatrix} O \\ \vdots \\ (I_n)_{j-1} \\ \vdots \\ O \end{pmatrix} j\text{th.}$$

Using Equations 3.7 and 3.8, we obtain

$$
L_n\left(I_n \otimes e_j^n + e_j^n \otimes I_n\right) =
\begin{pmatrix}
e_1^{n'} \otimes e_j^n \\
e_2^{n'} \otimes e_{j-1}^{n-1} \\
\vdots \\
e_j^{n'} \otimes e_1^{n-j+1} \\
O \\
\vdots \\
O
\end{pmatrix}
+
\begin{pmatrix}
O \\
O \\
\vdots \\
E_{j-1} \\
O \\
\vdots \\
O
\end{pmatrix}
= P_j,
$$

where P_j is the $\frac{1}{2}n(n+1) \times n$ matrix given by

$$
P_j =
\begin{pmatrix}
\begin{pmatrix}
e_j^n & & O \\
& \ddots & \\
O & & e_2^{n-j+2}
\end{pmatrix} & O \\
O & R_j \\
O & O
\end{pmatrix}
\begin{matrix} 1 \end{matrix}
\tag{3.16}
$$

for $j = 2, \ldots, n-1$, and R_j is the $n-j+1 \times n-j+1$ matrix given by

$$
R_j = e_1^{n-j+1} + E_{j-1} =
\begin{pmatrix}
2 & & & O \\
& 1 & & \\
& & \ddots & \\
O & & & 1
\end{pmatrix}
\tag{3.17}
$$

for $j = 1, 2, \ldots, n-1$.

Additionally, let

$$
P_1 = \begin{pmatrix} R_1 \\ O \end{pmatrix}.
\tag{3.18}
$$

and

$$
P_n =
\begin{pmatrix}
e_n^n & & & O \\
& \ddots & & \\
& & e_2^2 & \\
O & & & R_n
\end{pmatrix}
$$

with $R_n = 2$.

---

[1] The comments made with regard to E_j apply equally well for P_j and R_j.

Under this notation, an explicit expression for $L_n N_n$ is

$$L_n N_n = \frac{1}{2}(P_1 \quad \cdots \quad P_n).$$ (3.19)

For example,

$$L_3 N_3 = \frac{1}{2}(P_1 \quad P_2 \quad P_3)$$

where

$$P_1 = \begin{pmatrix} R_1 \\ O \end{pmatrix} = \begin{pmatrix} 2 & 0 & 0 \\ 0 & 1 & 0 \\ 0 & 0 & 1 \\ 0 & 0 & 0 \\ 0 & 0 & 0 \\ 0 & 0 & 0 \end{pmatrix}$$

$$P_2 = \begin{pmatrix} e_2^3 & O \\ 0 & R_2 \\ 0 & 0' \end{pmatrix} = \begin{pmatrix} 0 & 0 & 0 \\ 1 & 0 & 0 \\ 0 & 0 & 0 \\ 0 & 2 & 0 \\ 0 & 0 & 1 \\ 0 & 0 & 0 \end{pmatrix}$$

$$P_3 = \begin{pmatrix} e_3^3 & 0 & 0 \\ 0 & e_2^2 & 0 \\ 0 & 0 & R_3 \end{pmatrix} = \begin{pmatrix} 0 & 0 & 0 \\ 0 & 0 & 0 \\ 1 & 0 & 0 \\ 0 & 0 & 0 \\ 0 & 1 & 0 \\ 0 & 0 & 2 \end{pmatrix}$$

so

$$L_3 n_3 = \frac{1}{2} \begin{pmatrix} 2 & 0 & 0 & 0 & 0 & 0 & 0 & 0 & 0 \\ 0 & 1 & 0 & 1 & 0 & 0 & 0 & 0 & 0 \\ 0 & 0 & 1 & 0 & 0 & 0 & 1 & 0 & 0 \\ 0 & 0 & 0 & 0 & 2 & 0 & 0 & 0 & 0 \\ 0 & 0 & 0 & 0 & 0 & 1 & 0 & 1 & 0 \\ 0 & 0 & 0 & 0 & 0 & 0 & 0 & 0 & 2 \end{pmatrix}.$$

The explicit expression obtained for $L_n N_n$ writes this matrix as a 'row' of submatrices. An alternative expression for $L_n N_n$ writes the matrix as a 'column' of submatrices.

Write

$$L_n N_n = \frac{1}{2} L_n (I_{n^2} + K_{nn}) = \frac{1}{2}(L_n + L_n K_{nn}).$$

Now, from Equation 2.8 of Chapter 2, we have

$$L_n K_{nn} = L_n \left(I_n \otimes e_1^n \dots I_n \otimes e_n^n \right).$$

Using Theorem 3.1, we can then write $L_n K_{nn}$ as

$$
L_n K_{nn} = \begin{pmatrix}
e_1^{n'} \otimes e_1^n & \cdots & e_1^{n'} \otimes e_n^n \\
e_2^{n'} \otimes \left(e_1^n\right)_1 & \cdots & e_2^{n'} \otimes \left(e_n^n\right)_1 \\
\vdots & & \vdots \\
e_n^{n'} \otimes \left(e_1^n\right)_{n-1} & \cdots & e_n^{n'} \otimes \left(e_n^n\right)_{n-1}
\end{pmatrix}
$$

$$
= \begin{pmatrix}
e_1^n \otimes e_1^{n'} & \cdots & e_n^n \otimes e_1^{n'} \\
\left(e_1^n\right)_1 \otimes e_2^{n'} & \cdots & \left(e_n^n\right)_1 \otimes e_2^{n'} \\
\vdots & & \vdots \\
\left(e_1^n\right)_{n-1} \otimes e_n^{n'} & \cdots & \left(e_n^n\right)_{n-1} \otimes e_n^{n'}
\end{pmatrix}
= \begin{pmatrix}
I_n \otimes e_1^{n'} \\
\left(I_n\right)_1 \otimes e_2^{n'} \\
\vdots \\
\left(I_n\right)_{n-1} \otimes e_n^{n'}
\end{pmatrix}
$$

so if we write $2 L_n N_n$ as a 'column' of submatrices, the jth submatrix would be, using Equation 3.1

$$T_j = \begin{pmatrix} O & E_{j-1} & O \\ {}_{n-j+1 \times n(j-1)} & {}_{n-j+1 \times n} & {}_{n-j+1 \times n(n-j)} \end{pmatrix} + \left(I_n\right)_{j-1} \otimes e_j^{n'},$$

for $j = 2, \dots, n-1$.

But, we can write

$$\left(I_n\right)_{j-1} \otimes e_j^{n'} = \begin{pmatrix} e_j^{n'} \otimes e_j^{n'} \\ \left(I_n\right)_j \otimes e_j^{n'} \end{pmatrix}$$

and using Equation 3.9, we have that

$$\left(I_n\right)_{j-1} \otimes e_j^{n'} = \begin{pmatrix} 0' & e_j^{n'} & 0' & 0 & 0' & \cdots & 0' & 0 & 0' \\ O & O & O & e_1^{n-j} & O & \cdots & O & e_{n-j}^{n-j} & O \end{pmatrix}$$

$$= \begin{pmatrix} O & \begin{pmatrix} e_j^{n'} \\ O \end{pmatrix} & O & e_2^{n-j+1} & O & \cdots & O & e_{n-j+1}^{n-j+1} & O \end{pmatrix}$$

so

$$T_j = \begin{pmatrix} O & E_{j-1} + \begin{pmatrix} e_j^{n'} \\ O \end{pmatrix} & O & e_2^{n-j+1} & O & \cdots & O & e_{n-j+1}^{n-j+1} & O \end{pmatrix}.$$

Clearly, from Equation 3.2

$$E_{j-1} + \begin{pmatrix} e_j^{n'} \\ O \end{pmatrix} = (O \quad R_j)$$

where R_j is the $n - j + 1 \times n - j + 1$ matrix given by Equation 3.17.

If we let Z_i^j be the $n - j + 1 \times n$ matrix given by

$$Z_i^j = \begin{pmatrix} O & e_i^{n-j+1} & O \\ {}_{n-j+1 \times j-1} & & {}_{n-j+1 \times n-j} \end{pmatrix}^2 \tag{3.20}$$

for $i = 2, \ldots, n - j + 1$ and for $j = 2, \ldots, n - 1$ and we let

$$Z_i^1 = \begin{pmatrix} e_i^n & O \\ & {}_{n \times n-1} \end{pmatrix} \tag{3.21}$$

for the same values of i then we can write

$$T_j = \begin{pmatrix} O & (O \quad R_j) & Z_2^j & \cdots & Z_{n-j+1}^j \\ {}_{n-j+1 \times n(j-1)} & {}_{n-j+1 \times n} & & & \end{pmatrix} \tag{3.22}$$

for $j = 2, \ldots, n - 1$.

The other two submatrices are

$$T_1 = \begin{pmatrix} R_1 & Z_2^1 & \cdots & Z_n^1 \end{pmatrix} \tag{3.23}$$

and

$$\begin{aligned} T_n &= (0' \quad \cdots \quad 0' \quad E_{n-1}) + e_n' \otimes e_n' \\ &= (0' \quad \cdots \quad 0' \quad e_n^{n'}) + (0' \quad \cdots \quad 0' \quad e_n^{n'}) \\ &= \begin{pmatrix} 0' & 2e_n^{n'} \\ {}_{1 \times n(n-1)} & \end{pmatrix}. \end{aligned} \tag{3.24}$$

The second explicit expression for $L_n N_n$ is then

$$L_n N_n = \frac{1}{2} \begin{pmatrix} T_1 \\ \vdots \\ T_n \end{pmatrix}. \tag{3.25}$$

The matrices $Z_2^j \ldots Z_{n-j+1}^j$ are interesting in themselves but we reserve our study of the properties of these matrices until a future section on duplication matrices where they appear again. The reader may also be surprised that after all the trouble we have gone through to obtain explicit expressions for $L_n N_n$, we do not use them to get insights into how the elimination matrix $L_n N_n$

---

[2] Comments made about E_j apply equally well to Z_i^j. Each Z_i^j depends on n, but this parameter will be clear from the content.

interacts with Kronecker products. The mathematics is simpler if we use known properties of L_n and N_n. However, we shall certainly use the explicit expressions for $L_n N_n$ in the last subsection where we make comparisons between $2 L_n N_n$ and the duplication matrix D_n.

But first Kronecker products and $L_n N_n$. The notation introduced in Equations 3.3 and 3.4 is used extensively in the theorems that follow.

Theorem 3.5   *Let A, B, C, and D be $n \times p$, $n \times q$, $r \times n$, and $s \times n$ matrices, respectively. Then,*

$$L_n N_n (A \otimes B) = \frac{1}{2} \begin{pmatrix} a^{1'} \otimes B + A \otimes b^{1'} \\ a^{2'} \otimes (B)_1 + (A)_1 \otimes b^{2'} \\ \vdots \\ a^{n'} \otimes (B)_{n-1} + (A)_{n-1} \otimes b^{n'} \end{pmatrix}$$

and

$$(C \otimes D) N_n L_n'$$
$$= \frac{1}{2} \Big(c_1 \otimes D + C \otimes d_1 \quad c_2 \otimes (D)^1 + (C)^1 \otimes d_2 \quad \cdots \quad c_n \otimes (D)^{n-1}$$
$$+ (C)^{n-1} \otimes d_n \Big). \tag{3.26}$$

Proof: From the definition of N_n given in Section 2.5.7 of Chapter 2, we have

$$L_n N_n (A \otimes B) = \frac{1}{2} L_n (A \otimes B + K_{nn}(A \otimes B)) = \frac{1}{2} L_n (A \otimes B + (B \otimes A) K_{qp})$$

$$= \frac{1}{2} \left[\begin{pmatrix} a^{1'} \otimes B \\ a^{2'} \otimes (B)_1 \\ \vdots \\ a^{n'} \otimes (B)_{n-1} \end{pmatrix} + \begin{pmatrix} b^{1'} \otimes A \\ b^{2'} \otimes (A)_1 \\ \vdots \\ b^{n'} \otimes (A)_{n-1} \end{pmatrix} K_{qp} \right]$$

$$= \frac{1}{2} \begin{pmatrix} a^{1'} \otimes B + A \otimes b^{1'} \\ a^{2'} \otimes (B)_1 + (A)_1 \otimes b^{2'} \\ \vdots \\ a^{n'} \otimes (B)_{n-1} + (A)_{n-1} \otimes b^{n'} \end{pmatrix}$$

where we have used Theorem 3.2 and Equations 2.11 and 2.14 of Chapter 2 in our working.

In a similar manner, using Theorem 3.3

$$(C \otimes D)N_n L'_n = \frac{1}{2}(C \otimes D + K_{rs}(D \otimes C)L'_n$$

$$= \frac{1}{2}\Big[\big(c_1 \otimes D \quad c_2 \otimes (D)^1 \quad \cdots \quad c_n \otimes (D)^{n-1}\big)$$

$$+ K_{rs}\big(d_1 \otimes C \quad d_2 \otimes (C)^1 \quad \cdots \quad d_n \otimes (C)^{n-1}\big)\Big]$$

$$= \frac{1}{2}\Big(c_1 \otimes D + C \otimes d_1 \quad c_2 \otimes (D)^1$$

$$+ (C)^1 \otimes d_2 \quad \cdots \quad c_n \otimes (D)^{n-1} + (C)^{n-1} \otimes d_n\Big). \quad \blacksquare$$

Theorem 3.6 *Let A and B be $n \times n$ matrices and write*

$$L_n N_n (A \otimes B) N_n L'_n = \begin{pmatrix} C_1 \\ \vdots \\ C_n \end{pmatrix}.$$

Then, the jth submatrix C_j is the $n - j + 1 \times \frac{1}{2}n(n+1)$ matrix given by

$$C_j = \frac{1}{4}\Big[\big(a_{j1}(B)_{j-1} \quad a_{j2}((B)_{j-1})^1 \quad \cdots \quad a_{jn}((B)_{j-1})^{n-1}\big)$$

$$+ \big(b_{j1}(A)_{j-1} \quad b_{j2}((A)_{j-1})^1 \quad \cdots \quad b_{jn}((A)_{j-1})^{n-1}\big)$$

$$+ \big((a_1)_{j-1} \otimes b^{j'} \quad (a_2)_{j-1} \otimes (b^{j'})^1 \quad \cdots \quad (a_n)_{j-1} \otimes (b^{j'})^{n-1}\big)$$

$$+ \big((b_1)_{j-1} \otimes a^{j'} \quad (b_2)_{j-1} \otimes (a^{j'})^1 \quad \cdots \quad (b_n)_{j-1} \otimes (a^{j'})^{n-1}\big)\Big]$$

for $j = 1, \ldots, n$.

Proof: From Equation 2.50 of Chapter 2, we have

$$L_n N_n (A \otimes B) N_n L'_n = \frac{1}{4} L_n \begin{pmatrix} a^{1'} \otimes B + A \otimes b^{1'} & + & B \otimes a^{1'} + b^{1'} \otimes A \\ \vdots & & \vdots \\ a^{n'} \otimes B + A \otimes b^{n'} & + & B \otimes a^{n'} + b^{n'} \otimes A \end{pmatrix} L'_n$$

$$= \frac{1}{4} \begin{pmatrix} a^{1'} \otimes B + A \otimes b^{1'} + B \otimes a^{1'} + b^{1'} \otimes A \\ E_1(a^{2'} \otimes B + A \otimes b^{2'} + B \otimes a^{2'} + b^{2'} \otimes A) \\ \vdots \\ E_{n-1}(a^{n'} \otimes B + A \otimes b^{n'} + B \otimes a^{n'} + b^{n'} \otimes A) \end{pmatrix} L'_n$$

where we have used the representation of L_n given by Equation 3.1. Using the properties of E_j given by Equations 3.10 and 3.11, we write

$$L_n N_n (A \otimes B) N_n L_n'$$

$$= \frac{1}{4} \begin{pmatrix} a^{1'} \otimes B + A \otimes b^{1'} + B \otimes a^{1'} + b^{1'} \otimes A \\ a^{2'} \otimes (B)_1 + (A)_1 \otimes b^{2'} + (B)_1 \otimes a^{2'} + b^{2'} \otimes (A)_1 \\ \vdots \\ a^{n'} \otimes (B)_{n-1} + (A)_{n-1} \otimes b^{n'} + (B)_{n-1} \otimes a^{n'} + b^{n'} \otimes (A)_{n-1} \end{pmatrix} L_n'.$$

The jth submatrix of this matrix is

$$= \frac{1}{4} \left(a^{j'} \otimes (B)_{j-1} + (A)_{j-1} \otimes b^{j'} + (B)_{j-1} \otimes a^{j'} + b^{j'} \otimes (A)_{j-1} \right) L_n'.$$

Applying Theorem 3.1 gives the result. ∎

Often, in the application of matrix calculus to statistics, as we shall see in Chapter 6, we are confronted with matrices like $L_n N_n (A \otimes A) N_n L_n'$ and $L_n (A \otimes A) L_n'$.

It is informative to spend a little time comparing these two matrices for this special case. From the properties of N_n discussed in Section 2.5.7 of Chapter 2, we have that

$$L_n N_n (A \otimes A) N_n L_n' = L_n (A \otimes A) N_n L_n'$$

$$= \frac{1}{2} L_n (A \otimes A) L_n' + \frac{1}{2} L_n (A \otimes A) K_{nn} L_n'.$$

Using Theorem 3.2, we have

$$L_n (A \otimes A) K_{nn} L_n'$$

$$= \begin{pmatrix} a^{1'} \otimes A \\ a^{2'} \otimes (A)_1 \\ \vdots \\ a^{n'} \otimes (A)_{n-1} \end{pmatrix} K_{nn} L_n' = \begin{pmatrix} A \otimes a^{1'} \\ (A)_1 \otimes a^{2'} \\ \vdots \\ (A)_{n-1} \otimes a^{n'} \end{pmatrix} L_n'$$

$$= \begin{pmatrix} a_1 \otimes a^{1'} & a_2 \otimes (a^{1'})^1 & \cdots & a_n \otimes (a^{1'})^{n-1} \\ (a_1)_1 \otimes a^{2'} & (a_2)_1 \otimes (a^{2'})^1 & \cdots & (a_n)_1 \otimes (a^{2'})^{n-1} \\ \vdots & \vdots & & \vdots \\ (a_1)_{n-1} \otimes a^{n'} & (a_2)_{n-1} \otimes (a^{n'})^1 & \cdots & (a_n)_{n-1} \otimes (a^{n'})^{n-1} \end{pmatrix}.$$

Putting our pieces together, we have that

$$L_n N_n (A \otimes A) N_n L_n' = \frac{1}{2} L_n (A \otimes A) L_n'$$

$$+ \frac{1}{2} \begin{pmatrix} a_1 \otimes a^{1'} & a_2 \otimes (a^{1'})^1 & \cdots & a_n \otimes (a^{1'})^{n-1} \\ (a_1)_1 \otimes a^{2'} & (a_2)_1 \otimes (a^{2'})^1 & \cdots & (a_n)_1 \otimes (a^{2'})^{n-1} \\ \vdots & \vdots & & \vdots \\ (a_1)_{n-1} \otimes a^{n'} & (a_2)_{n-1} \otimes (a^{n'})^1 & \cdots & (a_n)_{n-1} \otimes (a^{n'})^{n-1} \end{pmatrix}.$$

$$(3.27)$$

Consider, for example, the case where A is a 2×2 matrix. By Theorem 3.4, we have

$$L_2 (A \otimes A) L_2' = \begin{pmatrix} a_{11} A & a_{12} (A)^1 \\ a_{21} (A)_1 & a_{22} ((A)_1)^1 \end{pmatrix}$$

$$= \begin{pmatrix} a_{11} \begin{pmatrix} a_{11} & a_{12} \\ a_{21} & a_{22} \end{pmatrix} & a_{21} \begin{pmatrix} a_{12} \\ a_{22} \end{pmatrix} \\ a_{21} \begin{pmatrix} a_{21} & a_{22} \end{pmatrix} & a_{22} a_{22} \end{pmatrix}$$

$$= \begin{pmatrix} a_{11}^2 & a_{11} a_{12} & a_{21} a_{12} \\ a_{11} a_{21} & a_{11} a_{22} & a_{21} a_{22} \\ a_{21}^2 & a_{21} a_{22} & a_{22}^2 \end{pmatrix}.$$

By Equation 3.27,

$$L_2 N_2 (A \otimes A) N_2 L_2' = \frac{1}{2} L_2 (A \otimes A) L_2' + \frac{1}{2} \begin{pmatrix} a_1 \otimes a^{1'} & a_2 \otimes (a^{1'})^1 \\ (a_1)_1 \otimes a^{2'} & (a_2)_1 \otimes (a^{2'})^1 \end{pmatrix}$$

$$= \frac{1}{2} L_2 (A \otimes A) L_2' + \frac{1}{2} \begin{pmatrix} a_{11} (a_{11} \ a_{12}) & a_{21} \ a_{12} \\ a_{21} (a_{11} \ a_{12}) & a_{22} \ a_{12} \\ a_{21} (a_{21} \ a_{22}) & a_{22} \ a_{22} \end{pmatrix}$$

$$= \frac{1}{2} L_2 (A \otimes A) L_2' + \frac{1}{2} \begin{pmatrix} a_{11}^2 & a_{11} \ a_{12} & a_{21} \ a_{12} \\ a_{21} a_{11} & a_{21} \ a_{12} & a_{22} \ a_{12} \\ a_{21}^2 & a_{21} \ a_{22} & a_{22}^2 \end{pmatrix}$$

$$= \begin{pmatrix} a_{11}^2 & a_{11} \ a_{12} & a_{21} \ a_{12} \\ a_{11} \ a_{21} & \dfrac{a_{11} a_{22} + a_{21} a_{12}}{2} & \dfrac{a_{21} a_{22} + a_{22} a_{12}}{2} \\ a_{21}^2 & a_{21} \ a_{22} & a_{22}^2 \end{pmatrix}.$$

$$(3.28)$$

Note if A is 2×2 and symmetric then only the $(2, 2)$ element differs in these two matrices.

3.2.3 The Elimination Matrices $\bar{L}_n$ and $\bar{L}_n N_n$

Comparing $\text{vec} A$ with $\bar{v}(A)$, we see that $\bar{L}_n$ is the $\frac{1}{2}n(n-1) \times n^2$ matrix given by

$$\bar{L}_n = \begin{pmatrix} E_1 & O & \cdots & & O \\ O & E_2 & \cdots & & O \\ \vdots & \vdots & \ddots & & \vdots \\ 0' & 0' & \cdots & E_{n-1} & 0' \end{pmatrix}.$$

For example,

$$\bar{L}_3 = \begin{pmatrix} E_1 & O & O \\ 0' & E_2 & 0' \end{pmatrix} = \begin{pmatrix} 0 & 1 & 0 & 0 & 0 & 0 & 0 & 0 & 0 \\ 0 & 0 & 1 & 0 & 0 & 0 & 0 & 0 & 0 \\ 0 & 0 & 0 & 0 & 0 & 1 & 0 & 0 & 0 \end{pmatrix}.$$

Properties of $\bar{L}_n$ can be obtained from the properties of E_j in much the same way as we derived properties for L_n.

If A, B, and C are the matrices given by Equations 3.12, 3.13, and 3.14, respectively, then

$$\bar{L}_n A = \begin{pmatrix} (A_1)_1 \\ (A_2)_2 \\ \vdots \\ (A_{n-1})_{n-1} \end{pmatrix}$$

$$B\bar{L}_n' = \left((B_1)^1 \cdots (B_{n-1})^{n-1} \right)$$

$$\bar{L}_n C \bar{L}_n' = \begin{pmatrix} ((C_{11})_1)^1 & \cdots & ((C_{1n-1})_1)^{n-1} \\ ((C_{21})_2)^1 & \cdots & ((C_{2n-1})_2)^{n-1} \\ \vdots & & \\ ((C_{n-11})_{n-1})^1 & \cdots & ((C_{n-1n-1})_{n-1})^{n-1} \end{pmatrix}.$$

If A and B are $n \times p$ and $n \times q$ matrices, respectively, then

$$\bar{L}_n (A \otimes B) = \begin{pmatrix} a^{1'} \otimes (B)_1 \\ \vdots \\ a^{n-1'} \otimes (B)_{n-1} \end{pmatrix}$$

and if C and D are $r \times n$ and $s \times n$ matrices, respectively, then

$$(C \otimes D)\bar{L}_n' = c_1 \otimes (D)^1 \quad \cdots \quad c_{n-1} \otimes (D)^{n-1}.$$

Finally, if A and B are both $n \times n$ matrices, then

$$\bar{L}_n(A \otimes B)\bar{L}'_n = \begin{pmatrix} a_{11}\big((B)_1\big)^1 & \cdots & a_{1n-1}\big((B)_1\big)^{n-1} \\ \vdots & & \vdots \\ a_{n-11}\big((B)_{n-1}\big)^1 & \cdots & a_{n-1n-1}\big((B)_{n-1}\big)^{n-1} \end{pmatrix}.$$

In a similar manner, properties can be obtained for the elimination matrix $\bar{L}_n N_n$. If A and B $n \times p$ and $n \times q$ matrices, respectively, then

$$\bar{L}_n N_n (A \otimes B) = \frac{1}{2} \begin{bmatrix} a^{1'} \otimes (B)_1 + (A)_1 \otimes b^{1'} \\ \vdots \\ a^{n-1'} \otimes (B)_{n-1} + (A)_{n-1} \otimes b^{n-1'} \end{bmatrix}.$$

If C and D are $r \times n$ and $s \times n$ matrices, respectively, then

$$(C \otimes D)N_n \bar{L}'_n = \frac{1}{2}\big[c_1 \otimes (D)^1 + (C)^1 \otimes d_1 \quad \cdots \quad c_{n-1} \otimes (D)^{n-1} \\ + (C)^{n-1} \otimes d_{n-1} \big].$$

If A and B are both $n \times n$ matrices and we write

$$\bar{L}_n N_n (A \otimes B)N_n \bar{L}'_n = \begin{pmatrix} C_1 \\ \vdots \\ C_{n-1} \end{pmatrix}$$

then the submatrix C_j is a the $n - j \times \frac{1}{2}n(n-1)$ given by

$$\begin{aligned} C_j = \frac{1}{4}\Big[& a_{j1}\big((B)_j\big)^1 & \cdots & a_{jn-1}\big((B)_j\big)^{n-1} \\ & + b_{j1}\big((A)_j\big)^1 & \cdots & b_{jn-1}\big((A)_j\big)^{n-1} \\ & + (b_1)_j \otimes (a^{j'})^1 & \cdots & (b_{n-1})_j \otimes (a^{j'})^{n-1} \\ & + (a_1)_j \otimes (b^{j'})^1 & \cdots & (a_{n-1})_j \otimes (b^{j'})^{n-1} \Big], \end{aligned}$$

for $j = 1, \ldots, n - 1$.

For the special case $A \otimes A$, we have

$$\begin{aligned} & \bar{L}_n N_n (A \otimes A)N_n \bar{L}'_n \\ &= \frac{1}{2}\bar{L}_n (A \otimes A)\bar{L}'_n + \frac{1}{2}\bar{L}_n (A \otimes A)K_{nn}\bar{L}'_n = \frac{1}{2}\bar{L}_n (A \otimes A)\bar{L}'_n \\ &\quad + \frac{1}{2}\begin{pmatrix} (a_1)_1 \otimes (a^{1'})^1 & \cdots & (a_{n-1})_1 \otimes (a^{1'})^{n-1} \\ \vdots & & \vdots \\ (a_1)_{n-1} \otimes (a^{n-1'})^1 & \cdots & (a_{n-1})_{n-1} \otimes (a^{n-1'})^{n-1} \end{pmatrix}. \end{aligned}$$

Consider $\bar{L}_n(A \otimes A)\bar{L}'_n$ and $\bar{L}_n N_n(A \otimes A)N_n\bar{L}'_n$ for the 3×3 case. First,

$$\bar{L}_3(A \otimes A)\bar{L}'_3 = \begin{pmatrix} a_{11}\big((A)_1\big)^1 & a_{12}\big((A)_1\big)^2 \\ a_{21}\big((A)_2\big)^1 & a_{22}\big((A)_2\big)^2 \end{pmatrix}$$

$$= \begin{pmatrix} a_{11}\begin{pmatrix} a_{22} & a_{23} \\ a_{32} & a_{33} \end{pmatrix} & a_{12}\begin{pmatrix} a_{23} \\ a_{33} \end{pmatrix} \\ a_{21}\begin{pmatrix} a_{32} & a_{33} \end{pmatrix} & a_{22}a_{33} \end{pmatrix}$$

$$= \begin{pmatrix} a_{11}a_{22} & a_{11}a_{23} & a_{12}a_{23} \\ a_{11}a_{32} & a_{11}a_{33} & a_{12}a_{33} \\ a_{21}a_{32} & a_{21}a_{33} & a_{22}a_{33} \end{pmatrix}.$$

Now,

$$\bar{L}_3(A \otimes A)K_{33}\bar{L}'_3 = \begin{pmatrix} (a_1)_1 \otimes \big(a^{1'}\big)^1 & (a_2)_1 \otimes \big(a^{1'}\big)^2 \\ (a_1)_2 \otimes \big(a^{2'}\big)^1 & (a_2)_2 \otimes \big(a^{2'}\big)^2 \end{pmatrix}$$

$$= \begin{pmatrix} a_{21}\begin{pmatrix} a_{12} & a_{13} \end{pmatrix} & a_{22}a_{13} \\ a_{31}\begin{pmatrix} a_{12} & a_{13} \end{pmatrix} & a_{32}a_{13} \\ a_{31}\begin{pmatrix} a_{22} & a_{23} \end{pmatrix} & a_{32}a_{23} \end{pmatrix}$$

$$= \begin{pmatrix} a_{21}a_{12} & a_{21}a_{13} & a_{22}a_{13} \\ a_{31}a_{12} & a_{31}a_{13} & a_{32}a_{13} \\ a_{31}a_{22} & a_{31}a_{23} & a_{32}a_{23} \end{pmatrix},$$

so

$$\bar{L}_3 N_3(A \otimes A)N_3\bar{L}'_3$$
$$= \frac{1}{2}\begin{pmatrix} a_{11}a_{22} + a_{21}a_{12} & a_{11}a_{23} + a_{21}a_{13} & a_{12}a_{23} + a_{22}a_{13} \\ a_{11}a_{32} + a_{31}a_{12} & a_{11}a_{33} + a_{31}a_{13} & a_{12}a_{33} + a_{32}a_{13} \\ a_{21}a_{32} + a_{31}a_{22} & a_{21}a_{33} + a_{31}a_{23} & a_{22}a_{33} + a_{32}a_{23} \end{pmatrix}.$$

The comments we made regarding L_n and $L_n N_n$ for a symmetric matrix A hold for $\bar{L}_n$ as well. If A is symmetric

$$\bar{L}_n \text{vec } A = \bar{L}_n N_n \text{vec } A = \bar{v}(A)$$

with $\bar{L}_n N_n$ the elimination matrix that recognizes the fact that A is symmetric.

To find an explicit expression for the matrix $\bar{L}_n N_n$, we take a different approach than the one we used for $L_n N_n$.

Using Equation 2.43 of Chapter 2, we write

$$\overline{L}_n N_n = \frac{1}{2} \begin{pmatrix} E_1 & & O & O \\ & \ddots & & \vdots \\ O & & E_{n-1} & 0' \end{pmatrix} \begin{pmatrix} I_n \otimes e_1^{n'} + e_1^{n'} \otimes I_n \\ \vdots \\ I_n \otimes e_n^{n'} + e_n^{n'} \otimes I_n \end{pmatrix}$$

$$= \frac{1}{2} \begin{pmatrix} E_1 \left(I_n \otimes e_1^{n'} + e_1^{n'} \otimes I_n \right) \\ \vdots \\ E_{n-1} \left(I_n \otimes e_{n-1}^{n'} + e_{n-1}^{n'} \otimes I_n \right) \end{pmatrix}$$

$$= \frac{1}{2} \begin{pmatrix} (I_n)_1 \otimes e_1^{n'} + e_1^{n'} \otimes (I_n)_1 \\ \vdots \\ (I_n)_{n-1} \otimes e_{n-1}^{n'} + e_{n-1}^{n'} \otimes (I_n)_{n-1} \end{pmatrix},$$

where we have used Equations 3.10 and 3.11.

We have seen that $(I_n)_j$ is the $n - j \times n$ matrix given by $(I_n)_j = \begin{pmatrix} O_{n-j \times j} & I_{n-j} \end{pmatrix} = E_j$, so the jth block of this matrix is the $n - j \times n^2$ matrix given by

$$\begin{pmatrix} O & I_{n-j} \end{pmatrix} \otimes e_j^{n'} + e_j^{n'} \otimes \begin{pmatrix} O & I_{n-j} \end{pmatrix}$$

$$= \begin{pmatrix} O_{n-j \times jn} & I_{n-j} \otimes e_j^{n'} \end{pmatrix} + \begin{pmatrix} O_{n-j \times (j-1)n} & \begin{pmatrix} O & I_{n-j} \end{pmatrix} & O_{n-j \times n(n-j)} \end{pmatrix}$$

$$= \begin{pmatrix} O_{(n-j) \times j(n+1)-n} & I_{n-j} & I_{n-j} \otimes e_j^{n'} \end{pmatrix} = Q_j, \qquad (3.29)$$

say, for $j = 1, \ldots, n - 1$. Our explicit expression for $\overline{L}_n N_n$ is then

$$\overline{L}_n N_n = \frac{1}{2} \begin{pmatrix} Q_1 \\ \vdots \\ Q_{n-1} \end{pmatrix}.$$

3.2.4 The Elimination Matrices L_n^*

Comparing vech A with $\overline{v}(A)$, we see that L_n^* is the $\frac{1}{2}n(n-1) \times \frac{1}{2}n(n+1)$ matrix given by

$$L_n^* = \begin{pmatrix} F_1 & O & \cdots & & \cdots & 0 \\ O & F_2 & \cdots & & \cdots & 0 \\ & & \ddots & & & \vdots \\ 0' & 0' & \cdots & F_{n-1} & 0 \end{pmatrix} \qquad (3.30)$$

where F_j is a $n - j \times n - j + 1$ matrix given by

$$F_j = \begin{pmatrix} O \\ n-j\times 1 & I_{n-j} \\ & n-j\times n-j \end{pmatrix},$$

for $j = 1, \ldots, n - 1$.

Clearly, if A is a $n - j + 1 \times p$ matrix, then

$$F_j A = (A)_1. \tag{3.31}$$

It follows then that

$$F_j E_{j-1} = (E_{j-1})_1 = E_j,$$

for $j = 2, \ldots, n - 1$ and that $F_1 = E_1$.

Using these properties, we have

$$L_n^* L_n = \begin{pmatrix} F_1 & O & \cdots & \cdots & 0 \\ O & F_2 & \cdots & & \vdots \\ \vdots & \vdots & \ddots & & \vdots \\ 0' & 0' & \cdots & F_{n-1} & 0 \end{pmatrix} \begin{pmatrix} I_n & \cdots & \cdots & O \\ \vdots & E_1 & & \vdots \\ \vdots & & \ddots & \vdots \\ O & \cdots & \cdots & E_{n-1} \end{pmatrix}$$

$$= \begin{pmatrix} E_1 & O & \cdots & \cdots & O \\ O & E_2 & \cdots & & O \\ \vdots & \vdots & \ddots & & \vdots \\ 0' & 0' & \cdots & E_{n-1} & 0' \end{pmatrix} = \bar{L}_n,$$

so

$$L_n^* L_n N = \bar{L}_n N \tag{3.32}$$

3.3 Duplication Matrices

3.3.1 The Duplication Matrix D_n

A matrix as complicated as $L_n N_n$ is the duplication matrix D_n (in fact, we shall see in the last section of this chapter that the two matrices bear many similarities). The duplication matrix D_n is the $n^2 \times n(n+1)/2$ zero-one matrix that takes us from $\text{vech}\,A$ to $\text{vec}\,A$ for the case where A is a symmetric matrix. Recall that $\text{vech}\,A$ is the $n(n+1)/2 \times 1$ vector given by

$$\text{vech}\,A = \begin{pmatrix} a_{11} \\ \vdots \\ a_{n1} \\ a_{22} \\ \vdots \\ a_{n2} \\ \vdots \\ a_{nn} \end{pmatrix}$$

whereas $\text{vec}\,A$ is $n^2 \times 1$ vector given by

$$\text{vec}\,A = \begin{pmatrix} a_{11} \\ \vdots \\ a_{n1} \\ \vdots \\ a_{1n} \\ \vdots \\ a_{nn} \end{pmatrix}.$$

Comparing $\text{vech}\,A$ with $\text{vec}\,A$, we see that we can write D_n as follows:

$$D_n = \begin{pmatrix} I_n & O & O & \cdots & O & 0 \\ e_2^{n'} & 0' & 0' & \cdots & 0' & 0 \\ O & I_{n-1} & O & \cdots & O & 0 \\ e_3^{n'} & 0' & 0' & \cdots & 0' & 0 \\ 0' & e_2^{n-1'} & 0' & \cdots & 0' & 0 \\ O & O & I_{n-2} & \cdots & O & 0 \\ & & \vdots & & & \vdots \\ e_n^{n'} & 0' & 0' & \cdots & 0' & 0 \\ 0' & e_{n-1}^{n-1'} & 0' & \cdots & 0' & 0 \\ \vdots & & & \ddots & & \vdots \\ \vdots & & & & \ddots & \vdots \\ & & & & e_2^{2'} & \\ 0' & 0' & 0' & \cdots & 0' & 1 \end{pmatrix}. \qquad (3.33)$$

For example,

$$
D_3 = \begin{pmatrix} I_3 & O & 0 \\ e_2^{3\prime} & 0' & 0 \\ O & I_2 & 0 \\ e_3^{3\prime} & 0' & 0 \\ 0' & e_2^{2\prime} & 0 \\ 0' & 0' & 1 \end{pmatrix} = \begin{pmatrix} 1 & 0 & 0 & 0 & 0 & 0 \\ 0 & 1 & 0 & 0 & 0 & 0 \\ 0 & 0 & 1 & 0 & 0 & 0 \\ 0 & 1 & 0 & 0 & 0 & 0 \\ 0 & 0 & 0 & 1 & 0 & 0 \\ 0 & 0 & 0 & 0 & 1 & 0 \\ 0 & 0 & 1 & 0 & 0 & 0 \\ 0 & 0 & 0 & 0 & 1 & 0 \\ 0 & 0 & 0 & 0 & 0 & 1 \end{pmatrix}.
$$

A close inspection of D_n shows that we can write the matrix in the following way:

$$
D_n = \begin{pmatrix} H_1 \\ \vdots \\ H_n \end{pmatrix} = (M_1 \quad \cdots \quad M_n) \tag{3.34}
$$

where H_1 is the $n \times \frac{1}{2}n(n+1)$ matrix given by

$$
H_1 = (I_n \quad O) \tag{3.35}
$$

where H_j is the $n \times \frac{1}{2}n(n+1)$ matrix given by

$$
H_j = (G_j \quad O) \tag{3.36}
$$

where G_j is the $n \times \frac{j}{2}(2n+1-j)$ matrix given by

$$
G_j = \begin{pmatrix} e_j^{n\prime} & & & & O \\ & e_{j-1}^{n-1\prime} & & & \\ & & \ddots & & \\ & & & e_2^{n-j+2\prime} & \\ O & & & & I_{n-j+1} \end{pmatrix}, \tag{3.37}
$$

for $j = 2, \ldots, n$.

In the alternate representation, M_j is the $n^2 \times n - j + 1$ matrix given by

$$
M_j = \begin{pmatrix} O \\ {\scriptstyle n(j-1)\times(n-j+1)} \\ O \\ {\scriptstyle (j-1)\times(n-j+1)} \\ I_{n-j+1} \\ O \\ {\scriptstyle (j-1)\times(n-j+1)} \\ e_2^{n-j+1'} \\ O \\ {\scriptstyle (n-j)\times(n-j+1)} \\ \vdots \\ O \\ e_{n-j+1}^{n-j+1'} \\ O \end{pmatrix} = \begin{pmatrix} O \\ O \\ I_{n-j+1} \\ Z_2^{j'} \\ \vdots \\ Z_{n-j+1}^{j'} \end{pmatrix}, \tag{3.38}
$$

for $j = 2, \ldots, n-1$ and

$$
M_1 = \begin{pmatrix} I_n \\ Z_2^{1'} \\ \vdots \\ Z_n^{1'} \end{pmatrix} \quad \text{and} \quad M_n = \begin{pmatrix} 0 \\ \vdots \\ E_{n-1}' \end{pmatrix}. \tag{3.39}
$$

The matrices $Z_2^j \ldots Z_{n-j+1}^j$ are given by Equations 3.20 and 3.21 for $j = 1, \ldots, n-1$.

The matrices H_j and M_j for $j = 1, \ldots, n$ are interesting in themselves and worthy of study. Consider the former one first. If A is a $n \times p$ matrix, then

$$
H_1'A = \begin{pmatrix} I_n \\ O \end{pmatrix} A = \begin{pmatrix} A \\ O \end{pmatrix} \tag{3.40}
$$

and

$$
H_j'A = \begin{pmatrix} G_j' \\ O \end{pmatrix} A = \begin{pmatrix} G_j'A \\ O \end{pmatrix} \tag{3.41}
$$

where

$$
G_j'A = \begin{pmatrix} e_j^n & & & & O \\ & e_{j-1}^{n-1} & & & \\ & & \ddots & & \\ & & & e_2^{n-j+2} & \\ O & & & & I_{n-j+1} \end{pmatrix} \begin{pmatrix} a^{1'} \\ \vdots \\ a^{j-1'} \\ (A)_{j-1} \end{pmatrix} = \begin{pmatrix} e_j^n a^{1'} \\ \vdots \\ e_2^{n-j+2} a^{j-1'} \\ (A)_{j-1} \end{pmatrix} \tag{3.42}
$$

for $j = 2, \ldots, n$. Also, if x is a $n \times 1$ matrix

$$H'_j(x' \otimes A) = x' \otimes H'_j A, \tag{3.43}$$

for $j = 1, \ldots, n$.

Taking the transposes of Equations 3.40, 3.41, 3.42, and 3.43, we get that if B is a $p \times n$ matrix, then

$$BH_1 = (B \quad O)$$

$$BH_j = (BG_j \quad O)$$

where

$$BG_j = \begin{pmatrix} b_1 e_j^{n'} \\ \vdots \\ b_{j-1} e_2^{n-j+2'} \\ (B)^{j-1} \end{pmatrix}'$$

for $j = 2, \ldots, n$. and

$$(x \otimes B)H_j = x \otimes BH_j$$

for $j = 1, \ldots, n$.

We write the other matrix M_j as

$$M_j = \begin{pmatrix} O \\ E'_{j-1} \\ Z_2^{j'} \\ \vdots \\ Z_{n-j+1}^{j'} \end{pmatrix}$$

for $j = 2, \ldots, n-1$, where from Equation 3.20 $Z_i^{j'}$ is the $n \times n - j + 1$ matrix given by

$$Z_i^{j'} = \begin{pmatrix} O \\ {}_{(j-1)\times(n-j+1)} \\ e_i^{n-j+1'} \\ O \\ {}_{(n-j)\times(n-j+1)} \end{pmatrix}^3$$

for $j = 2, \ldots, n - j + 1$.

---

[3] The remarks made about E_j clearly refer to H_j, G_j, M_j and Z_i^j as well. All these matrices are dependent on n, but for simplicity of notation, this is not indicated, the relevant n being clear from the content.

It is now time to investigate some of the properties of Z_i^j. First, if A is a $n \times p$ matrix, then

$$Z_i^j A = \begin{pmatrix} O & e_i^{n-j+1} & O \end{pmatrix} A = e_i^{n-j+1} a^{j'} = \begin{pmatrix} 0' \\ \vdots \\ a^{j'} \\ \vdots \\ 0' \end{pmatrix} i^{\text{th}} \qquad (3.44)$$

Clearly, if x is a $n \times 1$ vector

$$Z_i^j (x' \otimes A) = x' \otimes Z_i^{j'} A = x' \otimes e_i^{n-j+1} \otimes a^{j'}.$$

Taking the transposes, we get

$$BZ_i^{j'} = b_j e_i^{n-j+1'} = b_j \otimes e_i^{n-j+1'} = e_i^{n-j+1'} \otimes b_j = \begin{pmatrix} 0 & \cdots & b_j & \cdots & 0 \end{pmatrix}$$

and

$$(x \otimes B)Z_i^{j'} = x \otimes e_i^{n-j+1'} \otimes b_j.$$

If A is a $n^2 \times p$ matrix and we partition A as

$$A = \begin{pmatrix} A_1 \\ \vdots \\ A_n \end{pmatrix}$$

where each submatrix is $n \times p$, then

$$M_j' A = \begin{pmatrix} O & E_{j-1} & Z_2^j & \cdots & Z_{n-j+1}^j \end{pmatrix} \begin{pmatrix} A_1 \\ \vdots \\ A_j \\ A_{j+1} \\ \vdots \\ A_n \end{pmatrix}$$

$$= E_{j-1} A_j + Z_2^j A_{j+1} + \cdots + Z_{n-j+1}^j A_n$$

for $j = 1, \ldots, n-1$ and

$$M_n' A = E_{n-1} A_n.$$

Using Equations 3.3 and 3.44, we have

$$M'_j A = (A_j)_{j-1} + \begin{pmatrix} O \\ (A_{j+1})_{j \cdot} \\ O \\ \vdots \\ O \end{pmatrix} + \cdots + \begin{pmatrix} O \\ O \\ \vdots \\ (A_n)_{j \cdot} \end{pmatrix}$$

$$= \begin{pmatrix} (A_j)_{j \cdot} \\ (A_j)_{j+1 \cdot} \\ \vdots \\ (A_j)_{n \cdot} \end{pmatrix} + \begin{pmatrix} O \\ (A_{j+1})_{j \cdot} \\ \vdots \\ (A_n)_{j \cdot} \end{pmatrix}$$

$$= \begin{pmatrix} (A_j)_{j \cdot} \\ (A_j)_j + \left(A^{(j)}\right)_j \end{pmatrix} = \left((A_j)_{j-1} + \begin{pmatrix} 0' \\ \left(A^{(j)}\right)_j \end{pmatrix} \right) \quad (3.45)$$

for $j = 1, \ldots, n-1$, where we are using the notation introduced in Equation 1.8 of Chapter 1, and

$$M'_n A = (A_n)_{n-1}. \quad (3.46)$$

If A and B are $n \times p$ and $n \times q$ matrices, respectively,

$$M'_j (A \otimes B) = \begin{pmatrix} (a^{j'} \otimes B)_{j \cdot} \\ (a^{j'} \otimes B)_j + \left((A \otimes B)^{(j)}\right)_j \end{pmatrix}$$

for $j = 1, \ldots, n-1$ and

$$M'_n (A \otimes B) = (a^{n'} \otimes B)_{n-1}.$$

As pointed out in Section 1.2 of Chapter 1,

$$(a^{j'} \otimes B)_{j \cdot} = a^{j'} \otimes b^{j'}.$$

From Equation 3.6, we have

$$(a^{j'} \otimes B)_j = a^{j'} \otimes (B)_j$$

and from Equation 1.9 of Chapter 1, we have

$$(A \otimes B)^{(j)} = A \otimes b^{j'}$$

so using Equation 3.5, we have

$$\left((A \otimes B)^{(j)}\right)_j = (A)_j \otimes b^{j'}$$

for $j = 1, \ldots, n-1$. Hence, we write

$$M_j'(A \otimes B) = \begin{pmatrix} a^{j'} \otimes b^{j'} \\ a^{j'} \otimes (B)_j + (A)_j \otimes b^{j'} \end{pmatrix} = a^{j'} \otimes (B)_{j-1} + \begin{pmatrix} 0' \\ (A)_j \end{pmatrix} \otimes b^{j'}$$

(3.47)

for $j = 1, \ldots, n-1$ and

$$M_n'(A \otimes B) = a^{n'} \otimes (B)_{n-1}.$$

(3.48)

If we take the transposes of both sides of Equations 3.45, 3.46, 3.47, and 3.48, we have the following results. If B is a $p \times n^2$ matrix and we partition B as

$$B = \begin{pmatrix} B_1 & \cdots & B_n \end{pmatrix}$$

where each submatrix is $p \times n$, then

$$BM_j = \begin{pmatrix} (B_j)_{.j} & (B_j)^j + & (B_{(j)})^j \end{pmatrix}$$

(3.49)

for $j = 1, \ldots, n-1$, where we have used the notation introduced by Equation 2.67 of Chapter 2, and

$$BM_n = (B_n)^{n-1}.$$

If C and D are $p \times n$ and $q \times n$ matrices, respectively, then

$$(C \otimes D)M_j = \begin{pmatrix} c_j \otimes d_j & c_j \otimes (D)^j + (C)^j \otimes d_j \end{pmatrix}$$
$$= \begin{pmatrix} c_j \otimes (D)^{j-1} + (0 & (C)^j) \otimes d_j \end{pmatrix}$$

(3.50)

for $j = 1, \ldots, n-1$ and

$$(C \otimes D)M_n = c_n \otimes (D)^{n-1}.$$

Note that as special cases if x and y are both $n \times 1$ vectors

$$M_j'(x \otimes y) = \begin{pmatrix} x_j y_j \\ x_j(y)_j + (x)_j y_j \end{pmatrix} = \begin{pmatrix} x_j(y)_{j-1} + y_j \begin{pmatrix} 0 \\ (x)_j \end{pmatrix} \end{pmatrix}$$

for $j = 1, \ldots, n-1$ and

$$M_n'(x \otimes y) = x_n y_n$$

whereas

$$(x' \otimes y')M_j = \begin{pmatrix} x_j y_j & x_j(y')^j + y_j(x')^j \end{pmatrix} = \begin{pmatrix} x_j(y')^{j-1} + y_j (0' & (x')^j) \end{pmatrix}$$

(3.51)

for $j = 1, \ldots, n - 1$ and

$$(x' \otimes y')M_n = x_n y_n.$$

Now, consider the case where A and B are both $n \times n$ matrices, so we can form $M_j'(A \otimes B)M_\ell$. From Equation 3.47

$$M_j'(A \otimes B)M_\ell = \begin{pmatrix} a_j' \otimes b_j' \\ a_j' \otimes (B)_j + (A)_j \otimes b_j' \end{pmatrix} M_\ell$$

for $j = 1, \ldots, n - 1$. But using Equation 3.51, we can write

$$\left(a_j' \otimes b_j'\right)M_\ell = \begin{pmatrix} a_{j\ell} b_{j\ell} & a_{j\ell}\left(b_j'\right)^\ell + b_{j\ell}\left(a_j'\right)^\ell \end{pmatrix}$$

for $\ell = 1, \ldots, n - 1$, whereas using Equation 3.50, we have

$$\left(a_j' \otimes (B)_j\right)M_\ell = \begin{pmatrix} a_{j\ell}(b_\ell)_j & a_{j\ell}\left((B)_j\right)^\ell + \left(a_j'\right)^\ell \otimes (b_\ell)_j \end{pmatrix}$$

and

$$\left((A)_j \otimes b_j'\right)M_\ell = \begin{pmatrix} b_{j\ell}(a_\ell)_j & (a_\ell)_j \otimes \left(b_j'\right)^\ell + \left((A)_j\right)^\ell b_{j\ell} \end{pmatrix}$$

again for $j = 1, \ldots, n - 1$. Putting our pieces together we have that

$M_j'(A \otimes B)M_\ell$

$$= \begin{pmatrix} a_{j\ell} b_{j\ell} & a_{j\ell}(b^{j'})^\ell + b_{j\ell}(a^{j'})^\ell \\ a_{j\ell}(b_\ell)_j + b_{j\ell}(a_\ell)_j & a_{j\ell}\left((B)_j\right)^\ell + b_{j\ell}\left((A)_j\right)^\ell + (a^{j'})^\ell \otimes (b_\ell)_j + (a_\ell)_j \otimes (b^{j'})^\ell \end{pmatrix}$$

$$= \begin{pmatrix} a_{j\ell}(b_\ell)_{j-1} + b_{j\ell}\begin{pmatrix} 0 \\ (a_\ell)_j \end{pmatrix} & a_{j\ell}((B)_{j-1})^\ell + b_{j\ell}((A)_{j-1})^\ell + \begin{pmatrix} 0' \\ a^{j'} \end{pmatrix}^\ell \otimes (b_\ell)_j + \begin{pmatrix} 0 \\ (a_\ell)_j \end{pmatrix} \otimes (b^{j'})^\ell \end{pmatrix}$$

for $j = 1, \ldots, n - 1$, and $\ell = 1, \ldots, n - 1$.

The special cases are given by

$$M_n'(A \otimes B)M_\ell = \begin{pmatrix} a_{n\ell} b_{n\ell} & a_{n\ell}(b_n')^\ell + b_{n\ell}(a_n')^\ell \end{pmatrix}$$

$$= \begin{pmatrix} a_{n\ell}(b_n')^{\ell-1} + b_{n\ell}\begin{pmatrix} 0' \\ a_n' \end{pmatrix}^\ell \end{pmatrix}$$

for $\ell = 1, \ldots, n - 1$ and

$$M_j'(A \otimes B)M_n = \begin{pmatrix} a_{jn} b_{jn} \\ a_{jn}(b_n)_j + b_{jn}(a_n)_j \end{pmatrix} = \begin{pmatrix} a_{jn}(b_n)_{j-1} + b_{jn}\begin{pmatrix} 0 \\ (a_n)_j \end{pmatrix} \end{pmatrix}$$

for $j = 1, \ldots, n - 1$ and

$$M_n'(A \otimes B)M_n = a_{nn} b_{nn}.$$

Using these properties for $M_1, \ldots, M_n$, we can investigate how D_n interact with Kronecker products. Consider two matrices A and B, which are $n \times p$ and $n \times q$, respectively, then

$$D_n'(A \otimes B) = \begin{pmatrix} M_1'(A \otimes B) \\ \vdots \\ M_n'(A \otimes B) \end{pmatrix}.$$

Using the properties of M_j and M_n given by Equations 3.47 and 3.48, we can write

$$D_n'(A \otimes B) = \begin{pmatrix} a^{1'} \otimes b^{1'} \\ a^{1'} \otimes (B)_1 + (A)_1 \otimes b^{1'} \\ a^{2'} \otimes b^{2'} \\ a^{2'} \otimes (B)_2 + (A)_2 \otimes b^{2'} \\ \vdots \\ a^{n'} \otimes (B)_{n-1} \end{pmatrix}$$

$$= \begin{pmatrix} a^{1'} \otimes B + \begin{pmatrix} O \\ (A)_1 \end{pmatrix} \otimes b^{1'} \\ a^{2'} \otimes (B)_1 + \begin{pmatrix} O \\ (A)_2 \end{pmatrix} \otimes b^{2'} \\ \vdots \\ a^{n-1'} \otimes (B)_{n-2} + \begin{pmatrix} O \\ (A)_{n-1} \end{pmatrix} \otimes b^{n-1'} \\ a^{n'} \otimes (B)_{n-1} \end{pmatrix}$$

and if C and D are $r \times n$ and $s \times n$ matrices, respectively, then

$$(C \otimes D)D_n = \big(c_1 \otimes d_1 \quad c_1 \otimes (D)^1 + (C)^1 \otimes d_1 \quad \cdots$$
$$c_{n-1} \otimes d_{n-1} \quad c_{n-1} \otimes (D)^{n-1} + (C)^{n-1} \otimes d_{n-1} \quad c_n \otimes (D)^{n-1} \big)$$
$$= \big(c_1 \otimes D + (O \quad (C)^1) \otimes d_1 \quad \cdots$$
$$c_{n-1} \otimes (D)^{n-2} + (O \quad (C)^{n-1}) \otimes d_{n-1} \quad c_n \otimes (D)^{n-1} \big).$$

If A and B are both $n \times n$ matrices, so $D_n'(A \otimes B)D_n$ exists and if we write this matrix as

$$D_n'(A \otimes B)D_n = \begin{pmatrix} C_1 \\ \vdots \\ C_n \end{pmatrix},$$

then the submatrix C_j is the $n - j + 1 \times \frac{1}{2}n(n+1)$ matrix given by

$$C_j = \Big(a_{j1}(B)_{j-1} + \big(0' \quad (a^{j'})^1\big) \otimes (b_1)_{j-1} \cdots a_{jn-1}\big((B)_{j-1}\big)^{n-2}$$

$$+ \big(0' \quad (a^{j'})^{n-1}\big) \otimes (b_{n-1})_{j-1} \quad a_{jn}((B)_{j-1})^{n-1}\Big) + \Big(\binom{0}{(a_1)_j} \otimes b^{j'}$$

$$+ \Big(0 \quad \binom{0'}{(A)_j}^1\Big) b_{j1} \cdots \binom{0}{(a_{n-1})_j} \otimes (b^{j'})^{n-2}$$

$$+ \Big(0 \quad \binom{0'}{(A)_j}^{n-1}\Big) b_{jn-1} \binom{0}{(a_n)_j} \otimes (b^{j'})^{n-1}\Big) \tag{3.52}$$

for $j = 1, \ldots, n$ and

$$C_n = \Big(a_{n1}(B)_{n-1} + \big(0 \quad (a^{n'})^1\big) \otimes (b_1)_{n-1} \cdots a_{nn-1}\big((B)_{n-1}\big)^{n-2}$$

$$+ \big(0 \quad (a^{n'})^{n-1}\big) \otimes (b_{n-1})_{n-1} \, a_{nn}\big((B)_{n-1}\big)^{n-1}\Big)$$

$$= \Big(a_{n1}(B)_{n-1} + \big(0 \quad (a^{n'})^1\big) \otimes (b_1)_{n-1} \cdots a_{nn-1}\big((B)_{n-1}\big)^{n-2}$$

$$+ \big(0 \quad a_{nn}b_{n-1n}\big) \, a_{nn}b_{nn}\Big). \tag{3.53}$$

We see in Chapter 6 that the application of matrix calculus to statistics often gives rise to the matrix $D'_n(A \otimes A)D_n$ and in this expression, more often than not, A is a symmetric matrix. Consider the case where A is a 2×2 matrix, not necessarily symmetric. Then, by Equations 3.52 and 3.53

$$D'_2(A \otimes A)D_2 = \binom{C_1}{C_2}$$

where

$$C_1 = \Big(a_{11}(A)_0 + \big(0 \quad (a^{1'})^1\big) \otimes (a_1)_0 \quad a_{12}((A)_0)^1\big)$$

$$+ \Big(\binom{0}{(a_1)_1} \otimes a^{1'} + \Big(0 \quad \binom{0}{(A)_1}^1\Big) a_{11} \quad \binom{0}{(a_2)_1} \otimes (a^{1'})^1\Big)$$

$$= \Big(a_{11}\binom{a_{11} \quad a_{12}}{a_{21} \quad a_{22}} + \big(0 \quad a_{12}\big) \otimes \binom{a_{11}}{a_{21}} \quad a_{12}\binom{a_{12}}{a_{22}}\Big)$$

$$+ \Big(\binom{0}{a_{21}} \otimes \big(a_{11} \quad a_{12}\big) + \binom{0 \quad 0}{0 \quad a_{22}} a_{11} \quad \binom{0}{a_{22}} a_{12}\Big)$$

$$= \binom{a_{11}^2 \qquad\qquad 2a_{11}a_{12} \qquad\qquad a_{12}^2}{2a_{21}a_{11} \quad 2a_{11}a_{22} + 2a_{21}a_{12} \quad 2a_{12}a_{22}}$$

and

$$C_2 = \left(a_{21}(A)_1 + \left(0 \quad (a^{2'})^1\right)(a_1)_1 \quad a_{22}((A)_1)^1\right)$$
$$= \left(a_{21}(a_{21} \quad a_{22}) + \left(0 \quad a_{22}\right)a_{21} \quad a_{22}^2\right)$$
$$= \left(a_{21}^2 \quad 2a_{21}a_{22} \quad a_{22}^2\right)$$

so

$$D_2'(A \otimes A)D_2 = \begin{pmatrix} a_{11}^2 & 2a_{11}a_{12} & a_{12}^2 \\ 2a_{11}a_{21} & 2a_{11}a_{22} + 2a_{21}a_{12} & 2a_{12}a_{22} \\ a_{21}^2 & 2a_{21}a_{22} & a_{22}^2 \end{pmatrix}. \qquad (3.54)$$

Comparing Equation 3.54 with Equation 3.28, we see that there are a lot of similarities between $L_2N_2(A \otimes A)N_2L_2'$ and $D_2'(A \otimes A)D_2$ when A is symmetric. All the elements of these two matrices have the same combination of the a_{ij}s, though the number of these combinations differs in the 2nd row and the 2nd column. More will be made of this when we compare L_nN_n with D_n as we do in Section 3.4.

Using our explicit expression for L_n, L_nN_n, and D_n, it is simple to prove known results linking D_n with L_n and N_n.

For example,

$$L_nD_n = \begin{pmatrix} I_n & & & O \\ & E_1 & & \\ & & \ddots & \\ O & & & E_{n-1} \end{pmatrix} \begin{pmatrix} H_1 \\ \vdots \\ H_n \end{pmatrix} = \begin{pmatrix} H_1 \\ E_1H_2 \\ \vdots \\ E_{n-1}H_n \end{pmatrix}.$$

But using Equations 3.3, 3.35 and 3.36, the matrix E_jH_{j+1} is the $n-j \times \frac{1}{2}n(n+1)$ matrix given by

$$E_jH_{j+1} = \begin{pmatrix} O & I_{n-j} & O \\ (n-j)\times\frac{j}{2}(2n-j+1) & & (n-j)\times\frac{1}{2}(n-j+1)(n-j) \end{pmatrix},$$

so

$$L_nD_n = \begin{pmatrix} I_n & & & O \\ & I_{n-1} & & \\ & & \ddots & \\ O & & & 1 \end{pmatrix} = I_{\frac{1}{2}n(n+1)}.$$

Similarly,

$$L_n N_n D_n = \frac{1}{2}(P_1 \quad \cdots \quad P_n)\begin{pmatrix} H_1 \\ \vdots \\ H_n \end{pmatrix} = \frac{1}{2}(P_1 H_1 + \cdots + P_n H_n)$$

Now, from Equations 3.18 and 3.35,

$$P_1 H_1 = \begin{pmatrix} R_1 \\ O \end{pmatrix}(I_n \quad O) = \begin{pmatrix} R_1 & O \\ O & O \end{pmatrix}$$

and from Equations 3.16, 3.36, and 3.37.

$$P_j H_j = \begin{pmatrix} e_j^n & & & & O & \\ & e_{j-1}^{n-1} & & & & \\ & & \ddots & & & \\ O & & & e_2^{n-j+2} & & \\ & & & & R_j \\ O & & \cdots & & O \end{pmatrix}$$

$$\times \begin{pmatrix} e_j^{n'} & & & & O & & O \\ & e_{j-1}^{n-1'} & & & & & \\ & & \ddots & & & & \vdots \\ O & & & e_2^{n-j+2'} & & \\ O & & & & I_{n-j+1} & O \end{pmatrix}$$

$$= \begin{pmatrix} e_j^n e_j^{n'} & & & & O & & O \\ & e_{j-1}^{n-1} e_{j-1}^{n-1'} & & & & & \\ & & \ddots & & & & \vdots \\ O & & & e_2^{n-j+2} e_2^{n-j+2'} & & \\ & & & & & R_j \\ O & & \cdots & & & O & O \end{pmatrix}$$

for $j = 2, \ldots, n$, so

$$2L_n N_n D_n = \begin{pmatrix} R_1 & & & O \\ & O & & \\ & & \ddots & \\ O & & & O \end{pmatrix} + \begin{pmatrix} e_2^n e_2^{n'} & & & O \\ & R_2 & & \\ & & O & \\ O & & & O \end{pmatrix}$$

$$+ \begin{pmatrix} e_3^n e_3^{n'} & & & O \\ & e_2^{n-1} e_2^{n-1'} & & \\ & & R_3 & \\ & & & \ddots \\ O & & & O \end{pmatrix} + \cdots$$

$$+ \begin{pmatrix} e_n^n e_n^{n'} & & & O \\ & \ddots & & \\ & & e_2^2 e_2^{2'} & \\ O & & & R_n \end{pmatrix}$$

$$= 2 \begin{pmatrix} I_n & & & O \\ & I_{n-1} & & \\ & & \ddots & \\ O & & & 1 \end{pmatrix} = 2I_{\frac{1}{2}n(n+1)},$$

using Equation 3.17 and the fact that $R_n = 2$, which gives the result

$$L_n N_n D_n = I_{\frac{1}{2}n(n+1)}. \qquad (3.55)$$

But such proofs are highly inefficient. A far more elegant approach, which leads to simpler proofs is that of Magnus (1988), which concentrates on the roles played by the various matrices. For example, for a symmetric matrix A, we know that $N_n \text{vec } A = \text{vec } A$, $L_n N_n \text{vec } A = \text{vech } A$, and $D_n \text{vech } A = \text{vec } A$. Thus, it follows that

$$D_n L_n N_n \text{vec } A = N_n \text{vec } A,$$

which gives the result

$$D_n L_n N_n = N_n.$$

For numerous other results linking L_n, $L_n N_n$, $\bar{L}_n$, $\bar{L}_n N_n$ and D_n I can do no better than refer the reader to Magnus (1988).

Our approach, investigating explicit expression for elimination matrices and duplication matrices, comes into its own when we want to highlight the interaction of these matrices with Kronecker products. It also greatly facilitates comparisons of the various zero-one matrices, particularly $L_n N_n$ and D_n as we see in the next section.

But first a new result, involving as it does L_n^*.

Theorem 3.7

$$L_n^* D_n' = 2\overline{L}_n N_n = 2L_n^* L_n N_n$$

Proof: Using Equations 3.30 and 3.34, we write

$$
L_n^* D_n' = \begin{pmatrix} F_1 & & O & 0 \\ & \ddots & & \vdots \\ 0' & & F_{n-1} & 0' \end{pmatrix} \begin{pmatrix} M_1' \\ \vdots \\ M_n' \end{pmatrix} = \begin{pmatrix} F_1 M_1' \\ \vdots \\ F_{n-1} M_{n-1}' \end{pmatrix}.
$$

But using Equations 3.31 and 3.38,

$$
F_j M_j' = F_j \begin{pmatrix} O & O & I_{n-j+1} & O & e_2^{n-j+1} & O & \cdots & O & e_{n-j+1}^{n-j+1} & O \end{pmatrix}
$$

$$
= \begin{pmatrix} O & O & (I_{n-j+1})_1 & O & (e_2^{n-j+1})_1 & O & \cdots & O & (e_{n-j+1}^{n-j+1})_1 & O \end{pmatrix}
$$

$$
= \begin{pmatrix} O \\ {}_{(n-j)\times(j(n+1)-n)} & I_{n-j} & I_{n-j} \otimes e_j^{n'} \end{pmatrix} = Q_j,
$$

the matrix given by Equation 3.29.

In obtaining this result, we have used Theorem 1.1 of Chapter 1. The second part of the theorem was obtained earlier in Equation 3.32. ∎

Important consequences of Theorem 3.7 follow. If A and B are $n \times p$ and $n \times q$ matrices, respectively, then

$$L_n^* D_n'(A \otimes B) = 2L_n^* L_n N_n (A \otimes B)$$

and if C and D are $r \times n$ and $s \times n$ matrices respectively, then

$$(C \otimes D) D_n L_n^{*'} = 2(C \otimes D) N_n L_n' L_n^{*'}.$$

If, however, A and B are both $n \times n$ matrices, then

$$L_n^* D_n'(A \otimes B) D_n L_n^{*'} = 4L_n^* L_n N_n (A \otimes B) N_n L_n' L_n^{*'}.$$

3.3.2 The Elimination Matrix $L_n N_n$ and the Duplication Matrix D_n

If one compares Equations 3.19, 3.16, and 3.17 with Equations 3.34 and 3.39, or Equations 3.25, 3.22, 3.23, and 3.24 with Equations 3.34, 3.35,

3.36, and 3.37, one cannot help but notice the similarities between $2L_nN_n$ and D_n'.

In fact, these two matrices have most of their elements the same and the elements that differ are strategically placed in the two matrices being 2 in the matrix $2L_nN_n$ and being 1 in the matrix D_n'. The following theorem conveys this result.

Theorem 3.8   *The matrix $2L_nN_n - D_n'$ is the $\frac{1}{2}n(n+1)\times n^2$ block diagonal matrix given by*

$$2L_nN_n - D_n' = \begin{pmatrix} e_1^n e_1^{n'} & & & & O \\ & e_1^{n-1}e_2^{n'} & & & \\ & & e_1^{n-2}e_3^{n'} & & \\ & & & \ddots & \\ O & & & & e_n^{n'} \end{pmatrix}.$$

Proof: Consider L_nN_n and D_n as given by Equations 3.19 and 3.34, it follows that

$$2L_nN_n = (P_1 \quad \cdots \quad P_n)$$

and

$$D_n' = \begin{pmatrix} H_1' & \cdots & H_n' \end{pmatrix}.$$

Now, from Equations 3.18 and 3.35,

$$P_1 - H_1' = \begin{pmatrix} R_1 \\ O \end{pmatrix} - \begin{pmatrix} I_n \\ O \end{pmatrix},$$

where R_1 is the $n \times n$ matrix given by

$$R_1 = \begin{pmatrix} 2 & & & O \\ & 1 & & \\ & & \ddots & \\ O & & & 1 \end{pmatrix}.$$

It follows that $R_1 - I_n = e_1^n e_1^{n'}$, so

$$P_1 - H_1' = \begin{pmatrix} e_1^n e_1^{n'} \\ O \end{pmatrix}.$$

From Equations 3.16, 3.36, and 3.37,

$$P_j - H_j' = \begin{pmatrix} e_j^n & & & O \\ & \ddots & & \\ O & & e_2^{n-j+2} & \\ & & & R_j \\ O & \cdots & \cdots & O \end{pmatrix} - \begin{pmatrix} e_j^n & & & O \\ & \ddots & & \\ O & & e_2^{n-j+2} & \\ & & & I_{n-j+1} \\ O & \cdots & \cdots & O \end{pmatrix}$$

recalling that R_j is the $n - j + 1 \times n - j + 1$ matrix, given by

$$R_j = \begin{pmatrix} 2 & & & O \\ & 1 & & \\ & & \ddots & \\ O & & & 1 \end{pmatrix},$$

so

$$R_j - I_{n-j+1} = e_1^{n-j+1} e_1^{n-j+1'}$$

and

$$P_j - H_j' = \begin{pmatrix} O & & & \\ & \ddots & & \\ & & O & \\ O & \cdots & O & e_1^{n-j+1} e_1^{n-j+1'} \\ O & \cdots & \cdots & O \end{pmatrix}$$

for $j = 2, \ldots, n$. But,

$$\begin{pmatrix} O & \cdots & O & e_1^{n-j+1} e_1^{n-j+1'} \end{pmatrix} = e_1^{n-j+1} e_j^{n'}$$

for $j = 2, \ldots, n$. ∎

Theorem 3.8 can be used to investigate the different ways $2L_nN_n$ and D'_n interact with Kronecker products. For example,

$$
\left(2L_nN_n - D'_n\right)(A \otimes B) =
\begin{pmatrix}
e_1^n e_1^{n'} & & & O \\
& e_1^{n-1} e_2^{n'} & & \\
& & \ddots & \\
O & & & e_n^{n'}
\end{pmatrix}
\begin{pmatrix}
a^{1'} \otimes B \\
a^{2'} \otimes B \\
\vdots \\
a^{n'} \otimes B
\end{pmatrix}
$$

$$
=
\begin{pmatrix}
e_1^n a^{1'} \otimes e_1^{n'} B \\
e_1^{n-1} a^{2'} \otimes e_2^{n'} B \\
\vdots \\
a^{n'} \otimes e_n^{n'} B
\end{pmatrix}
=
\begin{pmatrix}
a^{1'} \otimes b^{1'} \\
O \\
a^{2'} \otimes b^{2'} \\
O \\
\vdots \\
a^{n'} \otimes b^{n'}
\end{pmatrix}.
$$

If we partition $L_nN_n(A \otimes B)$ as in Theorem 3.5, then the jth submatrix of $2L_nN_n(A \otimes B)$ is

$$
a^{j'} \otimes (B)_{j-1} + (A)_{j-1} \otimes b^{j'}.
$$

To obtain the equivalent jth submatrix of $D'_n(A \otimes B)$, we subtract $\begin{pmatrix} a^{j'} \otimes b^{j'} \\ O \end{pmatrix}$ from it. That is, $D'_n(A \otimes B)$ is the same matrix as $2L_nN_n(A \otimes B)$ except in the jth submatrix of $2L_nN_n(A \otimes B)$, the first row of $(A)_{j-1} \otimes b^{j'}$, which is $a^{j'} \otimes b^{j'}$, is replaced by the null vector.

By a similar analysis,

$$
(C \otimes D)D_n
$$
$$
= 2(C \otimes D)N_nL'_n - \begin{pmatrix} c_1 \otimes d_1 & O & \cdots & c_{n-1} \otimes d_{n-1} & O & c_n \otimes d_n \end{pmatrix}
$$

If we use the partitioning of $(C \otimes D)N_nL'_n$ given by Theorem 3.5, then the jth submatrix of $2(C \otimes D)N_nL'_n$ is $c_j \otimes (D)^{j-1} + (C)^{j-1} \otimes d_j$.

To obtain the equivalent jth submatrix for $(C \otimes D)D_n$, we subtract $\begin{pmatrix} c_j \otimes d_j & O \end{pmatrix}$.

In other words, $(C \otimes D)D_n$ is the same matrix as $(C \otimes D)N_nL'_n$ except in each jth submatrix the first column of $(C)^{j-1} \otimes d_j$, which is $c_j \otimes d_j$, is replaced by the null vector.

Further comparisons can be made. If we continue to write, $D'_n = (H'_1 \quad \cdots \quad H'_n)$ and $2L_nN_n = (P_1 \quad \cdots \quad P_n)$, then

$$
P_1 = \begin{pmatrix} R_1 \\ O \end{pmatrix} \quad \text{and} \quad H'_1 = \begin{pmatrix} I_n \\ O \end{pmatrix}
$$

so, clearly

$$
P_1 = H_1' \begin{pmatrix} 2e_1^{n'} \\ e_2^{n'} \\ \vdots \\ e_n^{n'} \end{pmatrix}.
$$

But,

$$
P_j = \begin{pmatrix} e_j^n & & & O \\ & \ddots & & \\ & & e_2^{n-j+2} & \\ O & & & R_j \\ O & \cdots & \cdots & O \end{pmatrix} \quad \text{and} \quad H_j' = \begin{pmatrix} e_j^n & & & O \\ & \ddots & & \\ & & e_2^{n-j+2} & \\ O & & & I_{n-j+1} \\ O & \cdots & \cdots & O \end{pmatrix}
$$

so

$$
P_j = H_j' \begin{pmatrix} e_1^{n'} \\ \vdots \\ 2e_j^{n'} \\ \vdots \\ e_n^{n'} \end{pmatrix}
$$

for $j = 2, \ldots, n$.

It follows that

$$
2L_n N_n = \begin{pmatrix} H_1' \begin{pmatrix} 2e_1^{n'} \\ e_2^{n'} \\ \vdots \\ e_n^{n'} \end{pmatrix} & \cdots & H_n' \begin{pmatrix} e_1^{n'} \\ e_2^{n'} \\ \vdots \\ 2e_n^{n'} \end{pmatrix} \end{pmatrix}
$$

$$
= D_n' \begin{pmatrix} \begin{pmatrix} 2e_1^{n'} \\ e_2^{n'} \\ \vdots \\ e_n^{n'} \end{pmatrix} & & O \\ & \ddots & \\ O & & \begin{pmatrix} e_1^{n'} \\ e_2^{n'} \\ \vdots \\ 2e_n^{n'} \end{pmatrix} \end{pmatrix}. \tag{3.56}
$$

Notice that the block diagonal matrix in Equation 3.56 is symmetric as its transpose is

$$
\begin{pmatrix}
\begin{pmatrix} 2e_1^n & e_2^n & \cdots & e_n^n \end{pmatrix} & & & O \\
& \ddots & & \\
O & & & \begin{pmatrix} e_1^n & \cdots & 2e_n^n \end{pmatrix}
\end{pmatrix}
$$

which is the matrix itself and it is also non-singular, its inverse being

$$
\begin{pmatrix}
\begin{pmatrix} \frac{1}{2}e_1^{n'} \\ e_2^{n'} \\ \vdots \\ e_n^{n'} \end{pmatrix} & & & O \\
& \ddots & & \\
O & & & \begin{pmatrix} e_1^{n'} \\ e_2^{n'} \\ \vdots \\ \frac{1}{2}e_n^{n'} \end{pmatrix}
\end{pmatrix},
$$

so we can write

$$
D_n' = L_n N_n
\begin{pmatrix}
\begin{pmatrix} e_1^{n'} \\ 2e_2^{n'} \\ \vdots \\ 2e_n^{n'} \end{pmatrix} & & & O \\
& \ddots & & \\
O & & & \begin{pmatrix} 2e_1^{n'} \\ 2e_2^{n'} \\ \vdots \\ e_n^{n'} \end{pmatrix}
\end{pmatrix}
$$

if we like.

Suppose now we use our other expression for $2L_n N_n$ and D_n', namely

$$
2L_n N_n = \begin{pmatrix} T_1 \\ \vdots \\ T_n \end{pmatrix}, \quad D_n' = \begin{pmatrix} M_1' \\ \vdots \\ M_n' \end{pmatrix}.
$$

Then, from Equations 3.24 and 3.39

$$T_n = \begin{pmatrix} 0' & 2e_n^{n'} \end{pmatrix}, \quad M_n = \begin{pmatrix} 0' & e_n^{n'} \end{pmatrix},$$

so, clearly

$$T_n = 2M'_n = R_n M'_n.$$

For $j = 2, \ldots, n-1$ from Equations 3.22 and 3.38

$$T_j = \begin{pmatrix} O & (O & R_j) & Z_2^j & \cdots & Z_{n-j+1}^j \end{pmatrix}$$

and

$$M'_j = \begin{pmatrix} O & (O & I_{n-j+1}) & Z_2^j & \cdots & Z_{n-j+1}^j \end{pmatrix}.$$

Consider for $i = 2, \ldots, n-j+1$

$$R_j Z_i = R_j \begin{pmatrix} O & e_i^{n-j+1} & O \end{pmatrix} = \begin{pmatrix} O & R_j e_i^{n-j+1} & O \end{pmatrix}$$

and

$$R_j e_i^{n-j+1} = \begin{pmatrix} 2 & & & O \\ & 1 & & \\ & & \ddots & \\ O & & & 1 \end{pmatrix} e_i^{n-j+1} = e_i^{n-j+1},$$

so $R_j Z_i = Z_i$ and $T_j = R_j M'_j$ for the values of the subscripts we consider. This comparison then gives

$$2L_n N_n = \begin{pmatrix} R_1 M'_1 \\ \vdots \\ R_n M'_n \end{pmatrix} = \begin{pmatrix} R_1 & & O \\ & \ddots & \\ O & & R_n \end{pmatrix} D'_n. \tag{3.57}$$

As R_j is a symmetric matrix, the block matrix in the right-hand side of Equation 3.57 is symmetric. It is also nonsingular, with its inverse being

$$\left(\begin{pmatrix} \frac{1}{2} & & & \\ & 1 & & \\ & & \ddots & \\ & & & 1 \end{pmatrix} \begin{matrix} & & O \\ & & \\ \end{matrix} \\ \begin{matrix} O & & \ddots & \\ & & & 1 \end{matrix} \right)$$

so if we like we could write

$$
D'_n = \left(\left(\begin{pmatrix} 1 & & & & \\ & 2 & & & \\ & & \ddots & & \\ & & & 2 \end{pmatrix} & \qquad O \\ \qquad O & \begin{pmatrix} \ddots & \\ & 2 \end{pmatrix} \end{array}\right)\right) L_n N_n.
$$

The matrix $L_n N_n$ and D_n are linked in another way. We saw in Section 2.5.7 of Chapter 2 that N_n is symmetric and idempotent, and in the previous section we saw that $L_n N_n D_n = I_{\frac{1}{2} n(n+1)}$ and $D_n L_n N_n = N_n$. These results mean that if A is a $n \times n$ nonsingular matrix, then

$$
\left(D'_n(A \otimes A)D_n \right)^{-1} = L_n N_n (A^{-1} \otimes A^{-1}) N_n L'_n. \tag{3.58}
$$

To establish this result, consider

$$
\begin{aligned}
& D'_n(A \otimes A)D_n L_n N_n (A^{-1} \otimes A^{-1}) N_n L'_n \\
&= D'_n(A \otimes A)N_n (A^{-1} \otimes A^{-1}) N_n L'_n \\
&= D'_n N_n (A \otimes A)(A^{-1} \otimes A^{-1}) N_n L'_n = D'_n N_n L'_n \\
&= I_{\frac{1}{2} n(n+1)},
\end{aligned}
$$

where we have used the fact that $N_n (A \otimes A) = (A \otimes A)N_n$.
Similarly,

$$
L_n N_n (A^{-1} \otimes A^{-1}) N_n L'_n D'_n (A \otimes A) D_n = I_{\frac{1}{2} n(n+1)}
$$

This result is found in Magnus (1988) and is important in the application of matrix calculus to statistical models, as discussed in Chapter 4.

3.3.3 The Duplication Matrix $\overline{D}_n$

There is another duplication matrix and we finish this chapter by quickly looking at this matrix. Fortunately, it is a far simpler matrix than D_n. It is associated with strictly lower triangular matrices rather than symmetric matrices as D_n. A $n \times n$ matrix A is strictly lower triangular if

$$
A = \begin{pmatrix}
0 & 0 & \cdots & \cdots & 0 \\
a_{21} & 0 & \cdots & \cdots & 0 \\
a_{31} & a_{32} & & & 0 \\
\vdots & \vdots & \ddots & & \vdots \\
a_{n1} & a_{n2} & \cdots & a_{nn-1} & 0
\end{pmatrix}.
$$

The vec of such a matrix is the $n^2 \times 1$ vector given by

$$
\text{vec } A = \begin{pmatrix} 0 \\ a_{21} \\ \vdots \\ a_{n1} \\ 0 \\ 0 \\ a_{32} \\ \vdots \\ a_{n2} \\ \vdots \\ 0 \\ 0 \\ \vdots \\ 0 \\ a_{nn-1} \\ 0 \\ \vdots \\ 0 \end{pmatrix}. \tag{3.59}
$$

As $\bar{v}(A)$ contains all the essential elements of A, there exists a $n^2 \times \frac{1}{2}n(n-1)$ duplication $\overline{D}_n$ such that $\overline{D}_n \bar{v}(A) = \text{vec } A$.

Comparing $\text{vec} A$ given by Equation 3.59 with $\bar{v}(A)$, we see that

$$
\overline{D}_n = \begin{pmatrix} \begin{pmatrix} 0' \\ I_{n-1} \end{pmatrix} & \cdots & \cdots & O \\ \vdots & \begin{pmatrix} O \\ I_{n-2} \end{pmatrix} & & \vdots \\ \vdots & & \ddots & \vdots \\ O & & & \begin{pmatrix} 0 \\ 1 \end{pmatrix} \\ 0' & 0' & \cdots & 0 \end{pmatrix} = \begin{pmatrix} E_1' & \cdots & \cdots & O \\ \vdots & E_2' & & \vdots \\ \vdots & & \ddots & \vdots \\ O & & & E_{n-1}' \\ 0' & \cdots & \cdots & 0 \end{pmatrix} = \overline{L}_n'.
$$

Properties of $\overline{D}_n$ can then be obtained from the properties we have already obtained for the elimination matrix $\overline{L}_n$.

FOUR

Matrix Calculus

4.1 Introduction

Let Y be an $p \times q$ matrix whose elements y_{ij}s are differentiable functions of the elements x_{rs}s of an $m \times n$ matrix X. We write $Y = Y(X)$ and say Y is a **matrix function** of X. Given such a setup, we have $mnpq$ partial derivatives that we can consider:

$$\frac{\partial y_{ij}}{\partial x_{rs}} \quad \begin{aligned} i &= 1, \ldots, p \\ j &= 1, \ldots, q \\ r &= 1, \ldots, m \\ s &= 1, \ldots, n. \end{aligned}$$

The question is how to arrange these derivatives. Different arrangements give rise to different concepts of derivatives in matrix calculus.

At least four concepts of a derivative of Y with respect to X are used in the literature. In the first part of this chapter, we show how the mathematical tools discussed in Chapters 1 and 2 can be used to analyze relationships that exist between the four concepts. In particular, generalized vec and rvec operators are useful concepts in establishing transformation principles that allow us to move from a result for one of the concepts of matrix derivatives to the corresponding results for the other three concepts.

In doing all this, it is not our intention to develop a table of known matrix calculus results. Such results are available elsewhere (see Rogers (1980), Graham (1981), Magnus and Neudecker (1988), Lutkepohl (1996) and Turkington (2005)).

Having said that, known matrix calculus results are presented without proof to illustrate the transformation principles we develop.

4.2 Different Concepts of a Derivative of a Matrix with Respect to Another Matrix

As mentioned in the introduction to this chapter, there are several concepts of the derivative of a $p \times q$ matrix Y with respect to another $m \times n$ matrix X depending on how we arrange the partial derivatives $\partial y_{ij}/\partial x_{rs}$.

The first concept we considered starts with a differentiable real value scalar function y of an $n \times 1$ vector x. It then defines the derivative of y with respect to vector x as the $1 \times n$ row vector

$$Dy = \left(\frac{\partial y}{\partial x_1} \cdots \frac{\partial y}{\partial x_n} \right)$$

where $x_1, \ldots, x_n$ are the elements of x. Consider now $y = \text{vec} Y$ where Y is our $p \times q$ matrix whose elements are differentiable functions of the elements, the x_{rs}s of a matrix X. Each element of vec Y is a differential function of x where $x = \text{vec} X$, so the derivative of the ith element with respect to x can be defined as

$$D(\text{vec } Y)_i = \left(\frac{\partial (\text{vec } Y)_i}{\partial x_{11}} \cdots \frac{\partial (\text{vec } Y)_i}{\partial x_{m1}} \cdots \frac{\partial (\text{vec } Y)_i}{\partial x_{1n}} \cdots \frac{\partial (\text{vec } Y)_i}{\partial x_{mn}} \right)$$

for $i = 1, \ldots, pq$. Stacking these row vectors under each other gives us our first concept of the derivative of Y with respect to X.

Concept 1 The derivative of the $p \times q$ matrix Y with respect to the $m \times n$ matrix X is the $pq \times mn$ matrix.

$$DY(X) = \begin{pmatrix}
\frac{\partial y_{11}}{\partial x_{11}} & \cdots & \frac{\partial y_{11}}{\partial x_{m1}} & \cdots & \frac{\partial y_{11}}{\partial x_{1n}} & \cdots & \frac{\partial y_{11}}{\partial x_{mn}} \\
\vdots & & \vdots & & \vdots & & \vdots \\
\frac{\partial y_{p1}}{\partial x_{11}} & \cdots & \frac{\partial y_{p1}}{\partial x_{m1}} & \cdots & \frac{\partial y_{p1}}{\partial x_{1n}} & \cdots & \frac{\partial y_{p1}}{\partial x_{mn}} \\
\vdots & & \vdots & & \vdots & & \vdots \\
\frac{\partial y_{1q}}{\partial x_{11}} & \cdots & \frac{\partial y_{1q}}{\partial x_{m1}} & \cdots & \frac{\partial y_{1q}}{\partial x_{1n}} & \cdots & \frac{\partial y_{1q}}{\partial x_{mn}} \\
\vdots & & \vdots & & \vdots & & \vdots \\
\frac{\partial y_{pq}}{\partial x_{11}} & \cdots & \frac{\partial y_{pq}}{\partial x_{m1}} & \cdots & \frac{\partial y_{pq}}{\partial x_{1n}} & \cdots & \frac{\partial y_{pq}}{\partial x_{mn}}
\end{pmatrix}.$$

Notice that under this concept the $mnpq$ derivatives are arranged in such a way that a row of $DY(X)$ gives the derivatives of a particular element of

Y with respect to each element of *X* and a column gives the derivatives of all the elements of *Y* with respect to a particular element of *X*. Notice also in talking about the derivatives of y_{ij}, we have to specify exactly where the ith row is located in this matrix. The device we first used in Theorem 2.1 of Section 2.2 of Chapter 2 comes in handy here. Likewise, when talking of the derivatives of all the elements of *Y* with respect to particular element x_{rs} of *X*, again, we have to specify exactly where the sth column is located in this matrix. Again, the device introduced in Section 2.2 of Chapter 2 comes in handy in doing this.

This concept of a matrix derivative is strongly advocated by Magnus and Neudecker (see, for example Magnus and Neudecker (1985) and Magnus (2010)). The feature they like about it is that $DY(X)$ is a straightforward matrix generalization of the Jacobian Matrix for $y = y(x)$ where *y* is a $p \times 1$ vector, which is a real value differentiable function of an $m \times 1$ vector *x*.

Consider now the case where the elements of the $p \times q$ matrix *Y* are all differentiable functions of a scalar *x*. Then, we could consider the derivative of *Y* with respect to *x* as the matrix of the derivatives of the elements of *Y* with respect to *x*.

Denote this $p \times q$ matrix as

$$\frac{\delta Y}{\delta x} = \begin{pmatrix} \dfrac{\partial y_{11}}{\partial x} & \cdots & \dfrac{\partial y_{1q}}{\partial x} \\ \vdots & & \vdots \\ \dfrac{\partial y_{p1}}{\partial x} & \cdots & \dfrac{\partial y_{pq}}{\partial x} \end{pmatrix}.$$

Return now to the case where each element of *Y* is a function of the elements of an $m \times n$ matrix *X*. We could then consider the derivative of *Y* with respect to *X* as made up of derivatives *Y* with respect to each element in *X*. That is, the $mp \times qn$ matrix

$$\frac{\delta Y}{\delta X} = \begin{pmatrix} \dfrac{\delta Y}{\delta x_{11}} & \cdots & \dfrac{\delta Y}{\delta x_{1n}} \\ \vdots & & \vdots \\ \dfrac{\delta Y}{\delta x_{m1}} & \cdots & \dfrac{\delta Y}{\delta x_{mn}} \end{pmatrix}.$$

This leads us to Concept 2 of the derivative of *Y* with respect to *X*.

Concept 2 The derivative of the $p \times q$ matrix Y with respect to the $m \times n$ matrix X is the $mp \times nq$ matrix

$$\frac{\delta Y}{\delta X} = \begin{pmatrix} \dfrac{\delta Y}{\delta x_{11}} & \cdots & \dfrac{\delta Y}{\delta x_{1n}} \\ \vdots & & \vdots \\ \dfrac{\delta Y}{\delta x_{m1}} & \cdots & \dfrac{\delta Y}{\delta x_{mn}} \end{pmatrix}$$

where $\delta Y / \delta x_{rs}$ is the $p \times q$ matrix given by

$$\frac{\delta Y}{\delta x_{rs}} = \begin{pmatrix} \dfrac{\partial y_{11}}{\partial x_{rs}} & \cdots & \dfrac{\partial y_{1q}}{\partial x_{rs}} \\ \vdots & & \vdots \\ \dfrac{\partial y_{p1}}{\partial x_{rs}} & \cdots & \dfrac{\partial y_{pq}}{\partial x_{rs}} \end{pmatrix}$$

for $r = 1, \ldots, m,\, s = 1, \ldots, n$.

This concept of a matrix derivative is discussed in Dwyer and MacPhail (1948), Dwyer (1967), Rogers (1980), and Graham (1981).

Suppose y is a scalar but a differentiable function of all the elements of an $m \times n$ matrix X. Then, we could conceive of the derivative of y with respect to X as the $m \times n$ matrix consisting of all the partial derivatives of y with respect to the elements of X. Denote this $m \times n$ matrix as

$$\frac{\gamma y}{\gamma X} = \begin{pmatrix} \dfrac{\partial y}{\partial x_{11}} & \cdots & \dfrac{\partial y}{\partial x_{1n}} \\ \vdots & & \vdots \\ \dfrac{\partial y}{\partial x_{m1}} & \cdots & \dfrac{\partial y}{\partial x_{mn}} \end{pmatrix}.$$

We could then conceive of the derivative of Y with respect to X as the matrix made up of the $\gamma y_{ij} / \gamma X$. Denote this $mp \times qn$ matrix by $\gamma y / \gamma X$. This leads to the third concept of the derivative of Y with respect to X.

Concept 3   The derivative of the $p \times q$ matrix Y with respect to the $m \times n$ matrix X is the $mp \times nq$ matrix

$$
\frac{\gamma Y}{\gamma X} = \begin{pmatrix} \dfrac{\gamma y_{11}}{\gamma X} & \cdots & \dfrac{\gamma y_{1q}}{\gamma X} \\ \vdots & & \vdots \\ \dfrac{\gamma y_{p1}}{\gamma X} & \cdots & \dfrac{\gamma y_{pq}}{\gamma X} \end{pmatrix}.
$$

This is the concept of a matrix derivative studied in detail by MacRae (1974) and discussed by Dwyer (1967), Roger (1980), Graham (1981), and others.

From a theoretical point of view, Parring (1992) argues that all three concepts are permissible as operators depending on which matrix or vector space we are operating in and how this space is normed.

Concept 4   Consider ℓ a scalar function of an $n \times 1$ vector x. This concept defines the derivative of ℓ with respect to x as the $n \times 1$ vector

$$
\frac{\partial \ell}{\partial x} = \begin{pmatrix} \dfrac{\partial \ell}{\partial x_1} \\ \vdots \\ \dfrac{\partial \ell}{\partial x_n} \end{pmatrix}.
$$

Let $y = (y_i)$ be an $s \times 1$ vector whose elements are differentiable functions of the elements of an $r \times 1$ vector $x = (x_i)$. We write $y = y(x)$ and say y is a **vector function of x.**

Then, consider this concept the derivative of y with respect to x as the $r \times s$ matrix

$$
\frac{\partial y}{\partial x} = \begin{pmatrix} \dfrac{\partial y_1}{\partial x_1} & \cdots & \dfrac{\partial y_s}{\partial x_1} \\ \vdots & & \vdots \\ \dfrac{\partial y_1}{\partial x_r} & \cdots & \dfrac{\partial y_s}{\partial x_r} \end{pmatrix}.
$$

For a $p \times q$ matrix Y which is a matrix function of X this concept considers the vectors $\text{vec}\, Y$ and $\text{vec}\, X$ and defines the derivative of Y with respect to X as

$$
\frac{\partial \text{vec}\, Y}{\partial \text{vec}\, X} =
\begin{pmatrix}
\dfrac{\partial y_{11}}{\partial x_{11}} & \cdots & \dfrac{\partial y_{p1}}{\partial x_{11}} & \cdots & \dfrac{\partial y_{1q}}{\partial x_{11}} & \cdots & \dfrac{\partial y_{pq}}{\partial x_{11}} \\
\vdots & & \vdots & & \vdots & & \vdots \\
\dfrac{\partial y_{11}}{\partial x_{m1}} & \cdots & \dfrac{\partial y_{p1}}{\partial x_{m1}} & \cdots & \dfrac{\partial y_{1q}}{\partial x_{m1}} & \cdots & \dfrac{\partial y_{pq}}{\partial x_{m1}} \\
\vdots & & \vdots & & \vdots & & \vdots \\
\dfrac{\partial y_{11}}{\partial x_{1n}} & \cdots & \dfrac{\partial y_{p1}}{\partial x_{1m}} & \cdots & \dfrac{\partial y_{1q}}{\partial x_{1n}} & \cdots & \dfrac{\partial y_{pq}}{\partial x_{1n}} \\
\vdots & & \vdots & & \vdots & & \vdots \\
\dfrac{\partial y_{11}}{\partial x_{mn}} & \cdots & \dfrac{\partial y_{p1}}{\partial x_{mn}} & \cdots & \dfrac{\partial y_{1q}}{\partial x_{mn}} & \cdots & \dfrac{\partial y_{pq}}{\partial x_{mn}}
\end{pmatrix}.
$$

This concept of a matrix derivative was used by Graham (1983) and Turkington (2005).

As this is just the transpose of Concept 1, we do not include it in our discussions on the different concepts of matrix derivatives. However, we take it up again in Chapter 5.

4.3 The Commutation Matrix and the Concepts of Matrix Derivatives

We saw in Equation 2.57 of Chapter 2 that the commutation matrix can be regarded as a twining matrix that intertwines a number of matrices taking one row at a time. Suppose we partition the $p \times q$ matrix Y into its columns, so $Y = (y_1 \ldots y_q)$. If we let $x = \text{vec} X$ and $y = \text{vec} Y$, then using Concept 1

$$
DY(X) =
\begin{pmatrix}
Dy_1 \\
\vdots \\
Dy_q
\end{pmatrix}
$$

and

$$K_{pq}DY(X) = \begin{pmatrix} Dy_{11} \\ \vdots \\ Dy_{1q} \\ \vdots \\ Dy_{p1} \\ \vdots \\ Dy_{pq} \end{pmatrix} = \begin{pmatrix} DY_{1\cdot} \\ \vdots \\ DY_{p\cdot} \end{pmatrix},$$

where $Y_{j\cdot}$ is the jth row of Y for $j = 1, \ldots, p$. If Y is an $p \times p$ symmetric matrix, so $y_{ij} = y_{ji}$, then

$$K_{pp}DY(X) = DY(X).$$

Referring to Concept 2

$$K_{pm}\frac{\delta Y}{\delta X} = K_{pm}\begin{pmatrix} \dfrac{\delta Y}{\delta x_{11}} & \cdots & \dfrac{\delta Y}{\delta x_{1n}} \\ \vdots & & \vdots \\ \dfrac{\delta Y}{\delta x_{m1}} & \cdots & \dfrac{\delta Y}{\delta x_{mn}} \end{pmatrix} = \begin{pmatrix} \dfrac{\delta Y_{1\cdot}}{\delta x_{11}} & \cdots & \dfrac{\delta Y_{1\cdot}}{\delta x_{1n}} \\ \vdots & & \vdots \\ \dfrac{\delta Y_{1\cdot}}{\delta x_{m1}} & \cdots & \dfrac{\delta Y_{1\cdot}}{\delta x_{mn}} \\ \vdots & & \vdots \\ \dfrac{\delta Y_{p\cdot}}{\delta x_{11}} & \cdots & \dfrac{\delta Y_{p\cdot}}{\delta x_{1n}} \\ \vdots & & \vdots \\ \dfrac{\delta Y_{p\cdot}}{\delta x_{m1}} & \cdots & \dfrac{\delta Y_{p\cdot}}{\delta x_{mn}} \end{pmatrix} = \begin{pmatrix} \dfrac{\delta Y_{1\cdot}}{\delta X} \\ \vdots \\ \dfrac{\delta Y_{p\cdot}}{\delta X} \end{pmatrix}.$$

In a similar manner,

$$K_{mp}\frac{\gamma Y}{\gamma X} = \begin{pmatrix} \dfrac{\gamma Y}{\gamma X_{1\cdot}} \\ \vdots \\ \dfrac{\gamma Y}{\gamma X_{m\cdot}} \end{pmatrix}.$$

4.4 Relationships Between the Different Concepts

Suppose X is a scalar, say x. This case is rather exceptional, but we include it for the sake of completeness. Then, it is easily seen that Concept 2 and Concept 3 are the same and Concept 1 is the vec of the others. That is, for x a scalar and Y an $p \times q$ matrix

$$\frac{\delta Y}{\delta x} = \frac{\gamma Y}{\gamma x} \quad \text{and} \quad DY(x) = \text{vec}\frac{\delta Y}{\delta x}.$$

As a vec can always be undone by taking the appropriate generalized rvec, rvec_p, in this case, we also have

$$\frac{\delta Y}{\delta x} = \text{rvec}_p DY(x) = \frac{\gamma Y}{\gamma x}.$$

Suppose Y is a scalar, say y. This case is far more common in statistics and econometrics. Then again, Concept 2 and Concept 3 are the same and Concept 1 is the transpose of the vec of either concept. That is, for y a scalar and X an $m \times n$ matrix

$$\frac{\delta y}{\delta X} = \frac{\gamma y}{\gamma X} \quad \text{and} \quad Dy(X) = \left(\text{vec}\frac{\delta y}{\delta X}\right)'. \tag{4.2}$$

As $\text{vec}\dfrac{\delta y}{\delta X} = (Dy(X))'$ and, again as a vec can always be undone by taking the appropriate generalized rvec, rvec_m, in this case, we have

$$\frac{\delta y}{\delta X} = \frac{\gamma y}{\gamma X} = \text{rvec}_m (Dy(X))'. \tag{4.3}$$

The last case, where Y is in fact a scalar is prevalent enough in statistics to warrant us looking at specific examples of the relationships between our three concepts. The matrix calculus results presented here, as indeed the results presented throughout this chapter, can be found in books such as Graham (1981), Lutkepohl (1996), Magnus and Neudecker (1988), Rogers (1980), and Turkington (2005).

Examples where Y is a scalar:

1. Suppose y is the determinant of a non-singular matrix. That is, $y = |X|$ where X is a non-singular matrix. Then,

$$Dy(X) = |X|\big[\text{vec}(X^{-1})'\big]'. \tag{4.4}$$

From Equation 4.3, it follows immediately that

$$\frac{\delta y}{\delta X} = \frac{\gamma y}{\gamma X} = |X|(X^{-1})'.$$

2. Consider $y = |Y|$ where $Y = X'AX$ is non-singular. Then,

$$\frac{\delta y}{\delta X} = |Y|(AXY^{-1} + A'XY^{-1'}).$$

It follows from Equation 4.2 that

$$Dy(X) = |Y|\{[(Y^{-1'} \otimes A) + (Y^{-1} \otimes A')]\text{vec } X\}'$$
$$= |Y|(\text{vec } X)'[(Y^{-1} \otimes A') + (Y^{-1'} \otimes A)]. \qquad (4.5)$$

3. Consider $y = |Z|$ where $Z = XBX'$. Then,

$$Dy(X) = |Z|(\text{vec } X)'[(B \otimes Z^{-1'}) + (B' \otimes Z^{-1})].$$

It follows from Equation 4.3 that

$$\frac{\delta y}{\delta X} = \frac{\gamma y}{\gamma X} = |Z|(Z^{-1}XB + Z^{-1'}XB').$$

4. Let $y = \text{tr}AX$. Then,

$$\frac{\delta y}{\delta X} = A'.$$

It follows from Equation 4.2 that

$$Dy(X) = (\text{vec } A')'. \qquad (4.6)$$

5. Let $y = \text{tr}X'AX$. Then,

$$Dy(X) = (\text{vec } (A'X + AX))'.$$

It follows from Equation 4.3 that

$$\frac{\delta y}{\delta X} = \frac{\gamma y}{\gamma X} = A'X + AX.$$

6. Let $y = \text{tr}XAX'B$. Then,

$$\frac{\delta y}{\delta X} = \frac{\gamma y}{\gamma X} = B'XA' + BXA.$$

It follows from Equation 4.2 that

$$Dy(X) = (\text{vec } (B'XA' + BXA))'.$$

These examples suffice to show that it is a trivial matter moving between the different concepts of matrix derivatives when Y is a scalar. In the next section, we derive transformation principles that allow us to move freely between the three different concepts of matrix derivatives in more complicated cases. These principles can be regarded as a generalization of the work done by Dwyer and Macphail (1948) and by Graham (1980). In deriving these principles, we call on the work we have done with regards to generalized vecs and rvecs in Chapter 2, particularly with reference to the selection of rows and columns of Kronecker products.

4.5 Tranformation Principles Between the Concepts

We can use our generalized vec and rvec operators to spell out the relationships that exist between our three concepts of matrix derivatives. We consider two concepts in turn.

4.5.1 Concept 1 and Concept 2

The submatrices in $\delta Y/\delta X$ are

$$
\frac{\delta Y}{\delta x_{rs}} = \begin{pmatrix} \dfrac{\partial y_{11}}{\partial x_{rs}} & \cdots & \dfrac{\partial y_{1q}}{\partial x_{rs}} \\ \vdots & & \vdots \\ \dfrac{\partial y_{p1}}{\partial x_{rs}} & \cdots & \dfrac{\partial y_{pq}}{\partial x_{rs}} \end{pmatrix}
$$

for $r = 1, \ldots, m$ and $s = 1, \ldots, n$. In forming the submatrix $\delta Y/\delta x_{rs}$, we need the partial derivatives of the elements of Y with respect to x_{rs}. When we turn to Concept 1, we note that these partial derivatives all appear in a column of $DY(X)$. Just as we did in locating a column of a Kronecker product, we have to specify exactly where this column is located in the matrix $DY(X)$. If s is 1, then the partial derivatives appear in the rth column, if s is 2, then they appear in the $m + r$th column, if s is 3 in the $2m + r$th column, and so on until s is n, in which case the partial derivatives appear in the $(n-1)m + r$th column. To cater for all these possibilities, we say x_{rs} appears in the ℓth column of $DY(X)$ where

$$
\ell = (s-1)m + r
$$

and $s = 1, \ldots, n$. The partial derivatives we seek appear in that column as the column vector

$$\begin{pmatrix} \dfrac{\partial y_{11}}{\partial x_{rs}} \\ \vdots \\ \dfrac{\partial y_{p1}}{\partial x_{rs}} \\ \vdots \\ \dfrac{\partial y_{1q}}{\partial x_{rs}} \\ \vdots \\ \dfrac{\partial y_{pq}}{\partial x_{rs}} \end{pmatrix} .$$

If we take the rvec_p of this vector, we get $\delta Y / \delta x_{rs}$, so

$$\delta Y / \delta x_{rs} = \mathrm{rvec}_p (DY(X))_{\cdot \ell} \qquad (4.7)$$

where $\ell = (s-1)m + r$, for $s = 1, \ldots, n$ and $r = 1, \ldots, m$.

Now, this generalized rvec can be undone by taking the vec, so

$$(DY(X))_{\cdot \ell} = \mathrm{vec} \left(\frac{\delta Y}{\delta x_{rs}} \right). \qquad (4.8)$$

If we are given $DY(X)$ and we can identify the ℓth column of this matrix, then Equation 4.7 allows us to move from Concept 1 to Concept 2. If, however, we have in hand $\delta Y / \delta X$, we can identify the submatrix $\delta Y / \delta x_{rs}$ then Equation 4.8 allows us to move from Concept 2 to Concept 1.

4.5.2 Concept 1 and Concept 3

The submatrices in $\gamma Y / \gamma X$ are

$$\frac{\gamma y_{ij}}{\gamma X} = \begin{pmatrix} \dfrac{\partial y_{ij}}{\partial x_{11}} & \cdots & \dfrac{\partial y_{ij}}{\partial x_{1n}} \\ \vdots & & \vdots \\ \dfrac{\partial y_{ij}}{\partial x_{m1}} & \cdots & \dfrac{\partial y_{ij}}{\partial x_{mn}} \end{pmatrix}$$

for $i = 1, \ldots, p$ and $j = 1, \ldots, q$. In forming the submatrix $\gamma y_{ij}/\gamma X$, we need the partial derivative of y_{ij} with respect to the elements of X. When we examine $DY(X)$, we see that these derivatives appear in a row of $DY(X)$.

Again, we have to specify exactly where this row is located in the matrix $DY(X)$. If j is 1, then the partial derivatives appear in the ith row, if $j = 2$, then they appear in the $p + i$th row, if $j = 3$, then in the $2p + i$th row, and so on until $j = q$, in which case the partial derivative appears in $(q - 1)p + i$th row. To cater for all possibilities, we say the partial derivatives appear in the tth row of $\partial Y/\partial X$ where

$$t = (j - 1)p + i$$

and $j = 1, \ldots, q$. In this row, they appear as the row vector

$$\left(\frac{\partial y_{ij}}{\partial x_{11}} \cdots \frac{\partial y_{ij}}{\partial x_{m1}} \cdots \frac{\partial y_{ij}}{\partial x_{1n}} \cdots \frac{\partial y_{ij}}{\partial x_{mn}} \right).$$

If we take the vec_m of this vector, we obtain the matrix

$$\begin{pmatrix} \dfrac{\partial y_{ij}}{\partial x_{11}} & \cdots & \dfrac{\partial y_{ij}}{\partial x_{m1}} \\ \vdots & & \vdots \\ \dfrac{\partial y_{ij}}{\partial x_{1n}} & \cdots & \dfrac{\partial y_{ij}}{\partial x_{mn}} \end{pmatrix}$$

which is $(\gamma y_{ij}/\gamma X)'$. So, we have

$$\frac{\gamma y_{ij}}{\gamma X} = (\text{vec}_m(DY(X))_{t\cdot})' \tag{4.9}$$

where $t = (j - 1)p + i$, for $j = 1, \ldots, q$ and $i = 1, \ldots, p$.

As

$$\text{vec}_m(DY(X))_{t\cdot} = \left(\frac{\gamma y_{ij}}{\gamma X} \right)'$$

and a generalized vec can be undone by taking the rvec, we have

$$(DY(X))_{t\cdot} = \text{rvec} \left(\frac{\gamma y_{ij}}{\gamma X} \right)'. \tag{4.10}$$

If we have in hand $DY(X)$ and if we can identify the tth row of this matrix, then Equation 4.9 allows us to move from Concept 1 to Concept 3. If, however, we have obtained $\gamma Y/\gamma X$ so we can identify the submatrix $\gamma y_{ij}/\gamma X$ of this matrix, then Equation 4.10 allows us to move from Concept 3 to Concept 1.

4.5.3 Concept 2 and Concept 3

Returning to Concept 3, the submatrices of $\gamma Y/\gamma X$ are

$$\frac{\gamma y_{ij}}{\gamma X} = \begin{pmatrix} \dfrac{\partial y_{ij}}{\partial x_{11}} & \cdots & \dfrac{\partial y_{ij}}{\partial x_{1n}} \\ \vdots & & \vdots \\ \dfrac{\partial y_{ij}}{\partial x_{m1}} & \cdots & \dfrac{\partial y_{ij}}{\partial x_{mn}} \end{pmatrix}$$

and the partial derivative $\dfrac{\partial y_{ij}}{\partial x_{rs}}$ is given by the (r, s)th element of this submatrix. That is,

$$\frac{\partial y_{ij}}{\partial x_{rs}} = \left(\frac{\gamma y_{ij}}{\gamma X} \right)_{rs}.$$

It follows that

$$\frac{\delta Y}{\delta x_{rs}} = \begin{pmatrix} \left(\dfrac{\gamma y_{11}}{\gamma X} \right)_{rs} & \cdots & \left(\dfrac{\gamma y_{1q}}{\gamma X} \right)_{rs} \\ \vdots & & \vdots \\ \left(\dfrac{\gamma y_{p1}}{\gamma X} \right)_{rs} & \cdots & \left(\dfrac{\gamma y_{pq}}{\gamma X} \right)_{rs} \end{pmatrix}. \qquad (4.11)$$

Starting now with Concept 2, the submatrices of $\delta Y/\delta X$ are

$$\frac{\delta Y}{\delta x_{rs}} = \begin{pmatrix} \dfrac{\partial y_{11}}{\partial x_{rs}} & \cdots & \dfrac{\partial y_{1q}}{\partial x_{rs}} \\ \vdots & & \vdots \\ \dfrac{\partial y_{p1}}{\partial x_{rs}} & \cdots & \dfrac{\partial y_{pq}}{\partial x_{rs}} \end{pmatrix}$$

and the partial derivative $\partial y_{ij}/\partial x_{rs}$ is the (i, j)th element of this submatrix. That is,

$$\frac{\partial y_{ij}}{\partial x_{rs}} = \left(\frac{\delta Y}{\delta x_{rs}} \right)_{ij}.$$

It follows that

$$\frac{\gamma y_{ij}}{\gamma X} = \begin{pmatrix} \left(\dfrac{\delta Y}{\delta x_{11}}\right)_{ij} & \cdots & \left(\dfrac{\delta Y}{\delta x_{1n}}\right)_{ij} \\ \vdots & & \vdots \\ \left(\dfrac{\delta Y}{\delta x_{m1}}\right)_{ij} & \cdots & \left(\dfrac{\delta Y}{\delta x_{mn}}\right)_{ij} \end{pmatrix}. \tag{4.12}$$

If we have in hand $\gamma y / \gamma X$, then Equation 4.11 allows us to build up the submatrices we need for $\delta Y / \delta X$. If, however, we have a result for $\delta Y / \delta X$, then Equation 4.12 allows us to obtain the submatrices we need for $\gamma Y / \gamma X$.

4.6 Transformation Principle One

Several matrix calculus results when we use Concept 1 involve Kronecker products whereas the equivalent results, using Concepts 2 and 3, involve the elementary matrices we looked at in the start of Chapter 2. In this section, we see that this is no coincidence.

We have just seen that

$$\frac{\delta Y}{\delta x_{rs}} = \text{rvec}_p(DY)._\ell \tag{4.13}$$

where $\ell = (s - 1)m + r$ and that

$$\frac{\gamma y_{ij}}{\gamma X} = (\text{vec}_m(DY)_t.)' \tag{4.14}$$

where $t = (j - 1)p + i$. Suppose now that $DY(X) = A \otimes B$ where A is a $q \times n$ matrix and B is an $p \times m$ matrix. Then, we can call on the work we did in Sections 2.2 and 2.3 of Chapter 2 to locate the ℓth column and tth row of this Kronecker product. Using Equation 2.6 of that chapter, we have

$$(A \otimes B)._\ell = \text{vec } B E_{rs}^{mn} A'.$$

Undoing the vec by taking the rvec_p, we have

$$\text{rvec}_p(A \otimes B)._\ell = B E_{rs}^{mn} A',$$

so using Equation 4.13, we have that

$$\frac{\delta Y}{\delta x_{rs}} = B E_{rs}^{mn} A'.$$

Using Equation 2.4 of Chapter 2, we have

$$(A \otimes B)_t. = \text{rvec } A' E_{ji}^{qp} B.$$

Undoing the rvec by taking the vec_m, we have

$$\text{vec}_m (A \otimes B)_{t.} = A' E_{ji}^{qp} B$$

so from Equation 4.14

$$\frac{\gamma y_{ij}}{\gamma X} = \left(A' E_{ji}^{qp} B \right)' = B' E_{ij}^{pq} A,$$

as

$$\left(E_{ji}^{qp} \right)' = E_{ij}^{pq}.$$

This leads us to our first transformation principle.

The First Transformation Principle

Let A be an $q \times n$ matrix and B be an $p \times m$ matrix. Whenever

$$DY(X) = A \otimes B$$

regardless of whether A and B are matrix functions of X or not

$$\frac{\delta Y}{\delta x_{rs}} = B E_{rs}^{mn} A'$$

and

$$\frac{\gamma y_{ij}}{\gamma X} = B' E_{ij}^{pq} A$$

and the converse statements are true also.

For this case,

$$' \frac{\delta Y}{\delta X} = \begin{pmatrix} B E_{11}^{mn} A' & \cdots & B E_{1n}^{mn} A' \\ \vdots & & \vdots \\ B E_{m1}^{mn} A' & \cdots & B E_{mn}^{mn} A' \end{pmatrix} = (I_m \otimes B) U_{mn} (I_n \otimes A'),$$

where U_{mn} is the $m^2 \times n^2$ matrix introduced in Section 2.6 of Chapter 2, given by

$$U_{mn} = \begin{pmatrix} E_{11}^{mn} & \cdots & E_{1n}^{mn} \\ \vdots & & \vdots \\ E_{m1}^{mn} & \cdots & E_{mn}^{mn} \end{pmatrix}.$$

We saw in Theorem 2.33 of Chapter 2 that

$$(A \otimes B) U_{mn} (C \otimes D) = (\text{vec } BA')(\text{rvec } C'D),$$

so

$$\frac{\delta Y}{\delta X} = (\text{vec } B)(\text{rvec } A').$$

In terms of Concept 3, for this case

$$\frac{\gamma Y}{\gamma X} = \begin{pmatrix} B'E_{11}^{pq}A & \cdots & B'E_{1q}^{pq}A \\ \vdots & & \vdots \\ B'E_{p1}^{pq}A & \cdots & B'E_{pq}^{pq}A \end{pmatrix} = (I_p \otimes B')U_{pq}(I_q \otimes A)$$

$$= (\text{vec } B')(\text{rvec } A).$$

In terms of the entire matrices, we can express the First Transformation Principle by saying that the following statements are equivalent:

$$DY(X) = A \otimes B$$

$$\frac{\delta Y}{\delta X} = (\text{vec } B)(\text{rvec } A')$$

$$\frac{\gamma Y}{\gamma X} = (\text{vec } B')(\text{rvec } A).$$

Examples of the Use of the First Transformation Principle

1. $Y = AXB$ for A $p \times m$ and B $n \times q$.
   Then, it is known that

$$D(AXB) = B' \otimes A. \tag{4.15}$$

It follows that

$$\frac{\delta AXB}{\delta x_{rs}} = AE_{rs}^{mn}B$$

and

$$\frac{\gamma(AXB)_{ij}}{\gamma X} = A'E_{ij}^{pq}B'.$$

Moreover,

$$\frac{\delta AXB}{\delta X} = (\text{vec } A)(\text{rvec } B)$$

$$\frac{\gamma AXB}{\gamma X} = (\text{vec } A')(\text{rvec } B').$$

2. If $Y = XAX$ where X is an $m \times n$ matrix, then

$$\frac{\delta XAX}{\delta x_{rs}} = E_{rs}^{mn} AX + XAE_{rs}^{mn}.$$

It follows that

$$\frac{\gamma(XAX)_{ij}}{\gamma X} = E_{ij}^{mn} X'A' + A'X'E_{ij}^{mn}$$

and that

$$D(XAX) = X'A' \otimes I_m + I_n \otimes XA \qquad (4.16)$$

$$\frac{\delta XAX}{\delta X} = (\text{vec } I_m)(\text{rvec } AX) + (\text{vec } XA)(\text{rvec } I_n)$$

$$\frac{\gamma XAX}{\gamma X} = (\text{vec } I_m)(\text{rvec } X'A') + (\text{vec } A'X')(\text{rvec } I_n).$$

3. $Y = X \otimes I_G$ where X is an $m \times n$ matrix.
We have seen in Equation 2.29 of Chapter 2 that $\text{vec}(X \otimes I_G) = (I_n \otimes \text{vec}_m K_{mG})\text{vec } X$, so

$$D(X \otimes I_G) = I_n \otimes \text{vec}_m K_{mG}.$$

It follows that

$$\frac{\delta(X \otimes I_G)}{\delta x_{rs}} = (\text{vec}_m K_{Gm}) E_{rs}^{mn}$$

and

$$\frac{\gamma(X \otimes I_G)_{ij}}{\gamma X} = (\text{vec}_m K_{Gm})' E_{ij}^{kn} \quad \text{where} \quad k = G^2 m.$$

Moreover,

$$\frac{\delta(X \otimes I_G)}{\delta X} = \text{vec}(\text{vec}_m K_{mG})(\text{rvec } I_n) = (\text{vec } I_{mG})(\text{rvec } I_n)$$

$$\frac{\gamma(X \otimes I_G)}{\gamma X} = \text{vec}(\text{vec}_m K_{mG})'(\text{rvec } I_n) = (\text{vec } I_{mG})(\text{rvec } I_n),$$

where we have used Theorem 2.20 of Section 2.5 in Chapter 2.

4. $Y = AX^{-1}B$ where A is $p \times n$ and B is $n \times q$. Then, it is known that

$$\frac{\gamma(AX^{-1}B)_{ij}}{\gamma X} = -X^{-1'}A'E_{ij}^{pq}B'X^{-1'}.$$

It follows straight away that

$$\frac{\delta AX^{-1}B}{\delta x_{rs}} = -AX^{-1}E_{rs}^{nn}X^{-1}B,$$

and that

$$D(AX^{-1}B) = -B'X^{-1'} \otimes AX^{-1}. \tag{4.17}$$

Moreover,

$$\frac{\delta AX^{-1}B}{\delta X} = -(\text{vec } AX^{-1})(\text{rvec } X^{-1}B)$$

and

$$\frac{\gamma AX^{-1}B}{\gamma X} = -(\text{vec } X^{-1'}A')(\text{rvec } B'X^{-1'}).$$

5. $Y = AXBXC$ where X is $m \times n$, A is $p \times m$, B is $n \times m$, and C is $n \times q$. Then, it is well known that

$$\frac{\delta AXBXC}{\delta x_{rs}} = AE_{rs}^{mn}BXC + AXBE_{rs}^{mn}C.$$

It follows that

$$\frac{\gamma(AXBXC)_{ij}}{\gamma X} = A'E_{ij}^{pq}C'X'B' + B'X'A'E_{ij}^{pq}C'$$

and

$$D(AXBXC) = (C'X'B' \otimes A) + (C' \otimes AXB).$$

Moreover,

$$\frac{\delta AXBXC}{\delta X} = (\text{vec } A)(\text{rvec } BXC) + (\text{vec } AXB)(\text{rvec } C).$$

and

$$\frac{\gamma AXBXC}{\gamma X} = (\text{vec } A')(\text{rvec } C'X'B') + (\text{vec } B'X'A')(\text{rvec } C').$$

I hope these examples make clear that this transformation principle ensures that it is a very easy matter to move from a result involving one of the concepts of matrix derivatives to the corresponding results for the other two concepts. Although this principle covers a lot of cases, it does not cover them all. Several matrix calculus results for Concept 1 involve multiplying a Kronecker product by a commutation matrix. The following transformation principle covers this case.

4.7 Transformation Principle Two

Suppose then that

$$DY(X) = K_{qp}(C \otimes E) = (E \otimes C)K_{mn}$$

where C is an $p \times n$ matrix and E is an $q \times m$ matrix. Forming $\partial Y / \partial x_{rs}$ from this matrix requires that we first obtain the ℓth column of this matrix where $\ell = (s-1)m + r$ and we take the rvec_p of this column. Again, we can call on the work we did in Chapter 2. From Equation 2.22 of that chapter

$$\frac{\delta Y}{\delta x_{rs}} = CE_{sr}^{nm}E'.$$

In forming $\gamma y_{ij}/\gamma X$ from DY, we first have to obtain the tth row of this matrix, for $t = (j-1)p + i$ and then we take the vec_m of this row. The required matrix $\gamma y_{ij}/\gamma X$ is the transpose of the matrix thus obtained. Again, we call on the work we did in Chapter 2. From Equation 2.19 of that chapter,

$$\frac{\gamma y_{ij}}{\gamma X} = \left(C'E_{ij}^{pq}E\right)' = E'E_{ji}^{qp}C.$$

This leads us to our second transformation principle.

The Second Transformation Principle
Let C be an $p \times n$ matrix and D be an $q \times m$ matrix. Whenever

$$DY(X) = K_{qp}(C \otimes E)$$

regardless of whether C and D are matrix functions of X or not

$$\frac{\delta Y}{\delta x_{rs}} = CE_{sr}^{nm}E'$$

$$\frac{\gamma y_{ij}}{\gamma X} = E'E_{ji}^{qp}C$$

and the converse statements are true also.

For this case,

$$\frac{\delta Y}{\delta X} = \begin{pmatrix} CE_{11}^{nm}E' & \cdots & CE_{n1}^{nm}E' \\ \vdots & & \vdots \\ CE_{1m}^{nm}E' & \cdots & CE_{nm}^{nm}E' \end{pmatrix}$$

$$= (I_m \otimes C) \begin{pmatrix} E_{11}^{nm} & \cdots & E_{n1}^{nm} \\ \vdots & & \vdots \\ E_{1m}^{nm} & \cdots & E_{nm}^{nm} \end{pmatrix} (I_n \otimes E') = (I_m \otimes C)K_{mn}(I_n \otimes E').$$

In terms of $\gamma Y/\gamma X$, we have

$$\frac{\gamma Y}{\gamma X} = \begin{pmatrix} E'E_{11}^{qp}C & \cdots & E'E_{q1}^{qp}C \\ \vdots & & \vdots \\ E'E_{1p}^{qp}C & \cdots & E'E_{qp}^{qp}C \end{pmatrix} = (I_p \otimes E')K_{pq}(I_q \otimes C).$$

In terms of the full matrices, we can express the Second Transformation Principle as saying that the following statements are equivalent:

$$DY(X) = K_{qp}(C \otimes E)$$

$$\frac{\delta Y}{\delta X} = (I_m \otimes C)K_{mn}(I_n \otimes E')$$

$$\frac{\gamma Y}{\gamma X} = (I_p \otimes E')K_{pq}(I_q \otimes C).$$

As an example of the use of this second transformation principle, let $Y = AX'B$ where A is $p \times n$ and B is $m \times q$. Then, it is known that

$$D(AX'B) = K_{pq}(A \otimes B').$$

It follows that

$$\frac{\delta AX'B}{\delta x_{rs}} = AE_{sr}^{mn}B$$

and that

$$\frac{\gamma(AX'B)_{ij}}{\gamma X} = BE_{ji}^{pq}A.$$

In terms of the entire matrices, we

$$\frac{\delta Y}{\delta X} = (I_n \otimes A)K_{nm}(I_m \otimes B)$$

$$\frac{\gamma Y}{\gamma X} = (I_q \otimes B)K_{qp}(I_p \otimes A).$$

Principle 2 comes into its own when it is used in conjunction with Principle 1. Many matrix derivatives come in two parts: one where Principle 1 is applicable and the other where Principle 2 is applicable.

For example, we often have

$$DY(X) = A \otimes B + K_{qp}(C \otimes E),$$

so we would apply Principle 1 to the $A \otimes B$ part and Principle 2 to the $K_{qp}(C \otimes E)$ part.

Examples of the Combined Use of Principles One and Two

1. Let $Y = X'AX$ where X is $m \times n$, A is $m \times m$. Then, it is well known that

$$D(X'AX) = K_{nn}(I_n \otimes X'A') + (I_n \otimes X'A).$$

It follows that

$$\frac{\delta X'AX}{\delta x_{rs}} = E_{sr}^{nm} AX + X'AE_{rs}^{mn}$$

and that

$$\frac{\gamma(X'AX)_{ij}}{\gamma X} = AXE_{ji}^{nn} + A'XE_{ij}^{nn}.$$

Moreover,

$$\frac{\delta X'AX}{\delta X} = K_{mn}(I_n \otimes AX) + (I_m \otimes X'A)U_{mn}$$

$$= K_{mn}(I_n \otimes AX) + (\text{vec } X'A)(\text{rvec } I_n).$$

$$\frac{\gamma X'AX}{\gamma X} = (I_n \otimes AX)K_{nn} + (I_n \otimes A'X)U_{nn}$$

$$= (I_n \otimes AX)K_{nn} + (\text{vec } A'X)(\text{rvec } I_n).$$

2. Let $Y = XAX'$ where X is $m \times n$ and A is $n \times n$. Then, it is known that

$$\frac{\delta XAX'}{\delta x_{rs}} = XAE_{sr}^{nm} + E_{rs}^{mn}AX'.$$

It follows that

$$\frac{\gamma(XAX')_{ij}}{\gamma X} = E_{ji}^{mm}XA + E_{ij}^{mm}XA'$$

and

$$D(XAX') = K_{mm}(XA \otimes I_m) + (XA' \otimes I_m). \qquad (4.18)$$

Moreover,

$$\frac{\delta XAX'}{\delta X} = (I_m \otimes XA)K_{mn} + U_{mn}(I_n \otimes AX')$$

$$= (I_m \otimes XA)K_{mn} + (\text{vec } I_m)(\text{rvec } AX'),$$

and

$$\frac{\gamma XAX'}{\gamma X} = K_{mm}(I_m \otimes XA') + U_{mm}(I_m \otimes XA)$$

$$= K_{mm}(I_m \otimes XA) + (\text{vec } I_m)(\text{rvec } AX').$$

3. Let $Y = BX'AXC$ where B is $p \times n$, A is $m \times m$ and C is $n \times q$. Then, it is known that

$$\frac{\gamma(BX'AXC)_{ij}}{\gamma X} = AXCE_{ji}^{qp}B + A'XB'E_{ij}^{pq}C'.$$

It follows using our principles that

$$\frac{\delta BX'AXC}{\delta x_{rs}} = BE_{sr}^{nm}AXC + BX'AE_{rs}^{mn}C$$

and that

$$D(BX'AXC) = K_{qp}(B \otimes C'X'A') + (C' \otimes BX'A).$$

In terms of the entire matrices, we have

$$\frac{\delta BX'AXC}{\delta X} = (I_m \otimes B)K_{mn}(I_n \otimes AXC) + (I_m \otimes BX'A)U_{mn}(I_n \otimes C)$$

$$= (I_m \otimes B)K_{mn}(I_n \otimes AXC) + (\text{vec } BX'A)(\text{rvec } C).$$

$$\frac{\gamma BX'AXC}{\gamma X} = (I_p \otimes AXC)K_{pq}(I_q \otimes B) + (I_p \otimes A'XB')U_{pq}(I_q \otimes C')$$

$$= (I_p \otimes AXC)K_{pq}(I_q \otimes B) + (\text{vec } A'XB')(\text{rvec } C').$$

4. Let $Y = BXAX'C$ where B is $p \times m$, A is $n \times n$, and C is $m \times q$. Then, it is well known that

$$D(BXAX'C) = K_{qp}(BXA \otimes C') + (C'XA' \otimes B).$$

Using our principles we obtain,

$$\frac{\delta BXAX'C}{\delta x_{rs}} = BXAE_{sr}^{nm}C + BE_{rs}^{mn}AX'C$$

and

$$\frac{\gamma(BXAX'C)_{ij}}{\gamma X} = CE_{ji}^{qp}BXA + B'E_{ij}^{pq}C'XA'.$$

Moreover, we have

$$\frac{\delta BXAX'C}{\delta X} = (I_m \otimes BXA)K_{mn}(I_n \otimes C) + (I_m \otimes B)U_{mn}(I_n \otimes AX'C)$$

$$= (I_m \otimes BXA)K_{mn}(I_n \otimes C) + (\text{vec } B)(\text{rvec } AX'C).$$

$$\frac{\gamma BXAX'C}{\gamma X} = (I_p \otimes C)K_{pq}(I_q \otimes A'X'B') + (I_p \otimes B')U_{pq}(I_q \otimes C'XA')$$

$$= (I_p \otimes C)K_{pq}(I_q \otimes BXA) + (\text{vec } B')(\text{rvec } C'XA').$$

Comparing Example 1 with Example 3, and Example 4 with Example 2, points to rules that pertain to the different concepts of derivatives themselves. If $Y(X)$ is an $p \times q$ matrix function of an $m \times n$ matrix X, and A, B, and C are matrices of constants, then

$$D(BYC) = (C' \otimes B)DY(X)$$

$$\frac{\delta BYC}{\delta x_{rs}} = B\frac{\delta Y}{\delta x_{rs}}C$$

$$\frac{\delta BYC}{\delta X} = (I_n \otimes B)\frac{\delta Y}{\delta X}(I_n \otimes C).$$

The third concept of a matrix derivative is not so accommodating. Certainly, there are rules that allow you to move from $\gamma Y_{ij}/\gamma X$ and $\gamma Y/\gamma X$ to $\gamma(BYC)_{ij}/\gamma X$ and $\gamma BYC/\gamma X$ respectively, but these are more complicated.

The following results are not as well known:

5. Let $Y = E'E$ where $E = A + BXC$ with A $p \times q$, B $p \times m$, and C $n \times q$. Then, from Lutkepohl (1996), p. 191, we have

$$D(E'E) = K_{qq}(C' \otimes E'B) + C' \otimes E'B.$$

Using our principles, we obtain

$$\frac{\partial E'E}{\partial x_{rs}} = C'E_{sr}^{nm}B'E + B'EE_{rs}^{mn}C$$

and

$$\frac{\gamma(E'E)_{ij}}{\gamma X} = B'EE_{ji}^{qq}C' + B'EE_{ij}^{qq}C'.$$

In terms of the complete matrices, we have

$$\frac{\delta E'E}{\delta X} = (I_m \otimes C')K_{mn}(I_n \otimes B'E) + (I_m \otimes E'B)U_{mn}(I_n \otimes C)$$

$$= (I_m \otimes C')K_{mn}(I_n \otimes B'E) + (\text{vec } E'B)(\text{rvec } C)$$

$$\frac{\gamma E'E}{\gamma X} = (I_q \otimes B'E)K_{qq}(I_q \otimes E') + (I_q \otimes B'E)U_{qq}(I_q \otimes C')$$

$$= (I_q \otimes B'E)K_{qq}(I_q \otimes C') + (\text{vec } B'E)(\text{rvec } C').$$

6. Let $Y = EE'$ where E is as in 5.

Then, from Lutkepohl (1996), p. 191, again we have

$$D(EE') = K_{pp}(EC' \otimes B) + (EC' \otimes B).$$

It follows that

$$l\frac{\delta EE'}{\delta x_{rs}} = EC'E_{sr}^{nm}B' + BE_{rs}^{mn}CE'$$

$$\frac{\gamma(EE')_{ij}}{\gamma X} = B'E_{ji}^{pp}EC' + B'E_{ij}^{pp}EC'$$

or in terms of complete matrices

$$\frac{\delta EE'}{\delta X} = (I_m \otimes EC')K_{mn}(I_n \otimes B') + (I_m \otimes B)U_{mn}(I_n \otimes CE')$$

$$= (I_m \otimes EC')K_{mn}(I_n \otimes B') + (\text{vec } B)(\text{rvec } CE')$$

$$\frac{\gamma EE'}{\gamma X} = (I_p \otimes B')K_{pp}(I_p \otimes EC') + (I_p \otimes B')U_{pp}(I_p \otimes EC')$$

$$= (I_p \otimes B')K_{pp}(I_p \otimes EC') + (\text{vec } B')(\text{rvec } EC').$$

The next chapter looks at some new matrix calculus results or at least old results expressed in a new way. We deal with matrix derivatives using Concept 4 that involves cross-products and generalized vecs and rvecs. As far as cross-products are concerned, we can apply our principles to the transpose of every Kronecker product in the cross-product to get the corresponding results for the other concepts of matrix derivatives.

4.8 Recursive Derivatives

Let $Y(x)$ be an $p \times q$ matrix function of an $m \times 1$ vector x. Then, Rilstone, Srivastava, and Ullah (1996) consider a derivative of Y with respect to x that is a variation of Concept 3. That is, they define this derivative as

$$\nabla Y = \begin{pmatrix} Dy_{11} & \cdots & Dy_{1q} \\ \vdots & & \vdots \\ Dy_{p1} & \cdots & D_{pq} \end{pmatrix} \tag{4.19}$$

where y_{ij} is the (i, j)th element of Y. As each submatrix,

$$Dy_{ij} = \begin{pmatrix} \dfrac{\partial y_{ij}}{\partial x_1} \cdots \dfrac{\partial y_{ij}}{\partial x_m} \end{pmatrix}$$

is $1 \times m$ this matrix is $p \times qm$. They then define a matrix of the second order partial derivatives, the $\partial^2 y_{ij}/\partial x_r \partial x_s$, as $\nabla^2 Y = \nabla(\nabla Y)$. That is, to form

$\nabla^2 Y$ we take D of every element in ∇Y so $\nabla^2 Y$ is $p \times qm^2$. Matrices of higher order partial derivatives can be defined recursively by

$$\nabla^\nu Y = \nabla(\nabla^{\nu-1} Y)$$

where $\nabla^\nu Y$ is an $p \times qm^\nu$ matrix. If we let $y_{ij}^{\nu-1}$ denote the (i, j) th element of $\nabla^{\nu-1} Y$ for $i = 1, \ldots, p$ and $j = 1, \ldots, qm^{\nu-1}$, then in $\nabla^\nu Y$ this becomes the $1 \times m$ vector $Dy_{ij}^{\nu-1}$.

In this section, we want to look at the relationships between ∇Y and higher order derivatives as defined by Rilstone, Srivastava, and Ullah (1996), on the one hand, with those derived using the more conventional concept of a matrix derivative, Concept 1 studied in the previous sections.

Consider Concept 1 for this case, which is the $pq \times m$ matrix

$$DY(x) = \begin{pmatrix} Dy_{11} \\ \vdots \\ Dy_{p1} \\ \vdots \\ Dy_{1q} \\ \vdots \\ Dy_{pq} \end{pmatrix}. \tag{4.21}$$

By comparing Equations 4.19 and 4.21, we see that

$$\nabla Y = \text{rvec}_p DY(x),$$

and

$$DY(x) = \text{vec} \nabla Y.$$

Two special cases come to mind. If Y is a scalar function of x, so $p = q = 1$, or if Y is a vector function of x, so $q = 1$, then

$$\nabla Y = DY(x).$$

Consider now the $p \times qm^2$ matrix,

$$\nabla^2 Y = \begin{pmatrix} D\left(\dfrac{\partial y_{11}}{\partial x_1}\right) & \cdots & D\left(\dfrac{\partial y_{11}}{\partial x_m}\right) & \cdots & D\left(\dfrac{\partial y_{1q}}{\partial x_1}\right) & \cdots & D\left(\dfrac{\partial y_{1q}}{\partial x_m}\right) \\ \vdots & & \vdots & & \vdots & & \vdots \\ D\left(\dfrac{\partial y_{p1}}{\partial x_1}\right) & \cdots & D\left(\dfrac{\partial y_{p1}}{\partial x_m}\right) & \cdots & D\left(\dfrac{\partial y_{pq}}{\partial x_1}\right) & \cdots & D\left(\dfrac{\partial y_{pq}}{\partial x_m}\right) \end{pmatrix} \tag{4.22}$$

and compare it with the matrix of second order partial derivatives that would have been formed using Concept 1, namely the $pqm \times m$ matrix, which written out in full is

$$D^2Y = D(\text{vec } D) = \begin{pmatrix} D\left(\dfrac{\partial y_{11}}{\partial x_1}\right) \\ \vdots \\ D\left(\dfrac{\partial y_{p1}}{\partial x_1}\right) \\ \vdots \\ D\left(\dfrac{\partial y_{1q}}{\partial x_1}\right) \\ \vdots \\ D\left(\dfrac{\partial y_{pq}}{\partial x_1}\right) \\ \vdots \\ D\left(\dfrac{\partial y_{11}}{\partial x_m}\right) \\ \vdots \\ D\left(\dfrac{\partial y_{p1}}{\partial x_m}\right) \\ \vdots \\ D\left(\dfrac{\partial y_{1q}}{\partial x_m}\right) \\ \vdots \\ D\left(\dfrac{\partial y_{pq}}{\partial x_m}\right) \end{pmatrix}. \tag{4.23}$$

Comparing Equations 4.22 and 4.23, we have that

$$D^2Y = \text{vec}_m[(\nabla^2 Y)T'_{m,m,\dots,m}],$$

where $T_{m,m,\dots,m}$ is the appropriate twining matrix. But from Equation 2.69 of Chapter 2,

$$T'_{m,m,\dots,m} = K_{qm} \otimes I_m$$

so, we have

$$D^2Y = \text{vec}_m[(\nabla^2 Y)(K_{qm} \otimes I_m)]. \tag{4.24}$$

Moreover, as a generalized vec can always be undone by a generalized rvec, rvec_p in this case, we have

$$\text{rvec}_p(D^2Y) = \nabla^2 Y(K_{qm} \otimes I_m)$$

so

$$\nabla^2 Y = \text{rvec}_p(D^2Y)(K_{mq} \otimes I_m). \tag{4.25}$$

If $Y(x) = y(x)$ is a vector function of x, so $q = 1$, then as $K_{1m} = K_{m1} = I_m$, we have

$$D^2y = \text{vec}_m \nabla^2 y$$

and

$$\nabla^2 y = \text{rvec}_p D^2 y.$$

If $Y(x) = \ell(x)$ is a scalar function of x, so $p = q = 1$, then we have

$$D^2\ell(x) = \text{vec}_m \nabla^2 \ell$$

and

$$\nabla^2 \ell = \text{rvec}\,(D^2\ell(x)).$$

Notice that using Concept 1

$$D(D\ell(x))'$$

is the **Hessian matrix** of the function $\ell(x)$. That is, it is the $m \times m$ symmetric matrix whose (i, j)th is $\partial^2\ell/\partial x_j \partial x_i = \partial^2\ell/\partial x_i \partial x_j$. Again, notice also that using Concept 1 if $\ell(x)$ is a scalar function of a $n \times 1$ vector x, b is an $p \times 1$ vector of constants, and A is an $m \times q$ matrix of constants, then

$$D(b\ell(x)) = bD(\ell(x)) \tag{4.28}$$

and

$$D(A\ell(x)) = \text{vec}AD(\ell(x)). \tag{4.29}$$

Continuing with the special case $Y(x) = y(x)$ further, suppose we denote the $pm^{v-2} \times m$ matrix of $v - 1$ order partial derivatives we get using Concept 1 by $D^{v-1}y(x)$. Then, the matrix of $pm^{v-1} \times m$ matrix of v order partial derivatives, we get using this concept is

$$D^vy = D(\text{vec}\,D^{v-1}y(x))$$

and a little reflection shows that

$$D^v y = \text{vec}_m \nabla^v y \tag{4.26}$$

and

$$\nabla^v y = \text{rvec}_p (D^v y) \tag{4.27}$$

for all higher order derivatives $v \geq 2$.

We illustrate these results by way of the example provided by Rilstone *et al.,* (1996). They consider the version of the exponential regression model where the probability density function for y_t is

$$f(y_t; \beta) = \exp(x_t' \beta - y_t \exp(x_t' \beta))$$

and x_t a $K \times 1$ vector of constants, and β is a $K \times 1$ vector of unknown parameters.[1]

The probability density function of our sample is

$$f(y; \beta) = \exp \sum_{t=1}^{n} [x_t' \beta - y_t \exp(x_t' \beta)],$$

so the log likelihood function is

$$\ell(\beta) = \sum_{t=1}^{n} [x_t' \beta - y_t \exp(x_t' \beta)].$$

Sticking with Concept 1

$$D(\ell(\beta)) = \sum_{t=1}^{n} D[x_t' \beta - y_t \exp(x_t' \beta)].$$

Using the chain rule of ordinary calculus and Equation 4.29, we obtain

$$D(\ell(\beta)) = \sum_{t=1}^{n} [x_t' - y_t \exp(x_t' \beta) x_t']. \tag{4.30}$$

Taking the transpose of Equation 4.30, the maximum likelihood estimator $\hat{\beta}$ of β solves

$$\frac{1}{n} \sum_{t=1}^{n} q_t(\hat{\beta}) = 0$$

[1] Rilstone *et al.* actually consider the case where x_t is a random vector and $f(y_t; \beta)$ is the conditional density function, but as we are illustrating matrix calculus techniques we take the simpler case.

where the $k \times 1$ vector $q_t(\beta)$ is given by

$$q_t(\beta) = x_t - y_t \exp(x_t'\beta)x_t.$$

Rilstone *et al.*, (1996) obtain successively higher order derivatives of $q_t(\beta)$ using their recursive operator ∇. Here, instead, the derivatives are obtained using Concept 1 and the corresponding results for ∇ are obtained using Equation 4.27.

Write

$$q_t(\beta) = x_t - x_t\mu_t(\beta),$$

where $\mu_t(\beta)$ is the scalar function of β given by $\mu_t(\beta) = y_t \exp(x_t'\beta)$. Using the chain rule of ordinary calculus and Equation 4.29, we have

$$D\mu_t(\beta) = y_t \exp(x_t'\beta)x_t' = x_t'\mu_t,$$

so using Concept 1 and Equation 4.28,

$$Dq_t(\beta) = -x_t x_t'\mu_t = \nabla q_t(\beta).$$

Differentiating again using Concept 1 gives

$$D^2 q_t(\beta) = D(\text{vec } x_t x_t'\mu) = -(\text{vec } x_t x_t')x_t'\mu_t.$$

But from Equation 1.11 of Chapter 1, $\text{vec} x_t x_t' = x_t \otimes x_t$, so

$$D^2 q_t(\beta) = A_1\mu_t,$$

where $A_1 = -x_t \otimes x_t x_t'$. Differentiating again using Equation 4.28 gives

$$D^3 q_t(\beta) = D \text{vec} A_1\mu_1 = (\text{vec } A_1)x_t'\mu_t.$$

Again, by Equation 1.11 of Chapter 1

$$\text{vec } A_1 = -\text{vec } (x_t \otimes x_t)x_t' = -x_t \otimes x_t \otimes x_t$$

so

$$D^3 q_1(\beta) = A_2\mu_t$$

where $A_2 = -x_t \otimes x_t \otimes x_t x_t'$. Continuing in this manner it is clear that

$$D^v q_1(\beta) = A_{v-1}\mu_t = -(x_t \otimes \ldots \otimes x_t)x_t'\mu_t$$

for $v \geq 2$ where

$$A_{v-1} = \underbrace{-x_t \otimes \ldots \otimes x_t}_{v-1} \otimes x_t x_t'.$$

Using Equation 4.27, we have

$$\nabla^v q_t(\beta) = (\mathrm{rvec}_k A_{v-1})\mu_t.$$

But from Equation 1.17 of Chapter 1,

$$\mathrm{rvec}_k A_{v-1} = -(x_t \otimes \ldots \otimes x_t)' \otimes x_t x_t' = -x_t' \otimes \ldots \otimes x_t' \otimes x_t x_t'$$
$$= -x_t(x_t' \otimes \ldots \otimes x_t'),$$

so

$$\nabla^v q_t(\beta) = -x_t(x_t' \otimes \ldots \otimes x_t')\mu_t, \ v \geq 2.$$

Notice that for this special example

$$\nabla^v q_t(\beta) = (D^v q_t(\beta))'.$$

FIVE

New Matrix Calculus Results

5.1 Introduction

In this chapter, we develop new matrix calculus results or at least view existing results in a new light. We concentrate on results that involve the mathematical concepts developed in Chapters 1 and 2, particularly results that involve generalized vecs and rvecs on the one hand and cross-products on the other.

We avoid as much as possible matrix calculus results that are well known. If the reader wants to familiarize themselves with these, then I refer them to Magnus and Neudecker (1999), Lutkepohl (1996), and Turkington (2005). Having said this, however, because I want this book to be self-contained, it is necessary for me to at least present matrix calculus results, which we use all the time in our derivations. These results on the whole form rules, which are the generalizations of the chain rule and the product rule of ordinary calculus.

We saw in the last chapter that at least four different concepts of matrix derivatives are prevalent in the literature and that using transformation principles is an easy matter to move from results derived for one concept to the corresponding results for the other concepts. That is not to say, however, that new results can be just as easily obtained regardless of what concept one chooses to work with. Experience has shown that by far the easiest concept to use in deriving results for difficult cases is Concept 1, or the transpose of this concept, which we called Concept 4. In the following sections, we develop basic rules for Concept 4.

5.2 Concept of a Matrix Derivative Used

In this chapter the concept of a matrix derivative used is Concept 4. Recall that if $y = y(x)$ is an $s \times 1$ vector function of x, an $r \times 1$ vector then under this concept we define $\partial y / \partial x$ as

$$
\frac{\partial y}{\partial x} = \begin{pmatrix} \dfrac{\partial y_1}{\partial x_1} & \cdots & \dfrac{\partial y_s}{\partial x_1} \\ \vdots & & \vdots \\ \dfrac{\partial y_1}{\partial x_r} & \cdots & \dfrac{\partial y_s}{\partial x_r} \end{pmatrix}. \tag{5.1}
$$

(See Graham 1981). If Y is an $p \times q$ matrix whose elements y_{ij} are differentiable functions of the elements x_{rs} of an $m \times n$ matrix X, then the derivative of Y with respect to X we work withis the $mn \times pq$ matrix

$$
\frac{\partial \text{vec } Y}{\partial \text{vec } X} = \begin{bmatrix} \dfrac{\partial y_{11}}{\partial x_{11}} & \cdots & \dfrac{\partial y_{p1}}{\partial x_{11}} & \cdots & \dfrac{\partial y_{1q}}{\partial x_{11}} & \cdots & \dfrac{\partial y_{pq}}{\partial x_{11}} \\ \vdots & & \vdots & & \vdots & & \vdots \\ \dfrac{\partial y_{11}}{\partial x_{m1}} & \cdots & \dfrac{\partial y_{p1}}{\partial x_{m1}} & \cdots & \dfrac{\partial y_{1q}}{\partial x_{m1}} & \cdots & \dfrac{\partial y_{pq}}{\partial x_{m1}} \\ \vdots & & \vdots & & \vdots & & \vdots \\ \dfrac{\partial y_{11}}{\partial x_{1n}} & \cdots & \dfrac{\partial y_{p1}}{\partial x_{1n}} & \cdots & \dfrac{\partial y_{1q}}{\partial x_{1n}} & \cdots & \dfrac{\partial y_{pq}}{\partial x_{1n}} \\ \vdots & & \vdots & & \vdots & & \vdots \\ \dfrac{\partial y_{11}}{\partial x_{mn}} & \cdots & \dfrac{\partial y_{p1}}{\partial x_{mn}} & \cdots & \dfrac{\partial y_{1q}}{\partial x_{mn}} & \cdots & \dfrac{\partial y_{pq}}{\partial x_{mn}} \end{bmatrix},
$$

where $\partial y_{ij} / \partial x_{rs}$ is the partial derivative of y_{ij} with respect to x_{rs}. A column of this matrix gives the derivatives of y_{ij} with respect to all the elements of X, $x_{11} \ldots x_{m1} \ldots x_{1n} \ldots x_{mn}$. A row of this matrix gives the derivatives of $y_{11} \cdots y_{p1} \cdots y_{1q} \ldots y_{pq}$ with respect to x_{rs}, a single element of X.

If y is a scalar, then $y(x)$ is a scalar function of x and $\partial y / \partial x$ is the $r \times 1$ vector given by

$$
\frac{\partial y}{\partial x} = \begin{pmatrix} \dfrac{\partial y}{\partial x_1} \\ \vdots \\ \dfrac{\partial y}{\partial x_r} \end{pmatrix}
$$

which is often called the **gradient vector** of y. Similarly, if x is a scalar $\partial y / \partial x$ is the $1 \times s$ vector

$$
\frac{\partial y}{\partial x} = \left(\frac{\partial y_1}{\partial x} \cdots \frac{\partial y_s}{\partial x} \right).
$$

For the general case given by Equation 5.1, where y and x are $s \times 1$ and $r \times 1$ vectors, respectively, the jth column of $\partial y/\partial x$ is the derivative of a scalar function with respect to a vector, namely $\partial y_j/\partial x$, whereas the ith row of the matrix $\partial y/\partial x$ is the derivative of a vector with respect to a scalar, namely $\partial y/\partial x_i$.

In deriving results, where $y = \text{vec } Y$ is a complicated vector function of $x = \text{vec } X$, we need a few basic rules for $\partial y/\partial x$, which I now intend to give with proofs. For a more complete list of known matrix calculus results, consult the references previously given.

The last section presents some simple theorems concerning $\partial \text{vec } Y/\partial \text{vec } X$. These theorems at first glance appear trivial, but taken together they give a very effective method of finding new matrix calculus results. This method is then applied to obtain new results for derivatives involving $\text{vec } A$, $\text{vech } A$, and $\bar{\text{v}}(A)$ where A is an $n \times n$ matrix.

5.3 Some Basic Rules of Matrix Calculus

Theorem 5.1 *Let x be an $r \times 1$ vector and let A be a matrix of constants; that is, the elements of $A = \{a_{ij}\}$ are not scalar functions, of x.*
  Then

$$\frac{\partial Ax}{\partial x} = A'$$

$$\frac{\partial x'Ax}{\partial x} = (A + A')x = 2Ax \quad \text{if } A \text{ is symmetric.}$$

Proof: The jth element of Ax is $\sum_k a_{jk} x_k$ so the jth column of $\partial Ax/\partial x$ is A'_j. and $\partial Ax/\partial x = A'$. The jth element of $\partial x'Ax/\partial x$ is $\partial x'Ax/\partial x_j = \sum_i a_{ij}x_i + \sum_\ell a_{j\ell}x_\ell$ so $\partial x'Ax/\partial x = (A + A')x$. Clearly, if A is symmetric, the result becomes $2Ax$. ∎

The next rule represents a generalization of the chain rule of ordinary calculus.

Theorem 5.2 (The Backward Chain Rule) *Let $x = (x_i)$, $y = (y_\ell)$, and $z = (z_j)$ be $r \times 1$, $s \times 1$, and $t \times 1$ vectors, respectively. Suppose z is a vector function of y, which in turn is a vector function of x, so we can write $z = z[y(x)]$.*

Then,

$$\frac{\partial z}{\partial x} = \frac{\partial y}{\partial x} \frac{\partial z}{\partial y}.$$

Proof: The (i, j)th element of the matrix $\partial z/\partial x$ is

$$\left(\frac{\partial z}{\partial x}\right)_{ij} = \frac{\partial z_j}{\partial x_i} = \sum_{k=1}^{s} \frac{\partial y_k}{\partial x_i} \frac{\partial z_j}{\partial y_k} = \left(\frac{\partial y}{\partial x}\right)_{i\cdot} \left(\frac{\partial z}{\partial y}\right)_{\cdot j} = \left(\frac{\partial y}{\partial x} \frac{\partial z}{\partial y}\right)_{ij}.$$

Hence,

$$\frac{\partial z}{\partial x} = \frac{\partial y}{\partial x} \frac{\partial z}{\partial y}. \qquad \blacksquare$$

In developing the next rule, the product rule, it is useful for us to refer to a generalization of the chain rule where z is a vector function of two vectors u and v. This generalization is given by the following theorem.

Theorem 5.3 (Generalized Chain Rule) *Let z be an $t \times 1$ vector function of two vectors u and v, which are $h \times 1$ and $k \times 1$, respectively. Suppose u and v are both vector functions of an $r \times 1$ vector x, so $z = z[u(x), v(x)]$. Then,*

$$\frac{\partial z}{\partial x} = \frac{\partial u}{\partial x} \frac{\partial z}{\partial u} + \frac{\partial u}{\partial x} \frac{\partial z}{\partial v} = \frac{\partial z}{\partial x}\bigg|_{v \, constant} + \frac{\partial z}{\partial x}\bigg|_{u \, constant}$$

Proof: Similar to that of Theorem 5.2. $\qquad \blacksquare$

Theorem 5.3 can now be used to obtain the following product rule.

Theorem 5.4 (The Product Rule) *Let X be an $m \times n$ matrix and Y be an $n \times p$ matrix, and suppose that the elements of both these matrices are scalar functions of a vector z. Then,*

$$\frac{\partial vec\, XY}{\partial z} = \frac{\partial vec\, X}{\partial z}(Y \otimes I_m) + \frac{\partial vec\, Y}{\partial z}(I_p \otimes X').$$

Proof: By Theorem 5.3, we have

$$\frac{\partial vec\, XY}{\partial z} = \frac{\partial vec\, XY}{\partial z}\bigg|_{vecY \, constant} + \frac{\partial vec\, XY}{\partial z}\bigg|_{vecX \, constant}$$

$$= \frac{\partial vec\, X}{\partial z} \frac{\partial vec\, XY}{\partial vec\, X}\bigg|_{vecY \, constant} + \frac{\partial vec\, Y}{\partial z} \frac{\partial vec\, XY}{\partial vec\, X}\bigg|_{vecX \, constant}$$

where this last equality follows from the backward chain rule. The result follows by noting that

$$\text{vec}\, XY = (Y' \otimes I_m)\text{vec}\, X = (I_p \otimes X)\text{vec}\, Y$$

and applying Theorem 5.1. ∎

Theorem 5.4 has the following useful corollary.

Corollary to Theorem 5.4 *Let x be an $n \times 1$ vector, $f(x)$ be a scalar function of x, $u(x)$ and $v(x)$ be $m \times 1$ vector functions of x, and $A(x)$ and $B(x)$ be $p \times m$ and $m \times q$ matrices, respectively, whose elements are scalar functions of x. Then,*

$$\frac{\partial f(x)x}{\partial x} = f(x) \otimes I_n + \frac{\partial f(x)}{\partial x}x' = f(x)I_n + \frac{\partial f(x)}{\partial x}x',$$

$$\frac{\partial f(x)u(x)}{\partial x} = \frac{\partial u(x)}{\partial x}(f(x) \otimes I_m) + \frac{\partial f(x)}{\partial x}u(x)'$$

$$= \frac{\partial u(x)}{\partial x}f(x) + \frac{\partial f(x)}{\partial x}u(x)',$$

$$\frac{\partial u(x)'v(x)}{\partial x} = \frac{\partial u(x)}{\partial x}v(x) + \frac{\partial v(x)}{\partial x}u(x),$$

$$\frac{\partial \,\text{vec}\, u(x)v(x)'}{\partial x} = \frac{\partial u(x)}{\partial x}(v(x)' \otimes I_m) + \frac{\partial v(x)}{\partial x}(I_m \otimes u(x)'),$$

$$\frac{\partial A(x)u(x)}{\partial x} = \frac{\partial \,\text{vec}\, A(x)}{\partial x}(u(x) \otimes I_p) + \frac{\partial u(x)}{\partial x}A(x)',$$

$$\frac{\partial \,\text{vec}\, u(x)'B(x)}{\partial x} = \frac{\partial B(x)'u(x)}{\partial x} = \frac{\partial \,\text{vec}\,[B(x)']}{\partial x}(u(x) \otimes I_q) + \frac{\partial u(x)}{\partial x}B(x).$$

These few basic results will suffice in the derivations that follow.

5.4 Matrix Calculus Results Involving Generalized Rvecs or Cross-Products

In this section, we obtain a number of matrix calculus results that can be expressed in terms of cross-products or generalized vecs and rvecs. In so doing, we call on the work we have done involving these operators together with work we did on generalized vecs and rvecs of the commutation matrix. These results pertain to the matrix differentiation of vecs of Kronecker products.

Recall from Section 2.5 of Chapter 2 that for an $m \times n$ matrix X, we can write

$$\text{vec}(X \otimes I_G) = (I_n \otimes \text{vec}_m K_{mG})\text{vec}\, X$$

and

$$\text{vec}(I_G \otimes X) = (\text{vec}_m K_{nG} \otimes I_m)\text{vec}\, X.$$

It follows using Theorem 5.1 that

$$\frac{\partial \text{vec}(X \otimes I_G)}{\partial \text{vec}\, X} = (I_n \otimes \text{vec}_m K_{mG})' = I_n \otimes (\text{vec}_m K_{mG})' = I_n \otimes \text{rvec}_m K_{Gm}$$

$$(5.2)$$

and that

$$\frac{\partial \text{vec}(I_G \otimes X)}{\partial \text{vec}\, X} = (\text{vec}_n K_{nG} \otimes I_m)' = (\text{vec}_n K_{nG})' \otimes I_m = \text{rvec}_n K_{Gn} \otimes I_m.$$

$$(5.3)$$

These two results are the building blocks of numerous other results involving the derivatives of the vecs of Kronecker products. We see that we can write these derivatives either in terms of generalized rvecs or in terms of cross-products and that both cases our results involve the commutation matrix.

Consider now an $p \times G$ matrix A whose elements are not functions of the elements of X. Then,

$$\text{vec}(X \otimes A) = \text{vec}[(I_m \otimes A)(X \otimes I_G)] = (I_{nG} \otimes I_m \otimes A)\text{vec}(X \otimes I_G).$$

Using the backward chain rule, Theorem 4.2, we have

$$\frac{\partial \text{vec}(X \otimes A)}{\partial \text{vec}\, X} = \frac{\partial \text{vec}(X \otimes I_G)}{\partial \text{vec}\, X}(I_{nGm} \otimes A').$$

From Equation 5.2, we can now write

$$\frac{\partial \text{vec}(X \otimes A)}{\partial \text{vec}\, X}$$
$$= (I_n \otimes \text{rvec}_m K_{Gm})(I_n \otimes I_{Gm} \otimes A') = I_n \otimes (\text{rvec}_m K_{Gm})(I_{Gm} \otimes A') \quad (5.4)$$
$$= I_n \otimes \text{rvec}_m[K_{Gm}(I_m \otimes A')], \quad (5.5)$$

using Equation 1.19 of Chapter 1, which gives the derivative in terms of generalized rvecs. If we want the equivalent result in terms of cross-products, we apply Theorem 2.28 of Chapter 2 to Equation 5.4 to obtain

$$\frac{\partial \text{vec}(X \otimes A)}{\partial \text{vec}\, X} = K_{Gn} \tau_{Gnm}[K_{Gm}(I_m \otimes A')]. \quad (5.6)$$

We can investigate this result further by applying Theorem 2.25 of Chapter 2 to Equation 5.5 to obtain

$$\frac{\partial \text{vec}(X \otimes A)}{\partial \text{vec}\, X} = I_n \otimes (I_m \otimes a_1' \ldots I_m \otimes a_G').$$

Alternatively, as

$$K_{Gn} = \begin{pmatrix} I_n \otimes e_1^{G'} \\ \vdots \\ I_n \otimes e_G^{G'} \end{pmatrix} \quad \text{and} \quad K_{Gm}(I_m \otimes A') = \begin{pmatrix} I_m \otimes a_1' \\ \vdots \\ I_m \otimes a_G' \end{pmatrix}$$

using Equation 5.6, we can write the same result as

$$\frac{\partial \text{vec}(X \otimes A)}{\partial \text{vec}\, X} = \left(I_n \otimes e_1^{G'} \right) \otimes \left(I_m \otimes a_1' \right) + \cdots + \left(I_n \otimes e_G^{G'} \right) \otimes \left(I_m \otimes a_G' \right).$$

In a similar manner,

$$\text{vec}(A \otimes X) = \text{vec}[(A \otimes I_m)(I_G \otimes X)] = (I_{Gn} \otimes A \otimes I_m)\text{vec}(I_G \otimes X).$$

Using the backward chain rule and Equation 5.3, we have

$$\frac{\partial \text{vec}(A \otimes X)}{\partial \text{vec}\, X}$$
$$= \frac{\partial \text{vec}(I_G \otimes X)}{\partial \text{vec}\, X}(I_{Gn} \otimes A' \otimes I_m) = (\text{rvec}_m K_{Gn} \otimes I_m)(I_{Gn} \otimes A' \otimes I_m) \tag{5.7}$$
$$= (\text{rvec}_m K_{Gn})(I_{Gn} \otimes A') \otimes I_m = \text{rvec}_m[K_{Gn}(I_n \otimes A')] \otimes I_m, \tag{5.8}$$

by Equation 1.19 of Chapter 1, which gives the derivative in terms of generalized rvecs. If we want the equivalent result in terms of cross-products, we apply Theorem 2.28 of Chapter 2 to Equation 5.7 to obtain

$$\frac{\partial \text{vec}(A \otimes X)}{\partial \text{vec}\, X} = I_{Gn} \tau_{Gnm}(A' \otimes I_m). \tag{5.9}$$

Again, we can investigate this result further by applying Theorem 2.25 of Chapter 2 to Equation 5.8 to obtain

$$\frac{\partial \text{vec}(A \otimes X)}{\partial \text{vec}\, X} = (I_n \otimes a_1' \ldots I_n \otimes a_G') \otimes I_m.$$

An alternative way of writing this result uses the cross-product given in Equation 5.9. Write

$$I_{Gn} = I_G \otimes I_n = \begin{pmatrix} e_1' \otimes I_n \\ \vdots \\ e_G' \otimes I_n \end{pmatrix}, \quad A' \otimes I_m = \begin{pmatrix} a_1' \otimes I_m \\ \vdots \\ a_G' \otimes I_m \end{pmatrix}$$

so

$$\frac{\partial \text{vec}(A \otimes X)}{\partial \text{vec}\, X} = I_{Gn} \tau_{Gnm} (A' \otimes I_m) = (e_1' \otimes I_n) \otimes (a_1' \otimes I_m)$$
$$+ \cdots + (e_G' \otimes I_n) \otimes (a_G' \otimes I_m).$$

Suppose now A and B are $mG \times p$ and $nG \times q$ matrices whose elements are not functions of the elements of the $m \times n$ matrix X. Consider

$$\text{vec}\, A'(I_G \otimes X)B = (B' \otimes A')\text{vec}(I_G \otimes X).$$

Applying the backward chain rule we have,

$$\frac{\partial \text{vec}\, A'(I_G \otimes X)B}{\partial \text{vec}\, X} = \frac{\partial \text{vec}(I_G \otimes X)}{\partial \text{vec}\, X}(B \otimes A) = (\text{rvec}_m K_{Gn} \otimes I_m)(B \otimes A)$$
$$= B\tau_{Gnm}A, \tag{5.10}$$

by Theorem 2.28 of Chapter 2.

If we partition A and B as follows,

$$A = \begin{pmatrix} A_1 \\ \vdots \\ A_G \end{pmatrix} \quad \text{and} \quad B = \begin{pmatrix} B_1 \\ \vdots \\ B_G \end{pmatrix}$$

where each submatrix A_i is $m \times p$ and each submatrix B_j is $n \times q$, then

$$\frac{\partial \text{vec}\, A'(I_G \otimes X)B}{\partial \text{vec}\, X} = (B_1 \otimes A_1) + \cdots + (B_G \otimes A_G).$$

The result for $A'(X \otimes I_G)B$ is easily obtained by writing

$$A'(X \otimes I_G)B = A'K_{mG}(I_G \otimes X)K_{Gn}B,$$

so using Equation 5.10, we have

$$\frac{\partial \text{vec}\, A'(X \otimes I_G)B}{\partial \text{vec}\, X} = K_{Gn}B\tau_{Gnm}K_{Gm}A. \tag{5.11}$$

If we want to expand this cross-product, recall from Theorem 2.10 of Chapter 2 that

$$K_{Gm}A = \begin{pmatrix} A^{(1)} \\ \vdots \\ A^{(G)} \end{pmatrix}$$

where the $A^{(j)}$s refer to the partitioning $A = (A_1' \ldots A_m')'$ where each A_i is $G \times p$. So

$$\frac{\partial \mathrm{vec}\, A'(X \otimes I_G)B}{\partial \mathrm{vec}\, X} = B^{(1)} \otimes A^{(1)} + \cdots + B^{(G)} \otimes A^{(G)}$$

where the $B^{(j)}$s refer to the partitioning $B = (B_1' \ldots B_n')$, in which each B_i is $G \times q$.

Special cases of the last two results are worthy of mention.

If a is an $mG \times 1$ vector and b is an $nG \times 1$ vector, then Equation 5.10 gives

$$\frac{\partial a'(I_G \otimes X)b}{\partial \mathrm{vec}\, X} = b\tau_{Gnm}a$$

whereas Equation 5.11 gives

$$\frac{\partial a'(X \otimes I_G)b}{\partial \mathrm{vec}\, X} = K_{Gn}b\tau_{Gnm}K_{Gm}a = \mathrm{vec}\, A'B$$

by Theorem 2.15 where $A = \mathrm{rvec}_G a$ and $B = \mathrm{rvec}_G b$.

Suppose D is an $G \times s$ matrix of constants and B is now an $ns \times q$ matrix, A and X as previously. Then, expressions such as $A'(D \otimes X)B$ are easily handled. We write

$$\mathrm{vec}\, A'(D \otimes X)B = \mathrm{vec}\, A'(D \otimes I_m)(I_s \otimes X)B$$

so, using Equation 5.10, we have

$$\frac{\partial \mathrm{vec}\, A'(D \otimes X)B}{\partial \mathrm{vec}\, X} = B\tau_{snm}(D' \otimes I_m)A.$$

If we partition B as,

$$B = \begin{pmatrix} B_1 \\ \vdots \\ B_s \end{pmatrix} \tag{5.12}$$

where each submatrix B_j is $n \times q$, then

$$\frac{\partial \text{vec}\, A'(D \otimes X)B}{\partial \text{vec}\, X} = (B_1 \otimes (d_1' \otimes I_m)A) + \cdots + (B_s \otimes (d_s' \otimes I_m)A)$$

where d_j is the jth column of D for $j = 1, \ldots, s$. Similarly, if A is now $ms \times p$, then

$$A'(X \otimes D)B = A'(I_m \otimes D)(X \otimes I_s)B$$

and from Equation 5.11

$$\frac{\partial \text{vec}\, A'(X \otimes D)B}{\partial \text{vec}\, X} = K_{sn}B\tau_{snm}K_{sm}(I_m \otimes D')A = B^{(1)} \otimes (I_m \otimes d_1')A$$
$$+ \cdots + B^{(s)} \otimes (I_m \otimes d_s')A.$$

when the $B^{(j)}$s refer to the previous partitioning given by Equation 5.12.

So far our results have been acquired with the application of Theorem 5.1 and Theorem 5.2, or the backward chain rule. Further results bring in the product rule as presented in Theorem 5.4.

Suppose that A is $m^2 \times p$ and B is $n^2 \times q$, and both these matrices are matrices of constants.

In obtaining the derivative of $A'(X \otimes X)B$, we write

$$A'(X \otimes X)B = A'(X \otimes I_m)(I_n \otimes X)B.$$

Applying the product rule, we have

$$\frac{\partial \text{vec}\, A'(X \otimes X)B}{\partial \text{vec}\, X} = \frac{\partial \text{vec}\, A'(X \otimes I_m)}{\partial \text{vec}\, X}((I_n \otimes X)B \otimes I_p)$$
$$+ \frac{\partial \text{vec}(I_n \otimes X)B}{\partial \text{vec}\, X}(I_q \otimes (X' \otimes I_m)A)$$
$$= (K_{mn}\tau_{mnm}K_{mm}A)((I_n \otimes X)B \otimes I_p)$$
$$+ (B\tau_{nnm}I_{mn})(I_q \otimes (X' \otimes I_m)A)$$

by applying Equations 5.10 and 5.11. It follows from Theorem 1.5 of Chapter 1 that

$$\frac{\partial \text{vec}\, A'(X \otimes X)B}{\partial \text{vec}\, X} = K_{mn}(I_n \otimes X)B\tau_{mnm}K_{mm}A + B\tau_{nnm}(X' \otimes I_m)A.$$

$$(5.13)$$

We could investigate this result further by expanding the cross-products to obtain

$$\frac{\partial \mathrm{vec}\, A'(X \otimes X)B}{\partial \mathrm{vec}\, X} = (I_n \otimes x^{1'})B \otimes A^{(1)} + \cdots + (I_n \otimes x^{m'})B \otimes A^{(m)}$$
$$+ B_1 \otimes (x_1' \otimes I_m)A + \cdots + B_n \otimes (x_n' \otimes I_m)A,$$

where we have partitioned A and B as

$$A = \begin{pmatrix} A_1 \\ \vdots \\ A_m \end{pmatrix} \qquad B = \begin{pmatrix} B_1 \\ \vdots \\ B_n \end{pmatrix}$$

with each submatrix A_j being $m \times p$ and each submatrix B_j being $n \times q$. With this basic result, we can easily obtain several others using the chain rule.

Suppose X is $n \times n$ and nonsingular, and A and B are $n^2 \times p$ and $n^2 \times q$ matrices of constants. Then, using the backward chain rule, we have

$$\frac{\partial \mathrm{vec}\, A'(X^{-1} \otimes X^{-1})B}{\partial \mathrm{vec}\, X} = \frac{\partial \mathrm{vec}\, X^{-1}}{\partial \mathrm{vec}\, X} \frac{\partial \mathrm{vec}\, A'(X^{-1} \otimes X^{-1})B}{\partial \mathrm{vec}\, X^{-1}}.$$

By Equation 4.17 of Chapter 4,

$$\frac{\partial \mathrm{vec}\, X^{-1}}{\partial \mathrm{vec}\, X} = -X^{-1} \otimes X^{-1'},$$

so, applying Equation 5.13, we have

$$\frac{\partial \mathrm{vec}\, A'(X^{-1} \otimes X^{-1})B}{\partial \mathrm{vec}\, X} = -(X^{-1} \otimes X^{-1'})[K_{nn}(I_n \otimes X^{-1})B\tau_{nnn}K_{nn}A$$
$$+ B\tau_{nnn}(X^{-1'} \otimes I_n)A].$$

Using Theorem 1.5 of Chapter 1 and Equation 2.11 of Chapter 2, we have

$$\frac{\partial \mathrm{vec} A'(X^{-1} \otimes X^{-1})B}{\partial \mathrm{vec}\, X} = -(I_n \otimes X^{-1})K_{nn}(I_n \otimes X^{-1})B\tau_{nnn}(I_n \otimes X^{-1'})K_{nn}A$$
$$- (I_n \otimes X^{-1})B\tau_{nnn}(I \otimes X^{-1'})(X^{-1'} \otimes I_n)A$$
$$= -(X^{-1} \otimes X^{-1})K_{nn}B\tau_{nnn}(I_n \otimes X^{-1'})K_{nn}A$$
$$- (I_n \otimes X^{-1})B\tau_{nnn}(X^{-1'} \otimes X^{-1'})A.$$

Several results can be achieved in a similar manner. In what follows, X is an $m \times n$ matrix and the orders of the matrices of constants, A and B, can be inferred from the example in hand.

For the derivative of $A'(X' \otimes X')B$, we write

$$\frac{\partial \text{vec } A'(X' \otimes X')B}{\partial \text{vec } X} = \frac{\partial \text{vec } X'}{\partial \text{vec } X} \frac{\partial \text{vec } A'(X' \otimes X')B}{\partial \text{vec } X'}. \qquad (5.14)$$

Recall that $K_{mn}\text{vec } X = \text{vec } X'$, so

$$\frac{\partial \text{vec } X'}{\partial \text{vec } X} = (K_{mn})' = K_{nm}.$$

By substituting in Equation 5.14 and appealing to Equation 5.13, we have

$$\frac{\partial \text{vec} A'(X' \otimes X')B}{\partial \text{vec } X} = K_{nm}[K_{nm}(I_m \otimes X')B\tau_{nmn}K_{nn}A + B\tau_{mmn}(X \otimes I_n)A].$$

If we wanted to break this derivative down further, we would appeal to Theorems 2.12 and 2.14 of Chapter 2 and Equation 1.10 of Chapter 1, which allow us to write

$$\frac{\partial \text{vec } A'(X' \otimes X')B}{\partial \text{vec } X} = \begin{pmatrix} K_{nm}(I_m \otimes X')B\tau_{nm1}A_1 \\ \vdots \\ K_{nm}(I_m \otimes X')B\tau_{nm1}A_n \end{pmatrix} + \begin{pmatrix} B\tau_{mm1}XA^{(1)} \\ \vdots \\ B\tau_{mm1}XA^{(n)} \end{pmatrix},$$

where $A^{(j)}$s refer to the partitioning $A = (A_1' \dots A_n')'$ and each A_j is $n \times p$, so

$$\frac{\partial \text{vec } A'(X' \otimes X')B}{\partial \text{vec } X}$$
$$= \begin{pmatrix} (I_m \otimes x_1')B \otimes (A_1)_{1.} + & \cdots & +(I_m \otimes x_n')B \otimes (A_1)_{n.} \\ \vdots & & \vdots \\ (I_m \otimes x_1')B \otimes (A_n)_{1.} + & \cdots & +(I_m \otimes x_n')B \otimes (A_n)_{n.} \end{pmatrix}$$
$$+ \begin{pmatrix} B_1 \otimes x^{1'}A^{(1)} + & \cdots & +B_m \otimes x^{m'}A^{(1)} \\ \vdots & & \vdots \\ B_1 \otimes x^{1'}A^{(n)} + & \cdots & +B_m \otimes x^{m'}A^{(n)} \end{pmatrix},$$

where $B = (B_1' \dots B_m')'$ and each submatrix B_j is $m \times q$.

Consider

$$A'(X' \otimes X)B = A'(X' \otimes I_m)(I_m \otimes X)B$$

so, applying the product rule yields

$$\frac{\partial \text{vec } A'(X' \otimes X)B}{\partial \text{vec } X} = \frac{\partial \text{vec } A'(X' \otimes I_m)}{\partial \text{vec } X}[(I_m \otimes X)B \otimes I_p]$$
$$+ \frac{\partial \text{vec}(I_m \otimes X)B}{\partial \text{vec } X}[I_q \otimes (X \otimes I_m)A]. \qquad (5.15)$$

The backward chain rule yields

$$\frac{\partial \text{vec} A'(X' \otimes I_m)}{\partial \text{vec} X} = \frac{\partial \text{vec} X'}{\partial \text{vec} X} \frac{\partial \text{vec} A'(X' \otimes I_m)}{\partial \text{vec} X'} = K_{nm}(K_{mm}\tau_{mmm}K_{mn}A)$$

(5.16)

where we have used Equation 5.11. Substituting Equation 5.16 in Equation 5.15 and using Equation 5.10 and Theorem 1.5 of Chapter 1, we obtain

$$\frac{\partial \text{vec} A'(X' \otimes X)B}{\partial \text{vec} X} = K_{nm}[K_{mm}(I_m \otimes X)B\tau_{mmn}K_{mn}A] + B\tau_{mnm}(X \otimes I_m)A.$$

We can expand this result further by appealing to Theorem 2.14 of Chapter 2 and Theorem 1.6 of Chapter 1 to obtain

$$\frac{\partial \text{vec} A'(X' \otimes X)B}{\partial \text{vec} X} = \begin{pmatrix} K_{mm}(I_m \otimes X)B\tau_{mm1}A_1 \\ \vdots \\ K_{mm}(I_m \otimes X)B\tau_{mm1}A_n \end{pmatrix} + \begin{pmatrix} B^{(1)}\tau_{m1m}(X \otimes I_m)A \\ \vdots \\ B^{(n)}\tau_{m1m}(X \otimes I_m)A \end{pmatrix}$$

where $A = (A_1' \dots A_n')'$ with each submatrix A_j being $m \times p$ and the $B^{(j)}$s refer to the partitioning $B = (B_1' \dots B_m')'$ where each submatrix is $n \times q$, so

$$\frac{\partial \text{vec} A'(X' \otimes X)B}{\partial \text{vec} X}$$

$$= \begin{pmatrix} (I_m \otimes x^{1'})B \otimes (A_1)_{1.} + \cdots + (I_m \otimes x^{m'})B \otimes (A_1)_{m.} \\ \vdots \qquad\qquad \vdots \\ (I_m \otimes x^{1'})B \otimes (A_n)_{1.} + \cdots + (I_m \otimes x^{m'})B \otimes (A_n)_{m.} \end{pmatrix}$$

$$+ \begin{pmatrix} (B_1)_{1.} \otimes (x^{1'} \otimes I_m)A + \cdots + (B_m)_{1.} \otimes (x^{m'} \otimes I_m)A \\ \vdots \qquad\qquad \vdots \\ (B_1)_{n.} \otimes (x^{1'} \otimes I_m)A + \cdots + (B_m)_{n.} \otimes (x^{m'} \otimes I_m)A \end{pmatrix}.$$

Consider

$$A'(X \otimes X')B = A'(X \otimes I_n)(I_n \otimes X')B$$

so, again applying the product rule gives

$$\frac{\partial \text{vec} A'(X \otimes X')B}{\partial \text{vec} X} = \frac{\partial \text{vec} A'(X \otimes I_n)}{\partial \text{vec} X}[(I_n \otimes X')B \otimes I_p]$$

$$+ \frac{\partial \text{vec}(I_n \otimes X')B}{\partial \text{vec} X}[I_q \otimes (X' \otimes I_n)A]. \quad (5.17)$$

Now,

$$\frac{\partial \text{vec}(I_n \otimes X')B}{\partial \text{vec} X} = \frac{\partial \text{vec} X'}{\partial \text{vec} X} \frac{\partial \text{vec}(I_n \otimes X')B}{\partial \text{vec} X'} = K_{nm}(B\tau_{nmn}I_{n^2}) \quad (5.18)$$

where we have used Equation 5.10. Substituting Equation 5.18 in Equation 5.17 and using Equation 5.11, we have

$$\frac{\partial \text{vec } A'(X \otimes X')B}{\partial \text{vec } X} = K_{nn}(I_n \otimes X')B \tau_{nnm} K_{nm} A + K_{nm}[B \tau_{nmn}(X' \otimes I_n)A].$$

Expanding this result requires a little work.

Using Theorem 2.13 of Chapter 2,

$$K_{nn}(I_n \otimes X')B \tau_{nnm} K_{nm} A = \begin{pmatrix} X'B_1 \tau_{n1m} K_{nm} A \\ \vdots \\ X'B_n \tau_{n1m} K_{nm} A \end{pmatrix}, \qquad (5.19)$$

where $B = (B'_1 \ldots B'_n)'$ and each submatrix is $m \times q$. From Equation 1.10 of Chapter 1,

$$((X' \otimes I_n)A)^{(j)} = X'A^{(j)}$$

where $A^{(j)}$ refers to the partitioning $A = (A'_1 \ldots A'_m)$ with each submatrix A_j being $n \times p$. Using Theorem 2.12 of Chapter 2, then

$$K_{nm}[B \tau_{nmn}(X' \otimes I_n)A] = \begin{pmatrix} B \tau_{nm1} X'A^{(1)} \\ \vdots \\ B \tau_{nm1} X'A^{(n)} \end{pmatrix}. \qquad (5.20)$$

Joining Equations 5.19 and 5.20 together, we have

$$\frac{\partial \text{vec } A'(X \otimes X')B}{\partial \text{vec } X} = \begin{pmatrix} X'B_1 \tau_{n1m} K_{nm} A \\ \vdots \\ X'B_n \tau_{n1m} K_{nm} A \end{pmatrix} + \begin{pmatrix} B \tau_{nm1} X'A^{(1)} \\ \vdots \\ B \tau_{nm1} X'A^{(n)} \end{pmatrix}$$

$$= \begin{pmatrix} x'_1 B_1 \otimes A^{(1)} + & \cdots & +x'_n B_1 \otimes A^{(n)} \\ \vdots & & \vdots \\ x'_1 B_n \otimes A^{(1)} + & \cdots & +x'_n B_n \otimes A^{(n)} \end{pmatrix}$$

$$+ \begin{pmatrix} B_1 \otimes x'_1 A^{(1)} + & \cdots & +B_n \otimes x'_1 A^{(1)} \\ \vdots & & \vdots \\ B_1 \otimes x'_1 A^{(n)} + & \cdots & +B_n \otimes x'_n A^{(n)} \end{pmatrix},$$

using Theorem 2.12 again.

5.5 Matrix Derivatives of Generalized Vecs and Rvecs

5.5.1 Introduction

When we take the rvec_m of an $mG \times p$ matrix A, we get an $m \times pG$ matrix. Whereas if we take the vec_m of $q \times mG$ matrix B, we get an $Gq \times m$ matrix and just like any other matrices we can envisage taking the matrix derivatives of these generalized rvecs and vecs. If Y is such a matrix, that is a generalized vec or generalized rvec and the elements of Y are differentiable functions of the elements of X, then as in the previous section we work with $\partial \text{vec} Y / \partial \text{vec } X$. For convenience, we divide this section into two parts. The first part deals with 'large X', where X is $mG \times p$ or $p \times mG$. The second part looks at generalized rvecs and vecs involving a 'small X' where X is, say, $p \times q$. As in the previous section, we call on the results derived in Chapters 1 and 2 on generalized vecs, rvecs, and cross-products together with results involving the rvec of the commutation matrix.

5.5.2 Large X

Results for Generalized rvecs

Suppose X is an $mG \times p$ matrix and we partition X as follows

$$X = \begin{pmatrix} X_1 \\ \vdots \\ X_G \end{pmatrix}$$

where each submatrix is $m \times p$. It follows that $\text{rvec}_m X$ is the $m \times pG$ matrix given by

$$\text{rvec}_m X = (X_1 \ldots X_G)$$

so

$$\text{vec}(\text{rvec}_m X) = \begin{pmatrix} \text{vec } X_1 \\ \vdots \\ \text{vec } X_G \end{pmatrix}.$$

From our work on selection matrices in Section 2.2 of Chapter 2, we know that

$$X_j = \left(e_j^{G'} \otimes I_m \right) X = S_j X$$

say, for $j = 1, \ldots G$, so

$$\text{vec } X_j = (I_p \otimes S_j)\text{vec } X$$

and

$$\text{vec}(\text{rvec}_m X) = \begin{pmatrix} I_p \otimes S_1 \\ \vdots \\ I_p \otimes S_G \end{pmatrix} \text{vec } X.$$

Using Theorem 5.1, we obtain

$$\frac{\partial \text{vec}(\text{rvec}_m X)}{\partial \text{vec } X} = \left(I_p \otimes S_1' \ldots I_p \otimes S_G'\right) = \left(I_p \otimes e_1^G \otimes I_m \ldots I_p \otimes e_G^G \otimes I_m\right)$$

$$= \left(I_p \otimes e_1^G \ldots I_p \otimes e_G^G\right) \otimes I_m = K_{pG} \otimes I_m. \tag{5.21}$$

This result is the basic building block from which several other matrix derivative results of generalized rvecs can be derived.

If X is now $p \times mG$, then using the backward chain rule

$$\frac{\partial \text{vec}(\text{rvec}_m X')}{\partial \text{vec } X} = \frac{\partial \text{vec } X'}{\partial \text{vec } X} \frac{\partial \text{vec}(\text{rvec}_m X')}{\partial \text{vec } X'}.$$

But $\dfrac{\partial \text{vec } X'}{\partial \text{vec } X} = K'_{p,mG} = K_{mG,p}$ so

$$\frac{\partial \text{vec}(\text{rvec}_m X')}{\partial \text{vec } X} = K_{mG,p}(K_{pG} \otimes I_m),$$

from Equation 5.21. But from Equation 2.9 of Chapter 2,

$$K_{mG,p}(K_{pG} \otimes I_m) = (I_G \otimes K_{mp})(K_{Gp} \otimes I_m)(K_{pG} \otimes I_m) = I_G \otimes K_{mp},$$

which gives our second result, namely

$$\frac{\partial \text{vec}(\text{rvec}_m X')}{\partial \text{vec } X} = I_G \otimes K_{mp}. \tag{5.22}$$

In a similar fashion, if X is $mG \times mG$ and nonsingular, then by the backward chain rule

$$\frac{\partial \text{vec}(\text{rvec}_m X^{-1})}{\partial \text{vec } X} = \frac{\partial \text{vec } X^{-1}}{\partial \text{vec } X} \frac{\partial \text{vec}(\text{rvec}_m X^{-1})}{\partial \text{vec } X^{-1}}.$$

But $\dfrac{\partial \text{vec } X^{-1}}{\partial \text{vec } X} = -(X^{-1} \otimes X^{-1'})$, by Equation 4.17 of Chapter 4 so using Equation 5.21, we have

$$\frac{\partial \text{vec}(\text{rvec}_m X^{-1})}{\partial \text{vec } X} = -(X^{-1} \otimes X^{-1'})(K_{mG,G} \otimes I_m).$$

If we want to breakdown this result further, we would partition X^{-1} as follows

$$X^{-1} = \begin{pmatrix} X^1 \\ \vdots \\ X^G \end{pmatrix}$$

where each submatrix is $m \times mG$, so

$$X^{-1'} = (X^{1'} \ldots X^{G'})$$

and we can call on Theorem 2.7 of Chapter 2 to write

$$\frac{\partial \text{vec}(\text{rvec}_m X^{-1})}{\partial \text{vec } X} = -(X^{-1} \otimes X^{1'} \ldots X^{-1} \otimes X^{G'}).$$

Matrices of constants can now be introduced. Let A be such a matrix. If X is $mG \times p$ and A is $p \times q$, then by Equation 1.19 of Chapter 1

$$\text{rvec}_m XA = (\text{rvec}_m X)(I_G \otimes A)$$

so

$$\text{vec}(\text{rvec}_m XA) = (I_G \otimes A' \otimes I_m)\text{vec}(\text{rvec}_m X)$$

and by Theorem 5.1 and Equation 5.21

$$\frac{\partial \text{vec}(\text{rvec}_m XA)}{\partial \text{vec } X} = (K_{pG} \otimes I_m)(I_G \otimes A \otimes I_m) = K_{pG}(I_G \otimes A) \otimes I_m.$$

We can expand this result further by calling on Theorem 2.3 of Chapter 2 to write

$$\frac{\partial \text{vec}(\text{rvec}_m XA)}{\partial \text{vec } X} = \begin{pmatrix} I_G \otimes a^{1'} \otimes I_m \\ \vdots \\ I_G \otimes a^{p'} \otimes I_m \end{pmatrix}.$$

In a similar manner, if X is $p \times mG$ and A is an $p \times q$ matrix of constants

$$\frac{\partial \text{vec}(\text{rvec}_m X'A)}{\partial \text{vec } X} = (I_G \otimes K_{mp})(I_G \otimes A \otimes I_m) = I_G \otimes K_{mp}(A \otimes I_m)$$

$$= I_G \otimes \begin{pmatrix} A \otimes e_1^{m'} \\ \vdots \\ A \otimes e_m^{m'} \end{pmatrix},$$

by Theorem 2.3 of Chapter 2.

By a similar analysis if X is a nonsingular $mG \times mG$ matrix and A is a $mG \times q$ matrix of constants,

$$\frac{\partial \text{vec}(\text{rvec}_m X^{-1} A)}{\partial \text{vec} X} = -(X^{-1} \otimes X^{-1})(K_{mG,G} \otimes I_m)(I_G \otimes A \otimes I_m)$$

$$= -(X^{-1} \otimes X^{1'} \ldots X^{-1} \otimes X^{G'})(I_G \otimes A \otimes I_m)$$

$$= -(X^{-1} \otimes X^{1'} \ldots X^{-1} \otimes X^{G'})\begin{pmatrix} A \otimes I_m & & O \\ & \ddots & \\ O & & A \otimes I_m \end{pmatrix}$$

$$= -(X^{-1} A \otimes X^{1'} \ldots X^{-1} A \otimes X^{G'})$$

Results for Generalized vecs

Suppose now X is an $p \times mG$ matrix and we partition X as $X = (X_1 \ldots X_G)$, where each submatrix is $p \times m$. It follows that $\text{vec}_m X$ is the $pG \times m$ matrix given by

$$\text{vec}_m X = \begin{pmatrix} X_1 \\ \vdots \\ X_G \end{pmatrix}.$$

From Theorem 2.40 of Chapter 2,

$$\text{vec}(\text{vec}_m X) = \text{vec} X K_{Gm} = (K_{mG} \otimes I_p)\text{vec} X$$

so using Theorem 5.1

$$\frac{\partial \text{vec}(\text{vec}_m X)}{\partial \text{vec} X} = (K_{mG} \otimes I_p)' = K_{Gm} \otimes I_p. \tag{5.23}$$

If X is an $mG \times p$ matrix, then by the backward chain rule

$$\frac{\partial \text{vec}(\text{vec}_m X')}{\partial \text{vec} X} = \frac{\partial \text{vec} X'}{\partial \text{vec} X} \frac{\partial \text{vec}_m X'}{\partial \text{vec} X'}.$$

But $K_{mG,p} \text{vec} X = \text{vec} X'$ so

$$\frac{\partial \text{vec} X'}{\partial \text{vec} X} = K'_{mG,p} = K_{p,mG}$$

and

$$\frac{\partial \text{vec}(\text{vec}_m X')}{\partial \text{vec} X} = K_{p,mG}(K_{Gm} \otimes I_p). \tag{5.24}$$

If X is an $mG \times mG$ nonsingular matrix, then

$$\frac{\partial \text{vec}(\text{vec}_m X^{-1})}{\partial \text{vec}\, X} = -(X^{-1} \otimes X^{-1'})(K_{Gm} \otimes I_{mG}) = -X^{-1} K_{Gm} \otimes X^{-1'}$$

$$= -\left(X_{(1)}^{-1} \otimes X^{-1'} \dots X_{(m)}^{-1} \otimes X^{-1'}\right) \qquad (5.25)$$

by Equation 2.66 of Section 2.7.7 of Chapter 2.

As with rvecs, we are now in a position to introduce a matrix of constants A. If X is an $p \times mG$ matrix and A is an $q \times p$ matrix of constants, then by Theorem 1.12 of Chapter 1

$$\text{vec}_m AX = (I_G \otimes A)\text{vec}_m X$$

so,

$$\text{vec}(\text{vec}_m AX) = (I_m \otimes I_G \otimes A)\text{vec}(\text{vec}_m X)$$

and by Theorem 5.1 and Equation 5.23

$$\frac{\partial \text{vec}(\text{vec}_m AX)}{\partial \text{vec}\, X} = \frac{\partial \text{vec}(\text{vec}_m X)}{\partial \text{vec}\, X}(I_m \otimes I_G \otimes A')$$

$$= (K_{Gm} \otimes I_p)(I_{mG} \otimes A') = K_{Gm} \otimes A'.$$

If X is an $mG \times p$ matrix and A is an $q \times p$ matrix of constants, then in a similar manner

$$\frac{\partial \text{vec}(\text{vec}_m AX')}{\partial \text{vec}\, X} = \frac{\partial \text{vec}(\text{vec}_m X')}{\partial \text{vec}\, X}(I_m \otimes I_G \otimes A')$$

$$= K_{p,mG}(K_{Gm} \otimes I_p)(I_{mG} \otimes A')$$

$$= K_{p,mG}(K_{Gm} \otimes A') = \begin{pmatrix} K_{Gm} \otimes a_1' \\ \vdots \\ K_{Gm} \otimes a_p' \end{pmatrix}$$

where in our analysis we have used Equation 5.24 and Theorem 2.3 of Chapter 2.

Finally, if X is an $mG \times mG$ nonsingular matrix and A is an $q \times mG$ matrix of constants, then

$$\frac{\partial \text{vec}(\text{vec}_m AX^{-1})}{\partial \text{vec}\, X}$$

$$= \frac{\partial \text{vec}(\text{vec}_m X^{-1})}{\partial \text{vec}\, X}(I_{mG} \otimes A') = -(X^{-1} K_{Gm} \otimes X^{-1'})(I_{mG} \otimes A')$$

$$= -(X^{-1} K_{Gm} \otimes X^{-1'} A') = \left(X_{(1)}^{-1} \otimes X^{-1'} A' \dots X_{(m)}^{-1} \otimes X^{-1'} A'\right)$$

where in our working we have made use of Equation 5.25 and Equation 2.66 of Chapter 2.

5.5.3 Small X

Results for Generalized rvecs

The matrix X may be part of a matrix product and it may also be the case that we are considering a generalized rvec of this product. The question is: what is the matrix derivative of such a matrix?

Suppose then that A and B are $mG \times p$ and $q \times r$ matrices of constants, respectively, and that X is an $p \times q$ matrix so it makes sense to take the rvec_m of AXB, which from Equation 1.19 of Chapter 1 is given by

$$\text{rvec}_m AXB = (\text{rvec}_m A)(I_G \otimes XB) = (\text{rvec}_m A)(I_G \otimes X)(I_G \otimes B),$$

so

$$\text{vec}(\text{rvec}_m AXB) = (I_G \otimes B' \otimes \text{rvec}_m A)\text{vec}(I_G \otimes X)$$

and by Theorem 5.1

$$\frac{\partial \text{vec}(\text{rvec}_m AXB)}{\partial \text{vec}\, X} = \frac{\partial \text{vec}(I_G \otimes X)}{\partial \text{vec}\, X}(I_G \otimes B \otimes (\text{rvec}_m A)').$$

Recall from Equation 5.3 that

$$\frac{\partial \text{vec}(I_G \otimes X)}{\partial \text{vec}\, X} = (\text{rvec}_q K_{Gq} \otimes I_p)$$

and from our work in Section 1.4 of Chapter 1 that

$$(\text{rvec}_m A)' = \text{vec}_m A'$$

so

$$\frac{\partial \text{vec}(\text{rvec}_m AXB)}{\partial \text{vec}\, X}$$

$$= (\text{rvec}_q K_{Gq} \otimes I_p)(I_G \otimes B \otimes \text{vec}_m A')$$

$$= \left(I_q \otimes e_1^{G'} \otimes I_p \ldots I_q \otimes e_G^{G'} \otimes I_p\right) \begin{pmatrix} B \otimes \text{vec}_m A' & & O \\ & \ddots & \\ O & & B \otimes \text{vec}_m A' \end{pmatrix}$$

$$= B \otimes \left(e_1^{G'} \otimes I_p\right) \text{vec}_m A' \ldots B \otimes \left(e_G^{G'} \otimes I_p\right) \text{vec}_m A'.$$

Now, if we partition A as follows

$$A = \begin{pmatrix} A_1 \\ \vdots \\ A_G \end{pmatrix}$$

where each submatrix is $m \times p$, then

$$A' = (A_1' \ldots A_G')$$

and

$$\text{vec}_m A' = \begin{pmatrix} A_1' \\ \vdots \\ A_G' \end{pmatrix}.$$

From our work of selection matrices in Section 2.2 of Chapter 2, we know that

$$\left(e_j^{G'} \otimes I_p\right)\text{vec}_m A' = A_j'$$

which gives our matrix derivative result:

$$\frac{\partial \text{vec}(\text{rvec}_m AXB)}{\partial \text{vec}\, X} = B \otimes A_1' \ldots B \otimes A_G'.$$

Using this result as our building block, we can derive others. If X is now $q \times p$, then by the backward chain rule

$$\frac{\partial \text{vec}(\text{rvec}_m AX'B)}{\partial \text{vec}\, X} = \frac{\partial \text{vec}\, X'}{\partial \text{vec}\, X} \frac{\partial (\text{rvec}_m AX'B)}{\partial \text{vec}\, X'} = K_{pq}(B \otimes A_1' \ldots B \otimes A_G')$$

$$= (A_1' \otimes B)K_{mr} \ldots (A_G' \otimes B)K_{mr} = (A' \otimes B)(I_G \otimes K_{mr}).$$

Finally, if X is $p \times p$ and nonsingular and B is $p \times r$, then

$$\frac{\partial \text{vec}(\text{rvec}_m AX^{-1}B)}{\partial \text{vec}\, X} = \frac{\partial \text{vec}\, X^{-1}}{\partial \text{vec}\, X} \frac{\partial \text{vec}(\text{rvec}_m AX^{-1}B)}{\partial \text{vec}\, X^{-1}}$$

$$= -(X^{-1} \otimes X^{-1'})(B \otimes A_1' \ldots B \otimes A_G')$$

$$= -(X^{-1}B \otimes X^{-1'}A_1' \ldots X^{-1}B \otimes X^{-1'}A_G').$$

Result for Generalized vecs

As with rvecs, we now want to take a generalized vec of a suitable product matrix that involves X. We then want to derive the matrix derivative of such a matrix.

Suppose that A and B are $s \times p$ and $q \times Gm$ matrices of constants, respectively, and that X is an $p \times q$ matrices. The product matrix AXB will then be an $s \times Gm$ matrix, so it makes sense that the vec_m of this product, which by Theorem 1.12 of Chapter 1 is given by

$$\text{vec}_m AXB = (I_G \otimes AX)\text{vec}_m B = (I_G \otimes A)(I_G \otimes X)\text{vec}_m B.$$

Taking the vec of this matrix renders

$$\text{vec}(\text{vec}_m AXB) = [(\text{vec}_m B)' \otimes (I_G \otimes A)]\text{vec}(I_G \otimes X),$$

so by Theorem 5.1

$$\frac{\partial \text{vec}(\text{vec}_m AXB)}{\partial \text{vec}\, X} = \frac{\partial \text{vec}(I_G \otimes X)}{\partial \text{vec}\, X}(\text{vec}_m B \otimes I_G \otimes A').$$

Applying Equation 5.3 allows us to write

$$\frac{\partial \text{vec}(\text{vec}_m AXB)}{\partial \text{vec}\, X} = (\text{rvec}_m K_{Gq} \otimes I_p)(\text{vec}_m B \otimes I_G \otimes A').$$

Applying Theorem 2.28 of Chapter 2, we obtain

$$\frac{\partial \text{vec}(\text{vec}_m AXB)}{\partial \text{vec}\, X} = \text{vec}_m B\, \tau_{Gqp}(I_G \otimes A'). \tag{5.26}$$

If we expand this derivative further by partitioning B as $B = (B_1 \ldots B_G)$, where each submatrix is $q \times m$, so writing out the cross-product of Equation 5.26 gives

$$\frac{\partial \text{vec}(\text{vec}_m AXB)}{\partial \text{vec}\, X} = B_1 \otimes e_1^{G'} \otimes A' + \cdots + B_G \otimes e_G^{G'} \otimes A'.$$

Suppose now X is $q \times p$ while A and B remain the same. Then, by the backward chain rule

$$\frac{\partial \text{vec}(\text{vec}_m AX'B)}{\partial \text{vec}\, X} = \frac{\partial \text{vec}\, X'}{\partial \text{vec}\, X}\frac{\partial \text{vec}(\text{vec}_m AX'B)}{\partial \text{vec}\, X'} = K_{pq}(\text{vec}_m B\tau_{Gqp}(I_G \otimes A'))$$

by Equation 5.26. But by Equation 1.9 of Chapter 1, $(I_G \otimes A')^{(j)} = I_G \otimes a'_j$ where a_j is the jth column of A, so using Theorem 2.12 of Chapter 2 we can write

$$\frac{\partial \text{vec}(\text{vec}_m AX'B)}{\partial \text{vec}\, X} = \begin{pmatrix} \text{vec}_m B\tau_{Gq1}(I_G \otimes a'_1) \\ \vdots \\ \text{vec}_m B\tau_{Gq1}(I_G \otimes a'_p) \end{pmatrix}.$$

To elaborate further, we can expand the cross-products to obtain

$$\frac{\partial \text{vec}(\text{vec}_m AX'B)}{\partial \text{vec}\, X} = \begin{pmatrix} B_1 \otimes e_1^{G'} \otimes a'_1 + \cdots + B_G \otimes e_G^{G'} \otimes a'_1 \\ \vdots \\ B_1 \otimes e_1^{G'} \otimes a'_p + \cdots + B_G \otimes e_G^{G'} \otimes a'_p \end{pmatrix}.$$

Finally, if X is $p \times p$ and nonsingular and B is $p \times Gm$, then

$$\frac{\partial \text{vec}(\text{vec}_m AX^{-1}B)}{\partial \text{vec} X} = \frac{\partial \text{vec} X^{-1}}{\partial \text{vec} X} \frac{\partial \text{vec}(\text{vec}_m AX^{-1}B)}{\partial \text{vec} X^{-1}}$$

$$= -(X^{-1} \otimes X^{-1'})\text{vec}_m B \tau_{Gpp}(I_G \otimes A')$$

$$= -(I_G \otimes X^{-1})\text{vec}_m B \tau_{Gpp}(I_G \otimes (AX^{-1})'),$$

using Equation 4.17 of Chapter 4, Equation 5.26, and Theorem 1.5 of Chapter 1 consecutively. Expanding this cross-product gives

$$\frac{\partial \text{vec}(\text{vec}_m AX^{-1}B)}{\partial \text{vec} X^{-1}} = -\left(X^{-1}B_1 \otimes e_1^{G'} \otimes (AX^{-1})'\right.$$

$$\left. + \cdots + X^{-1}B_G \otimes e_G^{G'} \otimes (AX^{-1})'\right).$$

5.6 Matrix Derivatives of Cross-Products

5.6.1 Basic Cross-Products

Cross-products, as we know, involve the sums of Kronecker products, so it follows that we can use the results obtained for the derivatives of vecs of Kronecker products in Section 5.3 to develop matrix derivatives of cross-products. This work will rely heavily on the results concerning selection matrices presented in Section 2.2 and the results about generalized vecs and rvecs of the commutation matrix presented in Section 2.5.

To get started, let X be an $mG \times p$ matrix and A be an $nG \times q$ matrix of constants and partition these matrices as follows:

$$X = \begin{pmatrix} X_1 \\ \vdots \\ X_G \end{pmatrix}, \quad A = \begin{pmatrix} A_1 \\ \vdots \\ A_G \end{pmatrix},$$

where in these partitions each submatrix X_i is $m \times p$ and each submatrix A_j is $n \times q$ for $i = 1, \ldots, G$ and $j = 1, \ldots, G$. Then, we know that

$$X \tau_{Gmn} A = X_1 \otimes A_1 + \cdots + X_G \otimes A_G$$

so

$$\text{vec}(X \tau_{Gmn} A) = \text{vec}(X_1 \otimes A_1) + \cdots + \text{vec}(X_G \otimes A_G),$$

and

$$\frac{\partial \text{vec}(X \tau_{Gmn} A)}{\partial \text{vec} X} = \frac{\partial \text{vec}(X_1 \otimes A_1)}{\partial \text{vec} X} + \cdots + \frac{\partial \text{vec}(X_G \otimes A_G)}{\partial \text{vec} X}.$$

Consider $\partial \text{vec}(X_1 \otimes A_1)/\partial \text{vec}\, X$, which using the backward chain rule, Theorem 5.2, we can write as

$$\frac{\partial \text{vec}(X_1 \otimes A_1)}{\partial \text{vec}\, X_1} = \frac{\partial \text{vec}\, X_1}{\partial \text{vec}\, X} \frac{\partial \text{vec}(X_1 \otimes A_1)}{\partial \text{vec}\, X_1}. \tag{5.27}$$

Using Equation 5.5 of Section 5.2, we can write

$$\frac{\partial \text{vec}(X_1 \otimes A_1)}{\partial \text{vec}\, X_1} = I_p \otimes (\text{rvec}_m K_{qm})(I_{qm} \otimes A_1'). \tag{5.28}$$

From our work on selection matrices in Section 2.2, we know that

$$X_1 = S_1 X$$

where $S_1 = e_G^{1'} \otimes I_m$ so $\text{vec}\, X_1 = (I_p \otimes S_1)\text{vec}\, X$ and

$$\frac{\partial \text{vec}\, X_1}{\partial \text{vec}\, X} = I_p \otimes S_1'. \tag{5.29}$$

Substituting Equations 5.29 and 5.28 in Equation 5.27, we have

$$\frac{\partial \text{vec}(X_1 \otimes A_1)}{\partial \text{vec}\, X} = I_p \otimes (S_1'\text{rvec}_m K_{qm})(I_{qm} \otimes A_1').$$

Now,

$$S_1'\text{rvec}_m K_{qm} = \left(e_G^1 \otimes I_m\right)\text{rvec}_m K_{qm} = e_G^1 \otimes \text{rvec}_m K_{qm}$$

so

$$\frac{\partial \text{vec}(X_1 \otimes A_1)}{\partial \text{vec}\, X} = I_p \otimes \left(e_G^1 \otimes \text{rvec}_m K_{qm}\right)\left(I_{qm} \otimes A_1'\right)$$

$$= I_p \otimes e_G^1 \otimes (\text{rvec}_m K_{qm})\left(I_{qm} \otimes A_1'\right)$$

$$= I_p \otimes \begin{pmatrix} (\text{rvec}_m K_{qm})\left(I_{qm} \otimes A_1'\right) \\ O \\ \vdots \\ O \end{pmatrix}.$$

It follows that

$$\frac{\partial \text{vec}\, X\, \tau_{Gmn} A}{\partial \text{vec}\, X} = I_p \otimes \begin{pmatrix} (\text{rvec}_m K_{qm})\left(I_{qm} \otimes A_1'\right) \\ \vdots \\ (\text{rvec}_m K_{qm})\left(I_{qm} \otimes A_G'\right) \end{pmatrix}.$$

But using Equation 1.19 of Chapter 1, we can write

$$(\text{rvec}_m K_{qm})\left(I_{qm} \otimes A_1'\right) = \text{rvec}_m\left[K_{qm}\left(I_m \otimes A_1'\right)\right]$$

so

$$\frac{\partial \text{vec}\, X\, \tau_{Gmn} A}{\partial \text{vec}\, X} = I_p \otimes \begin{pmatrix} \text{rvec}_m[K_{qm}(I_m \otimes A_1')] \\ \vdots \\ \text{rvec}_m[K_{qm}(I_m \otimes A_G')] \end{pmatrix}. \tag{5.30}$$

If we wanted to write this result more succinctly note that

$$\frac{\partial \text{vec}\, X\, \tau_{Gmn} A}{\partial \text{vec}\, X} = I_p \otimes (I_G \otimes \text{rvec}_m K_{qm}) \begin{pmatrix} I_{qm} \otimes A_1' \\ \vdots \\ I_{qm} \otimes A_G' \end{pmatrix}$$

and from Theorem 2.5 of Chapter 2

$$\begin{pmatrix} I_{qm} \otimes A_1' \\ \vdots \\ I_{qm} \otimes A_G' \end{pmatrix} = (K_{G,qm} \otimes I_q)(I_{qm} \otimes \text{vec}_m A'),$$

allowing us to write

$$\frac{\partial \text{vec}\, X\, \tau_{Gmn} A}{\partial \text{vec}\, X} = I_p \otimes (I_G \otimes \text{rvec}_m K_{qm})(K_{G,qm} \otimes I_q)(I_{qm} \otimes \text{vec}_n A').$$

But by Theorem 2.22 of Chapter 2,

$$(I_G \otimes \text{rvec}_m K_{qm})(K_{G,qm} \otimes I_q) = K_{Gm}\text{rvec}_{mG}K_{q,mG}$$

so, more succinctly

$$\frac{\partial \text{vec}\, X\, \tau_{Gmn} A}{\partial \text{vec}\, X} = I_p \otimes K_{Gm}\text{rvec}_{mG}K_{q,mG}(I_{qm} \otimes \text{vec}_m A'). \tag{5.31}$$

If, however, we wanted to break this result down further or write it another way, we could return to Equation 5.30 and appeal to Equation 2.11 of Chapter 2, which then allows us to write

$$\frac{\partial \text{vec}\, X\, \tau_{Gmn} A}{\partial \text{vec}\, X} = I_p \otimes \begin{pmatrix} I_m \otimes (A_1')_{1.} & \cdots & I_m \otimes (A_1')_{q.} \\ \vdots & & \vdots \\ I_m \otimes (A_G')_{1.} & \cdots & I_m \otimes (A_G')_{q.} \end{pmatrix}$$

$$= I_p \otimes \begin{pmatrix} \text{rvec}\, A_1' \otimes I_m \\ \vdots \\ \text{rvec}\, A_G' \otimes I_m \end{pmatrix}(I_q \otimes K_{nm}). \tag{5.32}$$

Consider now

$$\text{vec}\, A\, \tau_{Gnm} X = \text{vec}(A_1 \otimes X_1) + \cdots + \text{vec}(A_G \otimes X_G).$$

We could proceed as we did for $\text{vec } X \, \tau_{Gmn} A$ and compute

$$\frac{\partial \text{vec}(A_1 \otimes X_1)}{\partial \text{vec } X} = \frac{\partial \text{vec } X_1}{\partial \text{vec } X} \frac{\partial \text{vec}(A_1 \otimes X_1)}{\partial \text{vec } X_1}$$

and use Equation 5.8 to write

$$\frac{\partial \text{vec}(A_1 \otimes X_1)}{\partial \text{vec } X_1} = \left[\text{rvec}_m K_{qp} \left(I_{qp} \otimes A_1' \right) \right] \otimes I_m.$$

Alternatively, we could start by using the properties of cross-products as presented in Section 2.42 of Chapter 2. We saw in this section that

$$A \, \tau_{Gnm} X = K_{nm} (X \, \tau_{Gmn} A) K_{pq}$$

so

$$\text{vec } A \, \tau_{Gnm} X = (K_{qp} \otimes K_{nm}) \text{vec } X \, \tau_{Gmn} A$$

and

$$\frac{\partial \text{vec } A \, \tau_{Gnm} X}{\partial \text{vec } X} = \frac{\partial \text{vec } X \, \tau_{Gmn} A}{\partial \text{vec } X} (K_{pq} \otimes K_{mn}).$$

Using Equation 5.30, we can write

$$\frac{\partial \text{vec}(A \, \tau_{Gnm} X)}{\partial \text{vec } X} = (I_p \otimes C)(K_{pq} \otimes K_{mn})$$

where

$$C = \begin{pmatrix} \text{rvec}_m [K_{qm}(I_m \otimes A_1')] \\ \vdots \\ \text{rvec}_m [K_{qm}(I_m \otimes A_G')] \end{pmatrix}.$$

But from the definition of the commutation matrix given by Equation 2.8 of Chapter 2,

$$K_{pq} = I_p \otimes e_1^q \dots I_p \otimes e_q^q$$

so we write

$$\frac{\partial \text{vec}(A \, \tau_{Gnm} X)}{\partial \text{vec } X} = I_p \otimes C\left(e_1^q \otimes K_{mn}\right) \dots I_p \otimes C\left(e_q^q \otimes K_{mn}\right).$$

Consider the first block of the matrix $C(e_1^q \otimes K_{mn})$:

$$
\left(\text{rvec}_m\left[K_{qm}(I_m \otimes A_1')\right]\right)\left(e_1^q \otimes K_{mn}\right)
$$

$$
= (\text{rvec}_m K_{qm})(I_q \otimes I_m \otimes A_1')\left(e_1^q \otimes K_{mn}\right)
$$

$$
= (\text{rvec}_m K_{qm})\left(e_1^q \otimes (I_m \otimes A_1')K_{mn}\right)
$$

$$
= \left(I_m \otimes e_1^{q'} \ldots I_m \otimes e_q^{q'}\right)
\begin{pmatrix}
(I_m \otimes A_1')K_{mn} \\
O \\
\vdots \\
O
\end{pmatrix}
$$

$$
= \left(I_m \otimes e_1^{q'} A_1'\right)K_{mn} = \left(I_m \otimes (A_1')_1.\right)K_{mn} = (A_1')_1. \otimes I_m.
$$

It follows that the matrix in question can be written as

$$
C(e_1^q \otimes K_{mn}) =
\begin{pmatrix}
(A_1')_1. \otimes I_m \\
\vdots \\
(A_G')_1. \otimes I_m
\end{pmatrix}
= (\text{vec}_n A')^{(1)} \otimes I_m,
$$

and that

$$
\frac{\partial \text{vec}(A\,\tau_{Gnm}X)}{\partial \text{vec } X} = I_p \otimes (\text{vec}_n A')^{(1)} \otimes I_m \ldots I_p \otimes (\text{vec}_n A')^{(q)} \otimes I_m
$$

$$
= (I_p \otimes (\text{vec}_n A')^{(1)} \ldots I_p \otimes (\text{vec}_n A')^{(q)}) \otimes I_m. \tag{5.33}
$$

Appealing to Theorem 2.26 allows us to write this more succinctly as

$$
\frac{\partial \text{vec}(A\,\tau_{Gnm}X)}{\partial \text{vec } X} = (\text{rvec}_{pG}K_{q,pG})(I_{pq} \otimes \text{vec}_n A') \otimes I_m.
$$

5.6.2 Cross-Products Involving X'

Having obtained ways of writing the derivatives of basic cross-products, we can now expand our analysis for cross-products that involve X'.

Let X now be an $p \times mG$ matrix. Then,

$$
\frac{\partial \text{vec } X'\,\tau_{Gmn}A}{\partial \text{vec } X} = \frac{\partial \text{vec } X'}{\partial \text{vec } X}\frac{\partial \text{vec } X'\,\tau_{Gmn}A}{\partial \text{vec } X'}.
$$

Now,

$$
K_{p,mG}\text{vec } X = \text{vec } X'
$$

so

$$
\frac{\partial \text{vec } X'}{\partial \text{vec } X} = K_{p,mG}' = K_{mG,p},
$$

and using Equation 5.30, we have

$$\frac{\partial \text{vec}\, X'\, \tau_{Gm\,n}A}{\partial \text{vec}\, X} = K_{mG,p}\left(I_p \otimes \begin{pmatrix} \text{rvec}_m\big[K_{qm}\big(I_m \otimes A_1'\big)\big] \\ \vdots \\ \text{rvec}_m\big[K_{qm}\big(I_m \otimes A_G'\big)\big] \end{pmatrix}\right).$$

But from Equation 2.9 of Chapter 2,

$$K_{mG,p} = (I_G \otimes K_{mp})(K_{Gp} \otimes I_m)$$

and by Theorem 2.5 of Chapter 2

$$(K_{Gp} \otimes I_m)\left(I_p \otimes \begin{pmatrix} \text{rvec}_m\big[K_{qm}\big(I_m \otimes A_1'\big)\big] \\ \vdots \\ \text{rvec}_m\big[K_{qm}\big(I_m \otimes A_G'\big)\big] \end{pmatrix}\right)$$

$$= \begin{pmatrix} I_p \otimes \text{rvec}_m\big[K_{qm}\big(I_m \otimes A_1'\big)\big] \\ \vdots \\ I_p \otimes \text{rvec}_m\big[K_{qm}\big(I_m \otimes A_G'\big)\big] \end{pmatrix}$$

so

$$\frac{\partial \text{vec}\, X'\, \tau_{Gmn}A}{\partial \text{vec}\, X} = (I_G \otimes K_{mp})\begin{pmatrix} I_p \otimes \text{rvec}_m\big[K_{qm}\big(I_m \otimes A_1'\big)\big] \\ \vdots \\ I_p \otimes \text{rvec}_m\big[K_{qm}\big(I_m \otimes A_G'\big)\big] \end{pmatrix}.$$

Theorem 2.25 of Chapter 2 allows us to write this result another way and break it down further. Applying this theorem we have,

$$\text{rvec}_m\big[K_{qm}\big(I_m \otimes A_1'\big)\big] = \big(\text{rvec}\, A_1' \otimes I_m\big)\big(I_q \otimes K_{nm}\big)$$
$$= I_m \otimes \big(A_1'\big)_{1.} \cdots I_m \otimes \big(A_1'\big)_{q.}$$

so, another way of writing our result is

$$\frac{\partial \text{vec}\, X'\tau_{Gmn}A}{\partial \text{vec}\, X} = (I_G \otimes K_{mp})\begin{pmatrix} I_p \otimes \text{rvec}\, A_1' \otimes I_m \\ \vdots \\ I_p \otimes \text{rvec}\, A_G' \otimes I_m \end{pmatrix}(I_{pq} \otimes K_{nm})$$

$$= (I_G \otimes K_{mp})\begin{pmatrix} I_p \otimes \big(I_m \otimes \big(A_1'\big)_{1.} \cdots I_m \otimes \big(A_1'\big)_{q.}\big) \\ \vdots \\ I_p \otimes \big(I_m \otimes \big(A_G'\big)_{1.} \cdots I_m \otimes \big(A_G'\big)_{q.}\big) \end{pmatrix}.$$

$$(5.34)$$

Finally, appealing to Theorem 2.3 of Chapter 2, we can write

$$\frac{\partial \operatorname{vec} X' \tau_{Gmn} A}{\partial \operatorname{vec} X} = \begin{pmatrix} I_p \otimes \left(e_1^{m'} \otimes (A_1')_{1.} \cdots e_1^{m'} \otimes (A_1')_{q.} \right) \\ \vdots \\ I_p \otimes \left(e_m^{m'} \otimes (A_1')_{1.} \cdots e_m^{m'} \otimes (A_1')_{q.} \right) \\ \vdots \\ I_p \otimes \left(e_1^{m'} \otimes (A_G')_{1.} \cdots e_1^{m'} \otimes (A_G')_{q.} \right) \\ \vdots \\ I_p \otimes \left(e_m^{m'} \otimes (A_G')_{1.} \cdots e_m^{m'} \otimes (A_G')_{q.} \right) \end{pmatrix}$$

Appealing to the properties of cross-products, we now write

$$A \tau_{Gnm} X' = K_{nm} (X' \tau_{Gmn} A) K_{pq}$$

so

$$\operatorname{vec} A \tau_{Gnm} X' = (K_{qp} \otimes K_{nm}) \operatorname{vec} X' \tau_{Gmn} A$$

and

$$\frac{\partial \operatorname{vec} A \tau_{Gnm} X'}{\partial \operatorname{vec} X} = \frac{\partial \operatorname{vec} X' \tau_{Gmn} A}{\partial \operatorname{vec} X} (K_{pq} \otimes K_{mn}). \qquad (5.35)$$

Substituting Equation 5.34 into Equation 5.35 and noting that $K_{nm} K_{mn} = I_{mn}$, we have

$$\frac{\partial \operatorname{vec} A \tau_{Gmn} X'}{\partial \operatorname{vec} X} = (I_G \otimes K_{mp}) \begin{pmatrix} I_p \otimes \operatorname{rvec} A_1' \otimes I_m \\ \vdots \\ I_p \otimes \operatorname{rvec} A_G' \otimes I_m \end{pmatrix} (K_{pq} \otimes I_{mn}).$$

The first block of this matrix is

$$K_{mp} \left[\left(I_p \otimes \operatorname{rvec} A_1' \right) \left(K_{pq} \otimes I_n \right) \otimes I_m \right]$$

and appealing to Corollary 2.2 of Chapter 2, we can write this block as

$$K_{mp} \left[\left(I_p \otimes (A_1')_{1.} \cdots I_p \otimes (A_1')_{q.} \right) \otimes I_m \right].$$

Theorem 2.3 of Chapter 2 allows us to write this first block as

$$\begin{pmatrix} \left(I_p \otimes (A_1')_{1.} \cdots I_p \otimes (A_1')_{q.} \right) \otimes e_1^{m'} \\ \vdots \\ \left(I_p \otimes (A_1')_{1.} \cdots I_p \otimes (A_1')_{q.} \right) \otimes e_m^{m'} \end{pmatrix}$$

so the derivative can be broken down to give

$$\frac{\partial \text{vec } A\tau_{Gmn}X'}{\partial \text{vec } X} = \begin{pmatrix} (I_p \otimes (A_1')_1. \ldots I_p \otimes (A_1')_q.) \otimes e_1^{m'} \\ \vdots \\ (I_p \otimes (A_1')_1. \ldots I_p \otimes (A_1')_q.) \otimes e_m^{m'} \\ \vdots \\ (I_p \otimes (A_G')_1. \ldots I_p \otimes (A_G')_q.) \otimes e_1^{m'} \\ \vdots \\ (I_p \otimes (A_G')_1. \ldots I_p \otimes (A_G')_q.) \otimes e_m^{m'} \end{pmatrix}.$$

5.6.3 Cross-Products Involving X^{-1}

Cross-products can be formed from the inverse of X provided, of course, X is square and nonsingular. It is of some interest then to derive the derivative of such cross-products.

Suppose X is $mG \times mG$ and nonsingular. Then, by the backward chain rule and using Equation 5.32,

$$\frac{\partial \text{vec } X^{-1}\tau_{Gmn}A}{\partial \text{vec } X}$$

$$= \frac{\partial \text{vec } X^{-1}}{\partial \text{vec } X} \frac{\partial \text{vec } X^{-1}\tau_{Gmn}A}{\partial \text{vec } X^{-1}}$$

$$= -(X^{-1} \otimes X^{-1'}) \left[I_{mG} \otimes \begin{pmatrix} I_m \otimes (A_1')_1. \ldots I_m \otimes (A_1')_q. \\ \vdots \qquad \vdots \\ I_m \otimes (A_G')_1. \ldots I_m \otimes (A_G')_q. \end{pmatrix} \right].$$

If we partition X^{-1} as

$$X^{-1} = \begin{pmatrix} X^1 \\ \vdots \\ X^G \end{pmatrix}$$

where each submatrix X^j is $m \times mG$, then we can write

$$\frac{\partial \text{vec } X^{-1}\tau_{Gmn}A}{\partial \text{vec } X}$$

$$= -X^{-1} \otimes [X^{1'}(I_m \otimes (A_1')_1.) + \cdots$$

$$+ X^{G'}(I_m \otimes (A_G')_1.) \cdots X^{1'}(I_m \otimes (A_1')_q.) + \cdots + X^{G'}(I_m \otimes (A_G')_q.)].$$

If we want a more succinct expression, we can use Equation 5.31 to obtain

$$
\frac{\partial \text{vec} \, X^{-1} \tau_{Gm\,n} A}{\partial \text{vec} \, X} = -X^{-1} \otimes X^{-1'} K_{Gm} \text{rvec}_{mG} K_{q,mG} (I_{qm} \otimes \text{vec}_m A').
$$
(5.36)

In a similar manner,

$$
\frac{\partial \text{vec} \, A \tau_{Gnm} X^{-1}}{\partial \text{vec} \, X}
$$
$$
= -(X^{-1} \otimes X^{-1'}) \frac{\partial \text{vec} \, A \tau_{Gnm} X^{-1}}{\partial \text{vec} \, X^{-1}}
$$
$$
= -(X^{-1} \otimes X^{-1'})(I_{mG} \otimes (\text{vec}_n A')^{(1)} \otimes I_m \ldots I_{mG} \otimes (\text{vec}_n A')^{(q)} \otimes I_m)
$$
$$
= -X^{-1} \otimes X^{-1'}((\text{vec}_n A')^{(1)} \otimes I_m) \ldots - X^{-1} \otimes X^{-1'}(\text{vec}_n A')^{(q)} \otimes I_m
$$

where in our working we have used Equation 5.33.

Consider

$$
X^{-1'}((\text{vec}_n A')^{(1)} \otimes I_m) = (X^{1'} \ldots X^{G'}) \begin{pmatrix} (A'_1)_{1.} \otimes I_m \\ \vdots \\ (A'_G)_{1.} \otimes I_m \end{pmatrix}
$$
$$
= X^{1'}((A'_1)_{1.} \otimes I_m) + \cdots + X^{G'}((A'_G)_{1.} \otimes I_m).
$$

It follows then that

$$
\frac{\partial \text{vec} \, A \tau_{Gm\,n} X^{-1}}{\partial \text{vec} \, X}
$$
$$
= -X^{-1'} \otimes \left[X^{1'}((A'_1)_{1.} \otimes I_m) + \cdots + X^{G'}((A'_G)_{1.} \otimes I_m) \right] \ldots
$$
$$
-X^{-1'} \otimes \left[X^{1'}((A'_1)_{q.} \otimes I_m) + \cdots + X^{G'}((A'_G)_{q.} \otimes I_m) \right].
$$

A more succinct expression for this equation can be obtained using Equation 5.36 and the fact that

$$
\frac{\partial \text{vec} \, A \tau_{Gnm} X^{-1}}{\partial \text{vec} \, X} = \frac{\partial \text{vec} \, X^{-1} \tau_{Gmn} A}{\partial \text{vec} \, X} (K_{mG,q} \otimes K_{mn})
$$

to obtain

$$
\frac{\partial \text{vec} \, A \tau_{Gnm} X^{-1}}{\partial \text{vec} \, X}
$$
$$
= -(X^{-1} \otimes X^{-1'} K_{Gm} \text{rvec}_{mG} K_{q,mG} (I_{qm} \otimes \text{vec}_n A'))(K_{mG,q} \otimes K_{mn}).
$$

5.6.4 The Cross-Product $X\tau_{Gmm}X$

If X is $mG \times p$, then we can form the cross-product $X\tau_{Gmm}X$. In this section, we derive an expression for the derivative of this cross-product. Write

$$X = \begin{pmatrix} X_1 \\ \vdots \\ X_G \end{pmatrix}$$

where each submatrix in this partitioning is $m \times p$. Then,

$$X\tau_{Gmm}X = X_1 \otimes X_1 + \cdots + X_G \otimes X_G$$

and

$$\text{vec}(X\tau_{Gmm}X) = \text{vec}(X_1 \otimes X_1) + \cdots + \text{vec}(X_G \otimes X_G),$$

so

$$\frac{\partial \text{vec}(X\tau_{Gmm}X)}{\partial \text{vec}\,X} = \frac{\partial \text{vec}(X_1 \otimes X_1)}{\partial \text{vec}\,X} + \cdots + \frac{\partial \text{vec}(X_G \otimes X_G)}{\partial \text{vec}\,X}.$$

Consider $\dfrac{\partial \text{vec}(X_1 \otimes X_1)}{\partial \text{vec}\,X}$. By the backward chain rule,

$$\frac{\partial \text{vec}(X_1 \otimes X_1)}{\partial \text{vec}\,X} = \frac{\partial \text{vec}\,X_1}{\partial \text{vec}\,X}\frac{\partial \text{vec}(X_1 \otimes X_1)}{\partial \text{vec}\,X_1}.$$

By Equation 5.29,

$$\frac{\partial \text{vec}\,X_1}{\partial \text{vec}\,X} = I_p \otimes S_1'.$$

where S_1 is the $m \times mG$ selection matrix $e_1^{G'} \otimes I_m$.

From Equation 5.13 of Section 5.4,

$$\frac{\partial \text{vec}(X_1 \otimes X_1)}{\partial \text{vec}\,X_1} = K_{mp}(I_p \otimes X_1)\tau_{mpm}K_{mm} + I_{p^2}\tau_{ppm}(X_1' \otimes I_m).$$

But using Theorem 2.19 of Chapter 2,

$$K_{mp}(I_p \otimes X_1)\tau_{mpm}K_{mm} = I_p \otimes (X_1\tau_{m1m}K_{mm})$$

so

$$\frac{\partial \text{vec}(X_1 \otimes X_1)}{\partial \text{vec}\,X} = (I_p \otimes S_1')[I_p \otimes (X_1\tau_{m1m}K_{mm}) + I_{p^2}\tau_{ppm}(X_1' \otimes I_m)].$$

$$(5.37)$$

The second part of $\partial \mathrm{vec}(X_1 \otimes X_1)/\partial \mathrm{vec}\, X$ given by Equation 5.37 is

$$(I_p \otimes S_1')[I_{p^2}\tau_{ppm}(X_1' \otimes I_m)] = I_{p^2}\tau_{pp,Gm}(I_p \otimes S_1')(X_1' \otimes I_m)$$
$$= I_{p^2}\tau_{pp,Gm}(X_1' \otimes S_1')$$

so the corresponding second part of $\partial \mathrm{vec}(X\tau_{Gmm}X)/\partial \mathrm{vec}\, X$ is

$$I_{p^2}\tau_{p,p,Gm}(X_1' \otimes S_1') + \cdots + I_{p^2}\tau_{p,p,Gm}(X_G' \otimes S_G')$$
$$= I_{p^2}\tau_{p,p,Gm}[X_1' \otimes S_1' + \cdots + X_G' \otimes S_G'],$$

by Theorem 1.4 of Chapter 1 and where $S_j' = e_j^G \otimes I_m$ for $j = 1, \ldots, G$.
   If we write,

$$S = \begin{pmatrix} S_1 \\ \vdots \\ S_G \end{pmatrix}$$

then

$$X_1' \otimes S_1' + \cdots + X_G' \otimes S_G' = \mathrm{vec}_m X' \tau_{G,p,Gm}\mathrm{vec}_m S'$$

so this second part can be written as

$$I_{p^2}\tau_{p,p,Gm}(\mathrm{vec}_m X' \tau_{G,p,Gm}\mathrm{vec}_m S'). \tag{5.38}$$

   Consider the first matrix on this right-hand side of Equation 5.37, which we can write as

$$I_p \otimes S_1'(X_1\tau_{m1m}K_{mm}) = I_p \otimes \left(e_1^G \otimes I_m\right)(X_1\tau_{m1m}K_{mm})$$
$$= I_p \otimes e_1^G \otimes X_1\tau_{m1m}K_{mm}$$

so the corresponding part of $\partial \mathrm{vec}(X\tau_{Gmm}X)/\partial \mathrm{vec}\, X$ is

$$I_p \otimes e_1^G \otimes X_1\tau_{m1m}K_{mm} + \cdots + I_p \otimes e_G^G \otimes X_G\tau_{m1m}K_{mm}$$
$$= I_p \otimes \left(e_1^G \otimes X_1\tau_{m1m}K_{mm} + \cdots + e_G^G \otimes X_G\tau_{m1m}K_{mm}\right)$$
$$= I_p \otimes \begin{pmatrix} X_1\tau_{m1m}K_{mm} \\ \vdots \\ X_G\tau_{m1m}K_{mm} \end{pmatrix}.$$

But,

$$\begin{pmatrix} X_1\tau_{m1m}K_{mm} \\ \vdots \\ X_G\tau_{m1m}K_{mm} \end{pmatrix} = K_{mG}X\tau_{mGm}K_{mm},$$

by Theorem 2.13 of Chapter 2. We can write the first part of our derivative then as

$$I_p \otimes (K_{mG} X \tau_{mGm} K_{mm}). \qquad (5.39)$$

Adding our two parts given by Equations 5.38 and 5.39 together yields,

$$\frac{\partial \text{vec}(X \tau_{Gmm} X)}{\partial \text{vec}\, X}$$
$$= I_p \otimes (K_{mG} X \tau_{mGm} K_{mm}) + I_{p^2} \tau_{p,p,Gm} (\text{vec}_m X' \tau_{G,p,Gm} \text{vec}_m S'). \qquad (5.40)$$

To break this result down further consider,

$$I_{p^2} \tau_{p,p,Gm} (X_1' \otimes S_1')$$
$$= (e_1^{p'} \otimes I_p) \otimes ((X_1')_{1\cdot} \otimes S_1') + \cdots + (e_p^{p'} \otimes I_p) \otimes ((X_1')_{p\cdot} \otimes S_1')$$
$$= (I_p \otimes (X_1')_{1\cdot} \otimes S_1' \ldots I_p \otimes (X_1')_{p\cdot} \otimes S_1').$$

But $(X_1')_{1\cdot} \otimes S_1' = (X_1')_{1\cdot} \otimes e_1^G \otimes I_m = e_1^G (X_1')_{1\cdot} \otimes I_m$

so

$$I_{p^2} \tau_{p,p,Gm} (X_1' \otimes S_1') = (I_p \otimes e_1^G (X_1')_{1\cdot} \ldots I_p \otimes e_1^G (X_1')_{p\cdot}) \otimes I_m$$
$$= \left[I_p \otimes \begin{pmatrix} (X_1')_{1\cdot} \\ O \\ \vdots \\ O \end{pmatrix} \ldots I_p \otimes \begin{pmatrix} (X_1')_{p\cdot} \\ O \\ \vdots \\ O \end{pmatrix} \right] \otimes I_m.$$

It follows that the second part of $\partial \text{vec}(X \tau_{Gm\,m} X)/\partial \text{vec}\, X$ can be written as

$$\left[I_p \otimes \begin{pmatrix} (X_1')_{1\cdot} \\ \vdots \\ (X_G')_{1\cdot} \end{pmatrix} \ldots I_p \otimes \begin{pmatrix} (X_1')_{p\cdot} \\ \vdots \\ (X_G')_{p\cdot} \end{pmatrix} \right] \otimes I_m$$
$$= \left[I_p \otimes (\text{vec}_m X')^{(1)} \ldots I_p \otimes (\text{vec}_m X')^{(p)} \right] \otimes I_m. \qquad (5.41)$$

Also using Theorem 2.10 and Equation 2.8 of Chapter 2,

$$K_{mG} X \tau_{mGm} K_{mm} = X^{(1)} \otimes I_m \otimes e_1^{m'} + \cdots + X^{(m)} \otimes I_m \otimes e_m^{m'}. \qquad (5.42)$$

Combining Equations 5.41 and 5.42 allows us to write

$$\frac{\partial \text{vec}\, X \tau_{Gmm} X}{\partial \text{vec}\, X} = I_p \otimes (X^{(1)} \otimes I_m \otimes e_1^{m'} + \cdots + X^{(m)} \otimes I_m \otimes e_m^{m'})$$
$$+ \left[I_p \otimes (\text{vec}_m X')^{(1)} \ldots I_p \otimes (\text{vec}_m X')^{(p)} \right] \otimes I_m.$$

5.6.5 The Cross-Product $X'\tau_{Gm\,m}X'$

Suppose now X is $p \times mG$, so we can form $X'\tau_{Gm\,m}X'$. The derivative of this cross-product can be obtained from

$$\frac{\partial \text{vec}\, X'\tau_{Gm\,m}X'}{\partial \text{vec}\, X} = \frac{\partial \text{vec}\, X'}{\partial \text{vec}\, X} \frac{\partial \text{vec}\, X'\tau_{Gm\,m}X'}{\partial \text{vec}\, X'}.$$

As in the previous section,

$$\text{vec}\, X' = K_{p,mG}\text{vec}\, X$$

so

$$\frac{\partial \text{vec}\, X'}{\partial \text{vec}\, X} = K'_{p,mG} = K_{mG,p}$$

and using Equation 5.40, we have

$$\frac{\partial \text{vec}\, X'\tau_{Gm\,m}X'}{\partial \text{vec}\, X} = K_{mG,p}\big[I_p \otimes (K_{mG}X'\tau_{mGm}K_{mm})$$
$$+ I_{p^2}\tau_{p,p,Gm}(\text{vec}_m X\tau_{G,p,Gm}\text{vec}_m S')\big]. \qquad (5.43)$$

Now, from Equation 2.9 of Chapter 2,

$$K_{mG,p} = (I_G \otimes K_{mp})(K_{Gp} \otimes I_m)$$

and we can write the first matrix on the right-hand side of Equation 5.43 as

$$(I_G \otimes K_{mp})(K_{Gp} \otimes I_m)\big(I_p \otimes (K_{mG}X'\tau_{mGm}K_{mm})\big).$$

From Equation 2.8 of Chapter 2,

$$(K_{Gp} \otimes I_m)(I_p \otimes (K_{mG}X'\tau_{mGm}K_{mm}))$$
$$= \begin{pmatrix} I_p \otimes e_1^{G'} \otimes I_m \\ \vdots \\ I_p \otimes e_G^{G'} \otimes I_m \end{pmatrix} \big(I_p \otimes (K_{mG}X'\tau_{mGm}K_{mm})\big) \qquad (5.44)$$

and so the first block of this matrix is

$$\big(I_p \otimes (e_1^{G'} \otimes I_m)(K_{mG}X'\tau_{mGm}K_{mm})\big).$$

Now, from Theorem 1.5 of Chapter 1,

$$\left(e_1^{G'} \otimes I_m\right)\left(K_{mG}X'\tau_{mGm}K_{mm}\right) = \left(I_m \otimes e_1^{G'}\right)K_{mG}X'\tau_{m1m}K_{mm}$$
$$= \left(e_1^{G'} \otimes I_m\right)X'\tau_{m1m}K_{mm} = X_1'\tau_{m1m}K_{mm}$$

where we have partitioned X as $X = (X_1 \ldots X_G)$ each submatrix being $p \times m$, so we can write the right-hand side of Equation 5.44 as

$$\begin{pmatrix} I_p \otimes X_1'\tau_{m1m}K_{mm} \\ \vdots \\ I_p \otimes X_G'\tau_{m1m}K_{mm} \end{pmatrix},$$

and the first matrix on the right-hand side of Equation 5.43 as

$$\begin{pmatrix} K_{mp}\left(I_p \otimes X_1'\tau_{m1m}K_{mm}\right) \\ \vdots \\ K_{mp}\left(I_p \otimes X_G'\tau_{m1m}K_{mm}\right) \end{pmatrix} \tag{5.45}$$

The second matrix on the right-hand side of Equation 5.43 is

$$K_{mG,p}\left(I_{p^2}\tau_{p,p,Gm}\left(\text{vec}_m X \tau_{G,p,Gm}\text{vec}_m S'\right)\right)$$

which using Equation 5.41, we can write as

$$K_{mG,p}\left[I_p \otimes (\text{vec}_m X)^{(1)} \otimes I_m \ldots I_p \otimes (\text{vec}_m X)^{(p)} \otimes I_m\right]. \tag{5.46}$$

The first block of this matrix using Equation 2.9 of Chapter 2

$$\left(I_G \otimes K_{mp}\right)\left(K_{Gp} \otimes I_m\right)\left(I_p \otimes (\text{vec}_m X)^{(1)} \otimes I_m\right)$$
$$= \left(I_G \otimes K_{mp}\right)\left[K_{Gp}\left(I_p \otimes (\text{vec}_m X)^{(1)}\right) \otimes I_m\right].$$

Now, as

$$(\text{vec}_m X)^{(1)} = \begin{pmatrix} (X_1)_{1.} \\ \vdots \\ (X_G)_{1.} \end{pmatrix}$$

it follows from Theorem 2.3 of Chapter 2 that

$$K_{Gp}\left(I_p \otimes (\text{vec}_m X)^{(1)}\right) = \begin{pmatrix} I_p \otimes (X_1)_{1.} \\ \vdots \\ I_p \otimes (X_G)_{1.} \end{pmatrix}$$

so we can write our first block as

$$
\begin{pmatrix}
K_{mp}(I_p \otimes (X_1)_{1.} \otimes I_m) \\
\vdots \\
K_{mp}(I_p \otimes (X_G)_{1.} \otimes I_m)
\end{pmatrix}.
$$

Returning now to Equation 5.43, it is clear that we can write the second matrix of the right-hand side of Equation 5.43 as

$$
\begin{pmatrix}
K_{mp}(I_p \otimes (X_1)_{1.} \otimes I_m) & \cdots & K_{mp}(I_p \otimes (X_1)_{p.} \otimes I_m) \\
\vdots & & \vdots \\
K_{mp}(I_p \otimes (X_G)_{1.} \otimes I_m) & \cdots & K_{mp}(I_p \otimes (X_G)_{p.} \otimes I_m)
\end{pmatrix}.
$$

Combining this with Equation 5.45 gives the following result,

$$
\frac{\partial \operatorname{vec} X' \tau_{Gmm} X'}{\partial \operatorname{vec} X} =
\begin{pmatrix}
K_{mp}(I_p \otimes X_1' \tau_{m1m} K_{mm}) \\
\vdots \\
K_{mp}(I_p \otimes X_G' \tau_{m1m} K_{mm})
\end{pmatrix}
$$
$$
+
\begin{pmatrix}
K_{mp}(I_p \otimes (X_1)_{1.} \otimes I_m) & \cdots & K_{mp}(I_p \otimes (X_1)_{p.} \otimes I_m) \\
\vdots & & \vdots \\
K_{mp}(I_p \otimes (X_G)_{1.} \otimes I_m) & \cdots & K_{mp}(I_p \otimes (X_G)_{p.} \otimes I_m)
\end{pmatrix}. \tag{5.47}
$$

We can break this result down further by noting that

$$
K_{mp}(I_p \otimes X_1' \tau_{m1m} K_{mm}) = K_{mp}(I_p \otimes [(X_1')_{1.} \otimes I_m \otimes e_1^{m'}
$$
$$
+ \cdots + (X_1')_{m.} \otimes I_m \otimes e_m^{m'}])
$$

and by Theorem 2.3 of Chapter 2

$$
K_{mp}(I_p \otimes (X_1')_{1.} \otimes I_m \otimes e_1^{m'}) =
\begin{pmatrix}
I_p \otimes (X_1')_{1.} \otimes e_1^{m'} \otimes e_1^{m'} \\
\vdots \\
I_p \otimes (X_1')_{1.} \otimes e_m^{m'} \otimes e_1^{m'}
\end{pmatrix}
$$

so

$$K_{mp}\left(I_p \otimes X_1' \tau_{m1m} K_{mm}\right)$$

$$= \begin{pmatrix} I_p \otimes \left[(X_1')_{1\cdot} \otimes e_1^{m'} \otimes e_1^{m'} + \cdots + (X_1')_{m\cdot} \otimes e_1^{m'} \otimes e_m^{m'}\right] \\ \vdots \\ I_p \otimes \left[(X_1')_{1\cdot} \otimes e_m^{m'} \otimes e_1^{m'} + \cdots + (X_1')_{m\cdot} \otimes e_m^{m'} \otimes e_m^{m'}\right] \end{pmatrix}$$

$$= \begin{pmatrix} I_p \otimes \left[(X_1' \otimes e_1^{m'})\tau_{m1m} I_m\right] \\ \vdots \\ I_p \otimes \left[(X_1' \otimes e_m^{m'})\tau_{m1m} I_m\right] \end{pmatrix}.$$

The first matrix on the right-hand side of Equation 5.47 can then be broken down to

$$\begin{pmatrix} I_p \otimes \left((X_1' \otimes e_1^{m'})\tau_{m11} I_m\right) \\ \vdots \\ I_p \otimes \left((X_1' \otimes e_m^{m'})\tau_{m11} I_m\right) \\ \vdots \\ I_p \otimes \left((X_G' \otimes e_1^{m'})\tau_{m11} I_m\right) \\ \vdots \\ I_p \otimes \left((X_G' \otimes e_m^{m'})\tau_{m11} I_m\right) \end{pmatrix}.$$

To expand the second matrix on the right-hand side of Equation 5.47 note that by Equation 1.6 of Chapter 1,

$$(X_1')_{1\cdot} \otimes I_m = \begin{pmatrix} (X_1)_{1\cdot} \otimes e_1^{m'} \\ \vdots \\ (X_1)_{1\cdot} \otimes e_m^{m'} \end{pmatrix}$$

so, by Theorem 2.3 of Chapter 2

$$K_{mp}(I_p \otimes (X_1)_{1\cdot} \otimes I_m) = \begin{pmatrix} I_p \otimes (X_1)_{1\cdot} \otimes e_1^{m'} \\ \vdots \\ I_p \otimes (X_1)_{1\cdot} \otimes e_m^{m'} \end{pmatrix}.$$

It follows that this second matrix can be written as

$$
\begin{pmatrix}
I_p \otimes (X_1)_{1\cdot} \otimes e_1^{m'} & \cdots & I_p \otimes (X_1)_{p\cdot} \otimes e_1^{m'} \\
\vdots & & \vdots \\
I_p \otimes (X_1)_{1\cdot} \otimes e_m^{m'} & \cdots & I_p \otimes (X_1)_{p\cdot} \otimes e_m^{m'} \\
\vdots & & \vdots \\
I_p \otimes (X_G)_{1\cdot} \otimes e_1^{m'} & \cdots & I_p \otimes (X_G)_{p\cdot} \otimes e_1^{m'} \\
\vdots & & \vdots \\
I_p \otimes (X_G)_{1\cdot} \otimes e_m^{m'} & \cdots & I_p \otimes (X_G)_{p\cdot} \otimes e_m^{m'}
\end{pmatrix}.
$$

5.6.6 The Cross-Product $X^{-1}\tau_{Gmm}X^{-1}$

Suppose now X is $mG \times mG$ and nonsingular, so $X^{-1}\tau_{Gmm}X^{-1}$ can be formed. In this section, we obtain the derivative of this matrix.

By the backward chain rule,

$$
\frac{\partial \text{vec}\, X^{-1}\tau_{Gmm}X^{-1}}{\partial \text{vec}\, X} = \frac{\partial \text{vec}\, X^{-1}}{\partial \text{vec}\, X}\,\frac{\partial \text{vec}\, X^{-1}\tau_{Gmm}X^{-1}}{\partial \text{vec}\, X^{-1}}.
$$

We know that

$$
\frac{\partial \text{vec}\, X^{-1}}{\partial \text{vec}\, X} = -X^{-1} \otimes X^{-1'}
$$

and from Equation 5.40 that

$$
\frac{\partial \text{vec}\, X^{-1}\tau_{Gmn}X^{-1}}{\partial \text{vec}\, X^{-1}} = I_{mG} \otimes (K_{mG}X^{-1}\tau_{mGm}K_{mm})
$$
$$
+ I_{(mG)^2}\tau_{mG,mG,m}\left(\text{vec}_m X^{-1'}\tau_{G,Gm,Gm}\text{vec}_m S'\right)
$$

so

$$
\frac{\partial \text{vec}\, X^{-1}\tau_{Gmm}X^{-1}}{\partial \text{vec}\, X}
$$
$$
= -X^{-1} \otimes X^{-1'}(K_{mG}X^{-1}\tau_{mGm}K_{mm})
$$
$$
- (X^{-1} \otimes X^{-1'})(I_{(mG)^2}\tau_{mG,mG,m}(\text{vec}_m X^{-1'}\tau_{G,Gm,Gm}\text{vec}_m S')). \quad (5.48)
$$

Consider the first matrix on the right-hand side of this equation.

Suppose we write,

$$
X^{-1} = \begin{pmatrix} X^1 \\ \vdots \\ X^G \end{pmatrix}
$$

where each submatrix in this partitioning is $m \times mG$. It follows that

$$X^{-1'} = (X^{1'} \ldots X^{G'})$$

and using Theorem 2.13 of Chapter 2

$$X^{-1'}(K_{mG}X^{-1}\tau_{mGm}K_{mm})$$

$$= (X^{1'} \ldots X^{G'})\begin{pmatrix} X^1\tau_{m1m}K_{mm} \\ \vdots \\ X^G\tau_{m1m}K_{mm} \end{pmatrix}$$

$$= X^{1'}(X^1\tau_{m1m}K_{mm}) + \cdots + X^{G'}(X^G\tau_{m1m}K_{mm}).$$

By Theorem 1.8 of Chapter 1,

$$X^{1'}(X^1\tau_{m1m}K_{mm}) = X^1\tau_{m,1,mG}(I_m \otimes X^{1'})K_{mm} = (X^1 \otimes X^{1'})\tau_{m,mG,1}I_m$$

by Theorem 2.19 of Chapter 2.

It follows that the first matrix on the right-hand side of Equation 5.48 can be written as

$$-X^{-1} \otimes \left[(X^1 \otimes X^{1'})\tau_{m,mG,1}I_m + \cdots + (X^G \otimes X^{G'})\tau_{m,mG,1}I_m\right]$$

$$= -X^{-1'} \otimes \left[(X^1 \otimes X^{1'} + \cdots + X^G \otimes X^{G'})\tau_{m,mG,1}I_m\right]$$

$$= -X^{-1} \otimes \left[(X^{-1}\tau_{G,m,mG}\text{vec}_m X^{-1'})\tau_{m,mG,1}I_m\right]. \tag{5.49}$$

Consider now the second matrix on the right-hand side of Equation 5.48, which using Equation 5.41, we can write as

$$-(X^{-1} \otimes X^{-1'})\left[I_{mG} \otimes (\text{vec}_m X^{-1'})^{(1)} \otimes I_m \ldots I_{mG} \otimes (\text{vec}_m X^{-1'})^{(mG)} \otimes I_m\right]$$

$$= -X^{-1} \otimes X^{-1'}\left[(\text{vec}_m X^{-1'})^{(1)} \otimes I_m\right] \ldots$$

$$-X^{-1} \otimes X^{-1'}\left[(\text{vec}_m X^{-1'})^{(mG)} \otimes I_m\right].$$

By Theorem 1.18 of Chapter 1,

$$X^{-1'}\left((\text{vec}_m X^{-1'})^{(1)} \otimes I_m\right) = (\text{vec}_m X^{-1'})^{(1)}\tau_{G,1,mG}\text{vec}_m X^{-1'}$$

so we can write this second matrix as

$$-X^{-1} \otimes \left[(\text{vec}_m X^{-1'})^{(1)}\tau_{G,1,mG}\text{vec}_m X^{-1'}\right] \ldots$$

$$-X^{-1} \otimes \left[(\text{vec}_m X^{-1'})^{(mG)}\tau_{G,1,mG}\text{vec}_m X^{-1'}\right]. \tag{5.50}$$

Combining Equations 5.49 and 5.50 gives us our result, namely

$$
\frac{\partial \operatorname{vec} X^{-1} \tau_{Gm\,m} X^{-1}}{\partial \operatorname{vec} X}
$$
$$
= -X^{-1} \otimes \left[\left(X^{-1} \tau_{G,m,mG} \operatorname{vec}_m X^{-1'} \right) \tau_{m,mG,1} I_m \right]
$$
$$
- \left[X^{-1} \otimes \left(\operatorname{vec}_m X^{-1'} \right)^{(1)} \tau_{G,1,mG} \operatorname{vec}_m X^{-1'} \cdots \right.
$$
$$
\left. X^{-1} \otimes \left(\operatorname{vec}_m X^{-1'} \right)^{(mG)} \tau_{G,1,mG} \operatorname{vec}_m X^{-1'} \right].
$$

To break this result down further note that

$$
X^1 \otimes X^{1'} + \cdots + X^G \otimes X^{G'}
$$
$$
= \begin{pmatrix} (X^1)_{1.} \otimes X^{1'} + & \cdots & + (X^G)_{1.} \otimes X^{G'} \\ \vdots & & \vdots \\ (X^1)_{m.} \otimes X^{1'} + & \cdots & + (X^G)_{m.} \otimes X^{G'} \end{pmatrix},
$$

so the first matrix on the right-hand side of our result can be written as

$$
-X^{-1} \otimes \left[\left((X^1)_{1.} \otimes X^{1'} + \cdots + (X^G)_{1.} \otimes X^{G'} \right) \otimes e_1^{m'} \right.
$$
$$
\left. + \cdots + \left((X^1)_{m.} \otimes X^{1'} + \cdots + (X^G)_{m.} \otimes X^{G'} \right) \otimes e_m^{m'} \right]
$$

As far as the second matrix is concerned, note that

$$
\operatorname{vec}_m X^{-1'} = \begin{pmatrix} X^{1'} \\ \vdots \\ X^{G'} \end{pmatrix}
$$

so

$$
\left(\operatorname{vec}_m X^{-1'} \right)^{(1)} = \begin{pmatrix} (X^{1'})_{1.} \\ \vdots \\ (X^{G'})_{1.} \end{pmatrix} = \begin{pmatrix} X_{.1}^{1'} \\ \vdots \\ X_{.1}^{G'} \end{pmatrix}
$$

and

$$
\left(\operatorname{vec}_m X^{-1'} \right)^{(1)} \tau_{G,1,mG} \operatorname{vec}_m X^{-1'} = X_{.1}^{1'} \otimes X^{1'} + \cdots + X_{.1}^{G'} \otimes X^{G'}.
$$

We can break this second matrix of our result down as

$$
- \left[X^{-1} \otimes \left(X_{.1}^{1'} \otimes X^{1'} + \cdots + X_{.1}^{G'} \otimes X^{G'} \right) \ldots X^{-1} \otimes \left(X_{.mG}^{1'} \otimes X^{1'} \right. \right.
$$
$$
\left. \left. + \cdots + X_{.mG}^{G'} \otimes X^{G'} \right) \right].
$$

5.7 Results with Reference to $\partial \mathrm{vec}\, Y / \partial \mathrm{vec}\, X$

5.7.1 Introduction

One of the advantages of working with the concept of a matrix derivative given by $\partial \mathrm{vec}\, Y / \partial \mathrm{vec}\, X$ is that if $\mathrm{vec}\, Y = A \mathrm{vec}\, X$ where A is a matrix of constants, then $\partial \ell / \partial \mathrm{vec}\, Y = A \partial \ell / \partial \mathrm{vec}\, X$ for several of the vectors and matrices we encounter in our work. That is, often given the specialized matrices and vectors we work with if $y = Ax$, and A is a matrix of constants, then $\partial \ell / \partial y = A \partial \ell / \partial x$ for a scalar function ℓ. For example, if A is a selection matrix or a permutation matrix, then $y = Ax$ implies that $\partial \ell / \partial y = A \partial \ell / \partial x$, for an arbitrary scalar function ℓ as well. In this section, this property is investigated further. It is demonstrated that several theorems can be derived from this property. On the face of it, these theorems appear very simple and indeed their proofs are almost trivial. But taken together, they form a powerful tool for deriving matrix calculus results. By way of illustration, these theorems are used in Section 5.7.3 to derive results, some of which are new, for derivatives involving the vectors studied in Section 1.4.3 of Chapter 1, namely $\mathrm{vec}\, A$, $\mathrm{vech}\, A$, and $\bar{v}(A)$ for A a $n \times n$ matrix. They are also used in Section 5.7.4 to explain how results for derivatives involving $\mathrm{vec}\, X$ where X is a symmetric matrix can be derived from known results.

5.7.2 Simple Theorems Involving $\partial \mathrm{vec}\, Y / \partial \mathrm{vec}\, X$

Theorem 5.5   *Let x be an $n \times 1$ vector whose elements are distinct. Then,*

$$\frac{\partial x}{\partial x} = I_n.$$

Proof: Clearly,

$$\frac{\partial x}{\partial x} = \left(\frac{\partial x_1}{\partial x} \quad \cdots \quad \frac{\partial x_n}{\partial x} \right) = \left(e_1^n \quad \cdots \quad e_n^n \right) = I_n,$$

where e_j^n is the jth column of I_n.   ■

Theorem 5.6   *Suppose x and y are two column vectors such that $y = Ax$ and $\partial \ell / \partial y = A \partial \ell / \partial x$ for A a matrix of constants and ℓ a scalar function. Let z be a column vector. Then,*

$$\frac{\partial z}{\partial y} = A \frac{\partial z}{\partial x}.$$

Proof: We know that for any scalar ℓ,

$$\frac{\partial \ell}{\partial y} = A \frac{\partial \ell}{\partial x}.$$

Write

$$z = \begin{pmatrix} z_1 & \cdots & z_p \end{pmatrix}'.$$

Then,

$$\frac{\partial z}{\partial y} = \begin{pmatrix} \dfrac{\partial z_1}{\partial y} & \cdots & \dfrac{\partial z_p}{\partial y} \end{pmatrix} = \begin{pmatrix} A\dfrac{\partial z_1}{\partial x} & \cdots & A\dfrac{\partial z_p}{\partial x} \end{pmatrix}$$

$$= A \begin{pmatrix} \dfrac{\partial z_1}{\partial x} & \cdots & \dfrac{\partial z_p}{\partial x} \end{pmatrix} = A \frac{\partial z}{\partial x}. \qquad \blacksquare$$

Theorem 5.7   *Suppose x and y are two column vectors such that $y = Ax$ and $\partial \ell / \partial y = A \partial \ell / \partial x$ for A a matrix of constants and ℓ a scalar function. Suppose the elements of x are distinct. Then,*

$$\frac{\partial y}{\partial x} = \left(\frac{\partial x}{\partial y} \right)'.$$

Proof: Using the concept of a matrix derivative $\partial y / \partial x = A'$. But from Theorem 5.6,

$$\frac{\partial z}{\partial y} = A \frac{\partial z}{\partial x}$$

for any vector z. Taking $z = x$ gives

$$\frac{\partial x}{\partial y} = A \frac{\partial x}{\partial x}$$

and as the elements of x are distinct by Theorem 1, the derivative $\partial x / \partial x$ is the identity matrix

so

$$\frac{\partial x}{\partial y} = A = \left(\frac{\partial y}{\partial x} \right)'.$$

Taking transposes gives the result. $\blacksquare$

In using the concept of a matrix derivative we have, a backward chain rule applies, which is just the transpose of the chain rule reported by Magnus (see Magnus (2010)). That is, if y is a vector function of u and u is a vector function of x, so $y = y(u(x))$, then

$$\frac{\partial y}{\partial x} = \frac{\partial u}{\partial x}\frac{\partial y}{\partial u}.$$

Using this result gives us the following theorem.

Theorem 5.8 *For any vectors* x *and* y,

$$\frac{\partial y}{\partial x} = \frac{\partial x}{\partial x}\frac{\partial y}{\partial x}.$$

Proof: Write $y = y(x(x))$ and apply the backward chain rule. ∎

5.7.3 Theorems Concerning Derivatives Involving Vec A, Vech A, and $\bar{v}$

Let $A = \{a_{ij}\}$ be an $n \times n$ matrix and partition A into its columns, so $A = (a_1 \ \cdots \ a_n)$ where a_j is the jth column of A for $j = 1, \ldots, n$. Then, recall from Section 1.4.3 of Chapter 1 that vec A is the $n^2 \times 1$ vector given by vec $A = (a_1' \ \cdots \ a_n')'$, that is, to form vec A we stack the columns of A underneath each other. Vech A is the $\frac{1}{2}n(n+1) \times 1$ vector given by

$$\text{vech } A = (a_{11} \ \cdots \ a_{n1} \ a_{22} \ \cdots \ a_{n2} \ \cdots \ a_{nn})'.$$

That is, to form vech A we stack the elements of A on and below the main diagonal one underneath the other. The vector $\bar{v}(A)$ is the $\frac{1}{2}n(n-1) \times 1$ vector given by

$$\bar{v}(A) = (a_{21} \ \cdots \ a_{n1} \ a_{32} \ \cdots \ a_{n2} \ \cdots \ a_{nn-1})'.$$

That is, we form $\bar{v}(A)$ by stacking the elements of A below the main diagonal, one beneath the other. These vectors are important for statisticians and econometricians. If A is a covariance matrix, then vec A contains the variances and covariances but with the covariances duplicated. The vector vech A contains the variances and covariances without duplication and $\bar{v}(A)$ contains the covariances without the variances.

Regardless as to whether A is symmetric or not, the elements in vech A and $\bar{v}(A)$ are distinct. The elements in vec A are distinct provided A is not symmetric. If A is symmetric, the elements of vec A are not distinct.

So, from Theorem 5.5, we have

$$\frac{\partial \text{vech } A}{\partial \text{vech } A} = I_{\frac{1}{2}n(n+1)} \qquad \text{for all } A$$

$$\frac{\partial \bar{v}(A)}{\partial \bar{v}(A)} = I_{\frac{1}{2}n(n-1)} \qquad \text{for all } A$$

$$\frac{\partial \text{vec } A}{\partial \text{vec } A} = I_{n^2} \qquad \text{provided } A \text{ is not symmetric.}$$

What $\partial \text{vec } A/\partial \text{vec } A$ is in the case where A symmetric is discussed in Section 5.7.4.

In Section 3.2 of Chapter 3, we also saw that there exists $\frac{1}{2}n(n+1) \times n^2$ and $\frac{1}{2}n(n-1) \times n^2$ zero-one matrices L_n and $\bar{L}_n$, respectively, such that

$$L_n \text{vec } A = \text{vech } A$$

and

$$\bar{L}_n \text{vec } A = \bar{v}(A).$$

If A is symmetric, then

$$N_n \text{vec } A = \text{vec } A$$

where $N_n = \frac{1}{2}(I_{n^2} + K_{nn})$ and K_{nn} is a commutation matrix, so for this case

$$L_n N_n \text{vec } A = \text{vech } A$$

and

$$\bar{L}_n N_n \text{vec } A = \bar{v}(A).$$

The matrices $L_n N_n$ and $\bar{L}_n N_n$ are not zero-one matrices. However, as we know from Chapter 3 along with L_n and $\bar{L}_n$, they form a group of matrices known as elimination matrices. Finally, in Section 3.3 of Chapter 3, we saw that for special cases there exists zero-one matrices called duplication matrices, which take us back from vech A and $\bar{v}(A)$ to vec A. If A is symmetric, there exists an $n^2 \times \frac{1}{2}n(n+1)$ zero-one matrix D_n such that

$$D_n \text{vech } A = \text{vec } A.$$

Consider ℓ any scalar function. Then, reflexion shows that the same relationships exist between $\partial \ell/\partial \text{vec } A$, $\partial \ell/\partial \text{vech } A$, and $\partial \ell/\partial \bar{v}(A)$ as exist between vec A, vech A, and $\bar{v}(A)$, respectively.

Thus, for general A

$$\frac{\partial \ell}{\partial \text{vech } A} = L_n \frac{\partial \ell}{\partial \text{vec } A}$$

$$\frac{\partial \ell}{\partial \bar{\text{v}}(A)} = \bar{L}_n \frac{\partial \ell}{\partial \text{vec } A}.$$

For symmetric A,

$$\frac{\partial \ell}{\partial \text{vech } A} = L_n N_n \frac{\partial \ell}{\partial \text{vec } A}$$

$$\frac{\partial \ell}{\partial \bar{\text{v}}(A)} = \bar{L}_n N_n \frac{\partial \ell}{\partial \text{vec } A}$$

$$\frac{\partial \ell}{\partial \text{vec } A} = D_n \frac{\partial \ell}{\partial \text{vech } A}. \tag{5.51}$$

Using the Theorems of Section 3, we can prove the following results.

Theorem 5.9

$$\frac{\partial \text{vec } A}{\partial \text{vech } A} = D_n' \qquad \text{if } A \text{ is symmetric}$$

$$\frac{\partial \text{vec } A}{\partial \text{vech } A} = L_n \qquad \text{if } A \text{ is not symmetric.}$$

Proof: If A is symmetric vec $A = D_n$ vech A and the result follows. For the case where A is not symmetric, consider

$$\text{vech } A = L_n \text{vec } A.$$

By Theorem 5.6, we have that for any vector z

$$\frac{\partial z}{\partial \text{vech } A} = L_n \frac{\partial z}{\partial \text{vec } A}.$$

Taking $z = \text{vec } A$ gives

$$\frac{\partial \text{vec } A}{\partial \text{vech } A} = L_n \frac{\partial \text{vec } A}{\partial \text{vec } A}$$

and as A is not symmetric the elements of vec A are distinct, so by Theorem 5.5

$$\frac{\partial \text{vec } A}{\partial \text{vec } A} = I_{n^2}$$

and

$$\frac{\partial \text{vec } A}{\partial \text{vech } A} = L_n.$$

■

Theorem 5.10

$$\frac{\partial \text{vech } A}{\partial \text{vec } A} = D_n \qquad \text{if } A \text{ is symmetric}$$

$$\frac{\partial \text{vech } A}{\partial \text{vec } A} = L_n' \qquad \text{if } A \text{ is not symmetric}$$

Proof: A trivial application of Theorem 5.7.   ■

Theorem 5.6 can also be used to quickly derive results about elimination matrices, duplication matrices, and the matrix N_n. Consider, for example, the case where A is a symmetric $n \times n$ matrix, so

$$L_n N_n \text{vec } A = \text{vech } A.$$

By Theorem 5.6, for any vector z,

$$\frac{\partial z}{\partial \text{vech } A} = L_n N_n \frac{\partial z}{\partial \text{vec } A}.$$

Take $z = \text{vech } A$. Then,

$$\frac{\partial \text{vech } A}{\partial \text{vech } A} = L_n N_n \frac{\partial \text{vech } A}{\partial \text{vec } A} = L_n N_n D_n$$

by Theorem 5.10.

But as the elements of vech A are distinct,

$$\frac{\partial \text{vech } A}{\partial \text{vech } A} = I_{\frac{1}{2} n(n+1)},$$

so

$$L_n N_n D_n = I_{\frac{1}{2} n(n+1)},$$

a result we knew already from Equation 3.55 of Chapter 3.

5.7.4 Theorems Concerning Derivatives Involving Vec X where X Is Symmetric

Consider X an $n \times n$ symmetric matrix and let $x = \text{vec } X$. Then, the elements of x are not distinct and one of the implications of this is that

$$\frac{\partial x}{\partial x} \neq I_{n^2}.$$

Consider the 2×2 case. Then,

$$X = \begin{pmatrix} x_{11} & x_{21} \\ x_{21} & x_{22} \end{pmatrix}$$

and $x = (x_{11} \ \ x_{21} \ \ x_{21} \ \ x_{22})'$, so

$$\frac{\partial x}{\partial x} = \begin{pmatrix} \dfrac{\partial x_{11}}{\partial x} & \dfrac{\partial x_{21}}{\partial x} & \dfrac{\partial x_{21}}{\partial x} & \dfrac{\partial x_{22}}{\partial x} \end{pmatrix} = \begin{pmatrix} 1 & 0 & 0 & 0 \\ 0 & 1 & 1 & 0 \\ 0 & 1 & 1 & 0 \\ 0 & 0 & 0 & 1 \end{pmatrix}.$$

Clearly, this matrix is not the identity matrix. What it is, is given by the following theorem whose proof again calls on our results of Section 5.7.2.

Theorem 5.11   *Let X be an $n \times n$ symmetric matrix. Then,*

$$\frac{\partial \text{vec } X}{\partial \text{vec } X} = D_n D_n'.$$

Proof: As X is an $n \times n$ symmetric matrix,

$$\text{vec } X = D_n \text{vech } X$$

so it follows from Theorem 5.6 that for any vector z

$$\frac{\partial z}{\partial \text{vec } X} = D_n \frac{\partial z}{\partial \text{vech } X}.$$

Take $z = \text{vec } X$, so

$$\frac{\partial \text{vec } X}{\partial \text{vec } X} = D_n \frac{\partial \text{vec } X}{\partial \text{vech } X} = D_n D_n' \tag{5.52}$$

by Theorem 5.9.   ∎

The fact that in the case where X is an $n \times n$ symmetric matrix ∂vec X/∂vec $X = D_n D_n'$ means that all the usual rules of matrix calculus, regardless of what concept of a matrix derivative one is using, do not apply for vec X where X is symmetric. However, Theorem 5.8, coupled with Theorem 5.11, provide a quick and easy method for finding the results for this case using known matrix calculus results.

Consider again $x = \text{vec } X$ with X a symmetric matrix. Let $\phi y/\phi x$ denote the matrix derivative, we would get if we differentiated y with respect to x using the concept of differentiation advocated but *ignoring the fact that X is a symmetric matrix.* Then, the full import of Theorem 5.8 for this case is given by the equation

$$\frac{\partial y}{\partial x} = \frac{\partial x}{\partial x} \frac{\phi y}{\phi x}. \tag{5.53}$$

Combining Equations 5.51 and 5.52 give the following theorem.

Theorem 5.12 *Consider $y = y(x)$ with $x = \text{vec } X$ and X is a $n \times n$ symmetric matrix. Let $\phi y / \phi x$ denote the derivative of y with respect to x obtained when we ignore the fact that X is a symmetric matrix. Then,*

$$\frac{\partial y}{\partial x} = D_n D_n' \frac{\phi y}{\phi x}.$$

A few examples will suffice to illustrate the use of this theorem. (For the rules referred to in these examples, see Turkington (2004), Lutkepohl (1996), or Magnus and Neudecker (1999)).

For x with distinct elements and A a matrix of constants, we know that

$$\frac{\partial x' A x}{\partial x} = 2(A + A')x.$$

It follows that when $x = \text{vec } X$ and X is an $n \times n$ symmetric matrix

$$\frac{\partial x' A x}{\partial x} = 2 D_n D_n'(A + A')x.$$

For X non-singular, but non-symmetric matrix

$$\frac{\partial |X|}{\partial \text{vec } X} = |X| \text{vec}(X^{-1})'$$

so for X non-singular, but symmetric

$$\frac{\partial |X|}{\partial \text{vec } X} = |X| D_n D_n' \text{vec } X^{-1}.$$

For X an $n \times n$ non-symmetric matrix, A and B matrices of constants

$$\frac{\partial \text{vec } A X B}{\partial \text{vec } X} = B \otimes A'$$

so for X an $n \times n$ symmetric matrix

$$\frac{\partial \text{vec } A X B}{\partial \text{vec } X} = D_n D_n'(B \otimes A').$$

All results using either $\partial \text{vec}\, Y / \partial \text{vec}\, X$ or DY (in which case we have to take transposes) can be adjusted in this way to allow for the case where X is a symmetric matrix.

In the next chapter, the analysis of this section is brought together to explain precisely how one should differentiate a log-likelihood function using matrix calculus.

SIX

Applications

6.1 Introduction

As mentioned in the preface of this book, the main purpose of this work is to introduce new mathematical operators and to present known matrices that are important in matrix calculus in a new light. Much of this work has concentrated on cross-products, generalized vecs and rvecs, and how they interact and how they can be used to link different concepts of matrix derivatives. Well-known matrices such as elimination matrices and duplication matrices have been revisited and presented in a form that enables one to see precisely how these matrices interact with other matrices, particularly Kronecker products. New matrix calculus results have also been presented in this book.

Much of the work then has been of a theoretical nature and I hope it can stand on its own. Having said this, however, I feel the book would be incomplete without some indication as to how matrix calculus and the specialized properties associated with it can be applied.

Matrix calculus can be applied to any area that requires extensive differentiation. The advantage of using matrix calculus is that it substantially speeds up the differentiation process and stacks the partial derivatives in such a manner that one can easily identify the end result of the process. Multivariate optimization springs to mind. In Section 6.2, we illustrate the use of matrix calculus in a well-known optimization problem taken from the area of finance.

The traditional areas, however, that use matrix calculus are to a large extent statistics and econometrics. Classical statistical procedures centred around the log-likelihood function such as maximum likelihood estimation and the formation of classical test statistics certainly require extensive differentiation. It is here that matrix calculus comes into its own.

What has been said for statistics holds more so for econometrics, where the statistical models are complex and the log-likelihood function is a very complicated function. Applying classical statistical procedures then to econometric models is no trivial matter. Usually, it is beyond the scope of ordinary calculus and requires matrix calculus.

As shown in Chapter 4, four different concepts of matrix calculus have been used, particularly in statistics. In this chapter, as in Chapter 5, Concept 4 of Chapter 4 is used to derive the results.

No attempt is made in this chapter to provide an extensive list of the applications of matrix calculus and zero-one matrices to models in statistics and econometrics. For such applications, see Magnus and Neudecker (1999) and Turkington (2005). Instead, what is offered in Section 6.3 is a brief and non-rigorous summary of classical statistical procedures. Section 6.4 explains why these procedures are amenable to matrix calculus and the standard approach one should adopt when using matrix calculus to form the score vector and information matrix, the basic building blocks of classical statistical procedures. Sections 6.4, 6.5, and 6.6 present applications of our technique to a statistical model, where we are sampling from a multivariate normal distribution and to two econometric models, the limited information model and the full information matrix.

6.2 Optimization Problems

Consider scalar function of many variables $y = f(x)$ where x is an $n \times 1$ vector. Then using our concept of matrix derivative, the **score vector** is $\partial y / \partial x$ and the **Hessian matrix** is $\partial^2 y / \partial x \partial x = \partial (\partial y / \partial x) / \partial x$.

A critical point, (vectors are called points in this context), of the function is any point x such that

$$\frac{\partial y}{\partial x} = 0.$$

A given critical point is a local maximum if the Hessian matrix is negative definite when evaluated at that point whereas the point is a local minimum if the Hessian matrix is positive definite when evaluated at the point.

In complicated optimization problems, the rules of matrix calculus can be used to obtain both the score vector and the Hessian matrix usually far easier than if one was to use ordinary calculus. To illustrate, consider a well-known problem taken from finance, namely finding the optimal portfolio allocation. (This section is taken from Maller and Turkington

(2002)). Given an $n \times 1$ vector μ of expected asset returns and an associated $n \times n$ positive definite matrix Σ, the portfolio optimization problem is to choose a $n \times 1$ vector x of asset weights, whose elements add to one such that expected return $\mu_p = \mu' x$ is maximized when this return is discounted by the portfolio standard deviation $\sigma_p = \sqrt{x' \Sigma x}$. That is, our problem is as follows:

$$\text{Maximize} \quad f(x) = \frac{\mu' x}{\sqrt{x' \Sigma x}},$$

$$\text{subject to } i' x = 1,$$

where i is an $n \times 1$ vector whose elements are all 1. The ratio $\mu' x / \sqrt{x' \Sigma x}$ is called the **Sharpe ratio**.

As it stands, the problem is a constrained optimization problem, but it is easily converted to an unconstrained problem by using the constraint to eliminate one of the variables, say, the last one, x_n. We have

$$x_1 + \cdots + x_n = 1$$

so

$$x_n = 1 - x_1 - \cdots - x_{n-1} = 1 - i_R' x_R$$

where i_R is an $n - 1 \times 1$ vector whose elements are all ones and x_R is the $n - 1 \times 1$ vector given by $x_R = (x_1 \ldots x_{n-1})'$, and we can write

$$x = \begin{pmatrix} x_R \\ 1 - i_R' x_R \end{pmatrix} = A x_R + d,$$

where

$$A = \begin{pmatrix} I_{n-1} \\ -i_R' \end{pmatrix} \text{ and } d = \begin{pmatrix} 0 \\ 1 \end{pmatrix}.$$

The constrained optimization problem then becomes the following unconstrained optimization problem.

$$\underset{x_R}{\text{Max}} \; g(x_R) = \frac{y' \mu}{\sqrt{y' \Sigma y}} = y' \mu (y' \Sigma y)^{-\frac{1}{2}}$$

where $y = A x_R + d$. Using the product rule of ordinary calculus plus the backward chain rule of matrix calculus given by Theorem 5.2 of Chapter 5, we have that the score vector is given by

$$
\frac{\partial g(x_R)}{\partial x_R} = \frac{\partial y}{\partial x_R}\frac{\partial \mu' y}{\partial y}(y'\Sigma y)^{-\frac{1}{2}} + \frac{1}{2}y'\mu(y'\Sigma y)^{-\frac{3}{2}}\frac{\partial y}{\partial x_R}\frac{\partial y'\Sigma y}{\partial y}
$$

$$
= A'\mu(y'\Sigma y)^{-\frac{1}{2}} - y'\mu(y'\Sigma y)^{-\frac{3}{2}}A'\Sigma y
$$

$$
= \frac{A'\mu(y'\Sigma y) - y'\mu A'\Sigma y}{(y'\Sigma y)^{\frac{3}{2}}}.
$$

A critical point of $g(x_R)$ is any point x_R such that $\partial g(x_R)/\partial x_R = 0$, that is, any point x_R such that $A'\mu(y'\Sigma y) - y'\mu A'\Sigma y = 0$. Maller and Turkington (2002) shows that $g(x_R)$ has a unique critical point

$$
x_R^* = \frac{(\Sigma^{-1}\mu)_R}{i'\Sigma^{-1}\mu},
$$

where, following our notation $(\Sigma^{-1}\mu)_R$ denotes the vector consisting of the first $n-1$ elements of $\Sigma^{-1}\mu$. In terms of our original variables, the point x_R^* corresponds to

$$
x^{*'} = \Sigma^{-1}\mu/i'\Sigma^{-1}\mu
$$

which in turn is a critical point of $f(x)$.

Next, we want to determine the nature of this critical point by evaluating the Hessian matrix of $g(x_R)$ at x_R^*. Again, the rules of matrix calculus substantially help in determining this matrix. The Hessian matrix is

$$
\frac{\partial^2 g(x)}{\partial x_R \partial x_R} = \frac{\partial}{\partial x_R}\left(\frac{\partial g(x)}{\partial x_R}\right) = \frac{\partial}{\partial x_R}\left[(A'\mu y'\Sigma y - y'\mu A'\Sigma y)(y'\Sigma y)^{-\frac{3}{2}}\right].
$$

Using the product rule of ordinary calculus, the product rule of matrix calculus as presented in the corollary of Theorem 5.4 of Chapter 5 and the backward chain rule of matrix calculus Theorem 5.2 of that chapter, we have

$$
\frac{\partial^2 g(x)}{\partial x_R \partial x_R} = \left[\frac{\partial y}{\partial x_R}\frac{\partial y'\Sigma y}{\partial y}\mu'A - \frac{\partial y}{\partial x_R}\frac{\partial A'\Sigma y}{\partial y}y'\mu - \frac{\partial y}{\partial x_R}\frac{\partial \mu' y}{\partial y}y'\Sigma A\right](y'\Sigma y)^{-\frac{3}{2}}
$$

$$
- \frac{3}{2}\frac{\partial y}{\partial x_R}\frac{\partial y'\Sigma y}{\partial y}(y'\Sigma y)^{-\frac{5}{2}}(\mu'Ay'\Sigma y - y'\mu y'\Sigma A)
$$

$$
= \left\{(2A'\Sigma y\mu'A - A'\Sigma Ay'\mu - A'\mu y'\Sigma A)(y'\Sigma y)\right.
$$

$$
\left. - 3A'\Sigma y(\mu'Ay'\Sigma y - y'\mu y'\Sigma A)\right\}/(y'\Sigma y)^{\frac{5}{2}}
$$

$$
= -A'\left[y'\Sigma y(\Sigma y\mu' + \mu y'\Sigma + \Sigma\mu'y) - 3\mu'y\Sigma yy'\Sigma\right]A/(y'\Sigma y)^{\frac{5}{2}}.
$$

At the critical point x_R^*, $y = \Sigma^{-1}\mu/i'\Sigma^{-1}\mu$, so evaluating the Hessian matrix at x_R^*, we have

$$
\frac{\partial^2 g(x_R)}{\partial x_R \partial x_R}\Big|_{x_R^*}
$$

$$
= -A\left[\frac{\mu'\Sigma^{-1}\mu}{(i'\Sigma^{-1}\mu)^2}\left(\frac{\mu\mu'}{i'\Sigma^{-1}\mu} + \frac{\mu\mu'}{i'\Sigma^{-1}\mu} + \frac{\Sigma\mu'\Sigma^{-1}\mu}{i'\Sigma^{-1}\mu}\right)\frac{3\mu'\Sigma^{-1}\mu\mu'}{(i'\Sigma^{-1}\mu)^3}\right]A
$$

$$
\times \frac{(\mu'\Sigma^{-1}\mu)^{\frac{5}{2}}}{((i'\Sigma^{-1}\mu)^2)^{\frac{5}{2}}}.
$$

Now $((i'\Sigma^{-1}\mu)^2)^{\frac{5}{2}} = (|i'\Sigma^{-1}\mu|)^5 = \text{sign}(i'\Sigma^{-1}\mu)(i'\Sigma^{-1}\mu)^5$, so

$$
\frac{\partial^2 g(x_R)}{\partial x_R \partial x_R'}\Big|_{x_R^*} = -\frac{\text{sign}(i'\Sigma^{-1}\mu)(i'\Sigma^{-1}\mu)^2}{(\mu'\Sigma^{-1}\mu)^{\frac{1}{2}}}A'(\Sigma - \mu(\mu'\Sigma^{-1}\mu)^{-1}\mu')A.
$$

Well-known results from matrix algebra (see Horn and Johnson (1989)) ensure that the matrix $A'(\Sigma - \mu(\mu'\Sigma^{-1}\mu)^{-1}\mu')A$ is positive definite, so whether the Hessian matrix at x_R^* is negative definite or positive definitive depends crucially on the sign of $i'\Sigma^{-1}\mu$. If $i'\Sigma^{-1}\mu > 0$, then x_R^* is a maximum and converting back to our original variables, $x^* = \Sigma^{-1}\mu/i'\Sigma^{-1}\mu$ would be the unique maximum of the constrained problem. This gives the maximum Sharpe ratio of $f(x^*) = \sqrt{\mu'\Sigma^{-1}\mu}$. If $i'\Sigma^{-1}\mu < 0$, then x_R^* is a minimum and x^* gives a unique minimum of the constrained problem, namely $f(x^*) = -\sqrt{\mu'\Sigma^{-1}\mu}$ [1].

6.3 Summary of Classical Statistical Procedures

6.3.1 The Score Vector, the Information Model, and the Cramer-Rao Lower Bound

Let θ be an $k \times 1$ vector of unknown parameters associated with a statistical model and let $\ell(\theta)$ be the log-likelihood function of the model. We assume that this scalar function satisfies certain regularity conditions and that it is twice differentiable. Then, $\partial\ell/\partial\theta$ is an $k \times 1$ vector whose ith element is

---

[1] Maller and Turkington (2002) were the first to recognize the possibility that x^* may give rise to a minimum of the constrained problem rather than a maximum. Their expression for the Hessian matrix $\partial g(x_R)/\partial x_R \partial x_R$ contains a number of typos in it.

$\partial \ell / \partial \theta_i$. This vector we call the **score vector**. The Hessian matrix of $\ell(\theta)$ is the $k \times k$ matrix $\partial^2 \ell / \partial \theta \partial \theta = \partial(\partial \ell / \partial \theta) / \partial \theta$ whose (i, j)th element is $\partial^2 \ell / \partial \theta_i \partial \theta_j$. The asymptotic **information matrix** is

$$I(\theta) = - \lim_{n \to \infty} \frac{1}{n} E \left(\frac{\partial^2 \ell}{\partial \theta \partial \theta} \right)$$

where n denotes the sample size. Now, the limit of the expectation need not be the same as the probability limit, but for the models we consider in this chapter, based as they are on the multivariate normal distribution, the two concepts are the same. Often it is more convenient to regard the information matrix as

$$I(\theta) = -p \lim \frac{1}{n} \frac{\partial^2 \ell}{\partial \theta \partial \theta}.$$

The inverse of this matrix, $I^{-1}(\theta)$ is called the **asymptotic Cramer-Rao lower bound** and can be used in the following way. Suppose $\hat{\theta}$ is a consistent estimator of θ and that

$$\sqrt{n}(\hat{\theta} - \theta) \xrightarrow{d} N(0, V).^2$$

Then, the matrix V is the asymptotic covariance matrix of $\hat{\theta}$ and it exceeds the Cramer-Rao lower bound in the sense that $V - I^{-1}(\theta)$ is a positive-semidefinite matrix. If $V = I^{-1}(\theta)$, then $\hat{\theta}$ is an asymptotically efficient estimator and $\hat{\theta}$ is called a best asymptotically normally distributed estimator (BAN estimator for short).

6.3.2 Maximum Likelihood Estimators and Test Procedures

Classical statisticians prescribed a procedure for obtaining a BAN estimator, namely the maximum-likelihood procedure. Let $\oplus$ denote the parameter space. Then, any value of θ that maximizes $\ell(\theta)$ over $\oplus$ is called a maximum-likelihood estimate, and the underlying estimator is called the maximum-likelihood estimator (MLE). The first-order conditions for this maximization are given by

$$\frac{\partial \ell(\theta)}{\partial \theta} = 0.$$

[2] A shortcut notation is being used here. The more formally correct notation is $\sqrt{n}(\hat{\theta} - \theta) \xrightarrow{d} xN(0, V)$.

Let $\tilde{\theta}$ denote the MLE of θ. Then, $\tilde{\theta}$ is consistent, and $\tilde{\theta}$ is the BAN estimator so

$$\sqrt{n}(\tilde{\theta} - \theta) \overset{d}{\to} N\left[0, I^{-1}(\theta)\right].$$

Let h be a $G \times 1$ vector whose elements are differentiable functions of the elements of θ. That is, h is a vector function of θ, $h = h(\theta)$. Suppose we are interested in developing test statistics for the null hypothesis

$$H_0 : h(\theta) = 0$$

against the alternative

$$H_A : h(\theta) \neq 0.$$

Let $\tilde{\theta}$ denote the MLE of θ and $\bar{\theta}$ denote the constrained MLE of θ; that is, $\bar{\theta}$ is the MLE of θ after we impose H_0 in our model. Now, using our concept of a matrix derivative, $\partial h(\theta)/\partial \theta$ is the $k \times G$ matrix whose (i, j)th element is $\partial h_j/\partial \theta_i$. Then, classical statisticians prescribed three competing procedures for obtaining a test statistic for H_0. These are as follows.

Lagrangian Multiplier Test Statistic

$$T_1 = \frac{1}{n} \frac{\partial \ell(\bar{\theta})'}{\partial \theta} I^{-1}(\bar{\theta}) \frac{\partial \ell(\bar{\theta})}{\partial \theta}.$$

Note that the LMT statistic uses the constrained MLE of θ. If H_0 is true, $\bar{\theta}$ should be close to $\tilde{\theta}$ and as, by the first-order conditions, $\partial \ell(\tilde{\theta})/\partial \theta = 0$, the derivative $\partial \ell(\theta)/\partial \theta$ evaluated at $\bar{\theta}$ should also be close to the null vector. The test statistic is a measure of the distance $\partial \ell(\bar{\theta})/\partial \theta$ is from the null vector.

Wald Test Statistic

$$T_2 = nh(\tilde{\theta})' \left[\frac{\partial h(\tilde{\theta})'}{\partial \theta} I^{-1}(\tilde{\theta}) \frac{\partial h(\tilde{\theta})}{\partial \theta} \right]^{-1} h(\tilde{\theta}).$$

Note that the Wald test statistic uses the (unconstrained) MLE of θ. Essentially, it is based on the asymptotic distribution of $\sqrt{n}h(\tilde{\theta})$ under H_0, the statistic itself measuring the distance $h(\tilde{\theta})$ is from the null vector.

Likelihood Ratio Test Statistic

$$T_3 = 2\left[\ell(\tilde{\theta}) - \ell(\bar{\theta})\right].$$

Note that the likelihood ratio test (LRT) statistic uses both the unconstrained MLE $\tilde{\theta}$ and the constrained MLE $\bar{\theta}$. If H_0 is indeed true, it should not matter whether we impose it or not, so $\ell(\tilde{\theta})$ should be approximately the same as $\ell(\bar{\theta})$. The test statistic T_3 measures the distance between $\ell(\tilde{\theta})$ and $\ell(\bar{\theta})$.

All three test statistics are asymptotically equivalent in the sense that, under H_0, they all have the same limiting χ^2 distribution and under H_A, with local alternatives, they have the same limiting noncentral χ^2 distribution. Usually, imposing the null hypothesis on our model leads to a simpler statistical model, and thus constrained MLEs $\bar{\theta}$ are more obtainable than the $\tilde{\theta}$ MLEs. For this reason, the LMT statistic is often the easiest statistic to form. Certainly, it is the one that has been most widely used in econometrics.

6.3.3 Nuisance Parameters

Let us now partition θ into $\theta = (\alpha'\ \beta')'$, where α is an $k_1 \times 1$ vector of parameters of primary interest and β is an $k_2 \times 1$ vector of nuisance parameters, $k_1 + k_2 = k$. The terms used here do not imply that the parameters in β are unimportant to our statistical model. Rather, they indicate that the purpose of our analysis is to make statistical inference about the parameters in α instead of those in β.

In this situation, two approaches can be taken. First, we can derive the information matrix $I(\theta)$ and the Cramer-Rao lower bound $I^{-1}(\theta)$.

Let

$$I(\theta) = \begin{pmatrix} I_{\alpha\alpha} & I_{\alpha\beta} \\ I_{\beta\alpha} & I_{\beta\beta} \end{pmatrix}, \quad I^{-1}(\theta) = \begin{pmatrix} I^{\alpha\alpha} & I^{\alpha\beta} \\ I^{\beta\alpha} & I^{\beta\beta} \end{pmatrix}$$

be these matrices partitioned according to our partition of θ. As far as α is concerned, we can now work with $I_{\alpha\alpha}$ and $I^{\alpha\alpha}$ in place of $I(\theta)$ and $I^{-1}(\theta)$, respectively. For example, $I^{\alpha\alpha}$ is the Cramer-Rao lower bound for the asymptotic covariance matrix of a consistent estimator of α. If $\tilde{\alpha}$ is the MLE of α, then

$$\sqrt{n}(\tilde{\alpha} - \alpha) \xrightarrow{d} N(0, I^{\alpha\alpha}),$$

and so on.

A particular null hypothesis that has particular relevance for us is

$$H_0 : \alpha = 0$$

against

$$H_A : \alpha \neq 0.$$

Under this first approach, the classical test statistics for this null hypothesis would be the following test statistics.

Langrangian Test Statistic

$$T_1 = \frac{1}{n}\frac{\partial \ell(\overline{\theta})'}{\partial \alpha}I^{\alpha\alpha}(\overline{\theta})\frac{\partial \ell(\overline{\theta})}{\partial \alpha}.$$

Wald Test Statistic

$$T_2 = n\tilde{\alpha}' I^{\alpha\alpha}(\tilde{\theta})^{-1}\tilde{\alpha}.$$

Likelihood Ration Test Statistic

$$T_3 = 2\big[\ell(\tilde{\theta}) - \ell(\overline{\theta})\big].$$

Under H_0, all three test statistics would have a limiting χ^2 distribution with k_1 degrees of freedom, and the nature of the tests insists that we use the upper tail of this distribution to find the appropriate critical region.

The second approach is to work with the concentrated log-likelihood function. Here, we undertake a stepwise maximization of the log-likelihood function. We first maximize $\ell(\theta)$ with respect to the nuisance parameters β to obtain $\overline{\beta} = \overline{\beta}(\alpha)$. The vector $\overline{\beta}$ is then placed back in the log-likelihood function to obtain

$$\overline{\ell}(\alpha) = \ell\big[\alpha, \overline{\beta}(\alpha)\big].$$

The function $\overline{\ell}(\alpha)$ is called the **concentrated likelihood function**. Our analysis can now be reworked with $\overline{\ell}(\alpha)$ in place of $\ell(\theta)$.

For example, let

$$\overline{I} = -p\lim\frac{1}{n}\frac{\partial\overline{\ell}}{\partial\alpha\partial\alpha'}$$

and let $\hat{\alpha}$ be any consistent estimator of α such that

$$\sqrt{n}(\hat{\alpha} - \alpha) \xrightarrow{d} N\left(0, V_\alpha\right).$$

Then, $V_\alpha \geq \overline{I}^{-1}$ in the sense that their difference is a positive-semidefinite matrix. If $\tilde{\alpha}$ is the MLE of α, then $\tilde{\alpha}$ is obtained from

$$\frac{\partial\overline{\ell}}{\partial\alpha} = 0$$

$$\sqrt{n}(\tilde{\alpha} - \alpha) \xrightarrow{d} N(0, \overline{I}^{-1}),$$

and so on. As far as test procedures go for the null hypothesis $H_0 : \alpha = 0$, under this second approach we rewrite the test statistics by using $\overline{\ell}$ and $\overline{I}$ in place of $\ell(\theta)$ and $I(\theta)$, respectively. In our application in Sections 6.5 and

6.6, we use the second approach and form the concentrated log-likelihood function for our models.

6.4 Matrix Calculus and Classical Statistical Procedures

Classical statistical procedures involve much differentiation. The score vector $\partial \ell / \partial \theta$, the Hessian matrix $\partial^2 \ell / \partial \theta \partial \theta$, and $\partial h / \partial \theta$ all involve working out partial derivatives and it is at this stage that difficulties can arise in applying these procedures to econometric models. As noted in the introduction, the log-likelihood function $\ell(\theta)$ for most econometric models is a complicated function and it is no trivial matter to obtain the derivatives required for our application. Although in some cases it can be done (see, for example, Rothenberg and Lenders (1964)), what often happens when one attempts to do the differentiation using ordinary calculus is that one is confronted with a hopeless mess. It is here that matrix calculus comes into its own.

In most econometric models, we can partition θ, the vector containing the parameters of the model, as $\theta = (\delta' v')'$ where $v = \text{vech} \Sigma$ and Σ is a covariance matrix associated with the model. Usually, though not always, the vector v represents the nuisance parameters of the model and the primary aim of our analysis is to make statistical inference about the parameters in δ. Nuisance parameters or not, v represents a problem in that the log likelihood function is never expressed in terms of v. Rather, it is written up in terms of Σ.

The question is then how do we form $\partial \ell / \partial v$. The results of the last section of Chapter 5 present us with a method of doing this. As Σ is symmetric and assuming it is $G \times G$, then from Theorem 5.11 of Chapter 5, we have that

$$\frac{\partial \ell}{\partial \text{vec} \Sigma} = D_G D'_G \frac{\phi \ell}{\phi \text{vec} \Sigma} \tag{6.1}$$

recalling that $\phi \ell / \phi \text{vec} \Sigma$ is the derivative obtained when we ignore the fact that Σ is symmetric. But from Equation 5.51 of the same chapter,

$$\frac{\partial \ell}{\partial v} = L_G N_G \frac{\partial \ell}{\partial \text{vec} \Sigma} \tag{6.2}$$

so, combining Equations 6.1 and 6.2, we have that

$$\frac{\partial \ell}{\partial v} = L_G N_G D_G D'_G \frac{\phi \ell}{\phi \text{vec} \Sigma} = D'_G \frac{\phi \ell}{\phi \text{vec} \Sigma} \tag{6.3}$$

as by Equation 3.55 of Chapter 3, $L_G N_G D_G = I_{\frac{1}{2} G(G+1)}$.

Our method then is to differentiate the log-likelihood function with respect to $\text{vec}\Sigma$ ignoring the fact that Σ is symmetric. Then, premultiply the result obtained by D'_G.

Note from theorem of Chapter 5

$$\frac{\partial \text{vec}\Sigma}{\partial v} = D'_G$$

so we would write Equation 6.3 as

$$\frac{\partial \ell}{\partial v} = \frac{\partial \text{vec}\Sigma}{\partial v}\frac{\phi \ell}{\phi \text{vec}\Sigma}$$

which resembles a backward chain rule. This is the approach taken by Turkington (2005) in forming matrix derivatives associated with econometric models.

Consider now an $p \times 1$ vector $x = (x_1 \quad \cdots \quad x_p)'$ whose elements are differentiable functions of v but the vector itself is expressed in terms of Σ. Then, by Equation (6.3)

$$\frac{\partial x}{\partial v} = \left(\frac{\partial x_1}{\partial v} \quad \cdots \quad \frac{\partial x_p}{\partial v}\right) = \left(D'_G \frac{\phi x_1}{\phi v} \quad \cdots \quad D'_G \frac{\phi x_p}{\phi v}\right)$$
$$= D'_G \left(\frac{\phi x_1}{\phi v} \quad \cdots \quad \frac{\phi x_p}{\phi v}\right) = D'_G \frac{\phi x}{\phi v}. \tag{6.4}$$

Using Equation 6.4 allows us to form the Hessian matrix of $\ell(\theta)$. We have

$$\frac{\partial}{\partial v}\left(\frac{\partial \ell}{\partial \delta}\right) = D'_G \frac{\phi\,(\partial \ell/\partial \delta)}{\phi \text{vec}\Sigma}$$

so

$$\frac{\partial^2 \ell}{\partial \delta \partial v} = \left(\frac{\partial}{\partial v}\left(\frac{\partial \ell}{\partial \delta}\right)\right)' = \left(\frac{\phi\,(\partial \ell/\partial \delta)}{\phi \text{vec}\Sigma}\right)' D_G$$

and

$$\frac{\partial^2 \ell}{\partial v \partial v} = \frac{\partial}{\partial v}\left(\frac{\partial \ell}{\partial v}\right) = D'_G \frac{\phi}{\phi \text{vec}\Sigma}\left(D'_G \frac{\phi \ell}{\phi \text{vec}\Sigma}\right)$$
$$= D'_G \frac{\phi}{\phi \text{vec}\Sigma}\left(\frac{\phi \ell}{\phi \text{vec}\Sigma}\right) D_G = D'_G \frac{\phi^2 \ell}{\phi \text{vec}\Sigma \phi \text{vec}\Sigma} D_G \tag{6.5}$$

where in our working we have used Theorem 5.1 of Chapter 5.

The Hessian matrix of $\ell(\theta)$ is then

$$
H(\theta) = \begin{pmatrix}
\dfrac{\partial^2 \ell}{\partial \delta \partial \delta} & \left(\dfrac{\phi\,(\partial \ell/\partial \delta)}{\phi \mathrm{vec}\,\Sigma}\right)' D_G \\[2ex]
D_G' \dfrac{\phi(\partial \ell/\partial \delta)}{\phi \mathrm{vec}\,\Sigma} & D_G' \dfrac{\phi^2 \ell}{\phi \mathrm{vec}\,\Sigma \,\phi \mathrm{vec}\,\Sigma} D_G
\end{pmatrix}.
$$

As far as the asymptotic information matrix is concerned, if we assume the underlying distribution is the multivariate normal distribution, we know that we can write this matrix as

$$
I(\theta) = -p\lim \frac{1}{n}\frac{\partial^2 \ell}{\partial \theta \partial \theta'} = -p\lim \frac{1}{n} H(\theta).
$$

If we let

$$
A = -p\lim \frac{1}{n}\frac{\partial^2 \ell}{\partial \delta \partial \delta'}, \quad B = -p\lim \frac{1}{n}\left(\frac{\phi\,(\partial \ell/\partial \delta)}{\phi \mathrm{vec}\,\Sigma}\right)
$$

$$
C = -p\lim \frac{1}{n}\frac{\phi^2 \ell}{\phi \mathrm{vec}\,\Sigma \,\phi \mathrm{vec}\,\Sigma}.
$$

Then, we can write the information matrix as

$$
I(\theta) = \begin{pmatrix} A & B'D_G \\ D_G'B & D_G'CD_G \end{pmatrix}.
$$

Often, see for example Turkington (2005), the matrices B and C will be Kronecker products or at least involve Kronecker products, thus justifying our study in Chapter 3 of how the duplication matric D_G interacts with Kronecker products. In fact, in many econometric models $C = \frac{1}{2}(\Sigma \otimes \Sigma)$. Consider then the case where

$$
C = (E \otimes E)
$$

where we assume that E is nonsingular. Then, we saw in Equation 3.58 of Section 3.4 of Chapter 3 that

$$
(D_G'(E \otimes E)D_G)^{-1} = L_G N_G (E^{-1} \otimes E^{-1}) N_G L_G'.
$$

In some statistical and econometric models, B is the null matrix. In this special case, the information matrix is

$$
I^{-1}(\theta) = \begin{pmatrix} A^{-1} & O \\ O & L_G N_G \left(E^{-1} \otimes E^{-1}\right) N_G L_G' \end{pmatrix}
$$

thus justifying our study in Section 3.2.2 of Chapter 3 of how the elimination matrix $L_G N_G$ interacts with Kronecker products. In the case where B is not the null matrix, then

$$I^{-1}(\theta) = \begin{pmatrix} G & S \\ S' & J \end{pmatrix}$$

where

$$G = (A - B'D_G L_G N_G (E^{-1} \otimes E^{-1}) N_G L'_G D'_G B)^{-1}$$
$$= (A - B'N_G (E^{-1} \otimes E^{-1}) N_G B)^{-1}$$

as in Section 3.2.2, we saw that $D_G L_G N_G = N_G$, $S = -GB'D_G L_G N_G (E^{-1} \otimes E^{-1}) N_G L'_G = -GB'N_G (E^{-1} \otimes E^{-1}) N_G L'_G$
and

$$J = L_G N_G (E^{-1} \otimes E^{-1}) N_G L'_G - L_G N_G (E^{-1} \otimes E^{-1}) N_G S.$$

Again, we see that application of classical statistical procedures justifies the study, in some detail of $N_G (A \otimes B) N_G$, $L_G N_G (A \otimes B) N_G L'_G$ and $D_G (A \otimes B) D'_G$ as was conducted in Sections 3.2 and 3.3 of Chapter 3.

6.5 Sampling from a Multivariate Normal Distribution

A simple example shows how our analysis works in practice. The matrix calculus rules used in this example are found by taking the transposes of the equivalent rules reported in Section 4.3 of Chapter 4. We consider a sample of size n from the G dimensional distribution of a random vector y with mean vector μ and a positive definite covariance matrix Σ. The parameters of this model are $\theta = (\mu' v')'$ where $v = \text{vech}\Sigma$ and the log-likelihood function, apart from a constant is

$$\ell(\theta) = \frac{1}{2} n \log |\Sigma| - \frac{1}{2} \sum_{i=1}^{n} (y_i - \mu)' \Sigma^{-1} (y_i - \mu)$$
$$= \frac{1}{2} n \log |\Sigma| - \frac{1}{2} \text{tr } \Sigma^{-1} Z$$

with

$$Z = \sum_{i=1}^{n} (y_i - \mu)(y_i - \mu)'.$$

The Score Vector

Now, using Theorem 5.1 of Chapter 5

$$\frac{\partial \ell}{\partial \mu} = -\frac{1}{2}\sum_{i=1}^{n}\frac{\partial}{\partial \mu}(y_i - \mu)'\Sigma^{-1}(y_i - \mu) = \Sigma^{-1}\sum_{i=1}^{n}(y_i - \mu). \quad (6.6)$$

The next derivative in the score vector, namely $\partial \ell/\partial v$, uses the technique explained in the previous section. Consider

$$\frac{\phi \ell}{\phi \mathrm{vec}\Sigma} = -\frac{1}{2}n\frac{\phi \log|\Sigma|}{\phi \mathrm{vec}\Sigma} - \frac{1}{2}\frac{\phi}{\phi \mathrm{vec}\Sigma}\mathrm{tr}\,\Sigma^{-1}Z.$$

Now, from Equation 4.4 of Chapter 4

$$\frac{\phi \log|\Sigma|}{\phi \mathrm{vec}\Sigma} = \mathrm{vec}\Sigma^{-1}$$

and using the backward chain rule together with Equations 4.5 and 4.16 of Chapter 4

$$\frac{\phi\,\mathrm{tr}\,\Sigma^{-1}Z}{\phi \mathrm{vec}\Sigma} = \frac{\phi \mathrm{vec}\Sigma^{-1}}{\phi \mathrm{vec}\Sigma}\frac{\phi\,\mathrm{tr}\,\Sigma^{-1}Z}{\phi \mathrm{vec}\Sigma^{-1}} = -(\Sigma^{-1}\otimes\Sigma^{-1})\mathrm{vec}Z$$

so

$$\frac{\phi \ell}{\phi \mathrm{vec}\Sigma} = -\frac{1}{2}n\,\mathrm{vec}\Sigma^{-1} + \frac{1}{2}(\Sigma^{-1}\otimes\Sigma^{-1})\mathrm{vec}Z$$

$$= \frac{1}{2}(\Sigma^{-1}\otimes\Sigma^{-1})\mathrm{vec}\,(Z - n\Sigma)$$

and

$$\frac{\partial \ell}{\partial v} = \frac{1}{2}D_G'(\Sigma^{-1}\otimes\Sigma^{-1})\mathrm{vec}(Z - n\Sigma). \quad (6.7)$$

Together, Equations 6.6 and 6.7 give the components of the score vector

$$\frac{\partial \ell}{\partial \theta} = \left(\frac{\partial \ell'}{\partial \mu}\ \frac{\partial \ell'}{\partial v}\right)'.$$

The Hessian Matrix

The first component of this matrix is

$$\frac{\partial}{\partial \mu}\left(\frac{\partial \ell}{\partial \mu}\right) = -\Sigma^{-1}\sum_{i=1}^{n}\frac{\partial \mu}{\partial \mu} = -n\Sigma^{-1},$$

and using the backward chain rule, we can write

$$\frac{\phi}{\phi vec\Sigma}\left(\frac{\partial\ell}{\partial\mu}\right) = \frac{\phi vec\Sigma^{-1}}{\phi vec\Sigma}\frac{\phi vec\Sigma^{-1}a}{\phi vec\Sigma^{-1}}$$

with $a = \sum_{i=1}^{n}(y_i - \mu)$.

But using Theorem 5.1 of Chapter 5,

$$\frac{\phi vec\Sigma^{-1}a}{\phi vec\Sigma^{-1}} = \frac{\phi(a' \otimes I_G)vec\Sigma^{-1}}{\phi vec\Sigma^{-1}} = a \otimes I_G,$$

so the second component of the Hessian matrix is

$$\frac{\partial^2\ell}{\partial\mu\partial v} = -(\Sigma^{-1}a \otimes \Sigma^{-1})'D_G = -(a'\Sigma^{-1} \otimes \Sigma^{-1})D_G.$$

The last component of the Hessian matrix is computed by first considering

$$\frac{\phi}{\phi vec\Sigma}\left(\frac{\phi\ell}{\phi vec\Sigma}\right) = -\frac{n}{2}\frac{\phi vec\Sigma^{-1}}{\phi vec\Sigma} + \frac{1}{2}\frac{\phi vec\Sigma^{-1}Z\Sigma^{-1}}{\phi vec\Sigma}$$

$$= -\frac{\phi vec\Sigma^{-1}}{\phi vec\Sigma}\left(\frac{nI_{G^2}}{2} - \frac{1}{2}\frac{\phi vec\Sigma^{-1}Z\Sigma^{-1}}{\phi vec\Sigma^{-1}}\right). \qquad (6.8)$$

But from Equation 4.15 of Chapter 4,

$$\frac{\phi vec\Sigma^{-1}Z\Sigma^{-1}}{\phi vec\Sigma^{-1}} = \Sigma^{-1}Z \otimes I_G + I_G \otimes \Sigma^{-1}Z \qquad (6.9)$$

so from Equations 6.8 and 6.9,

$$\frac{\partial^2\ell}{\partial v\partial v} = D_G'(\Sigma^{-1} \otimes \Sigma^{-1})\left[\frac{nI_{G^2}}{2} - \frac{(\Sigma^{-1}Z \otimes I_G)}{2} - \frac{(I_G \otimes \Sigma^{-1}Z)}{2}\right]D_G.$$

The Information Matrix

From basic statistics,

$$\frac{1}{n}E(a) = 0 \qquad \frac{1}{n}E(Z) = \Sigma,$$

so the information matrix is

$$I(\theta) = -\lim_{n\to\infty}\frac{1}{n}E(H(\theta)) = \begin{pmatrix} \Sigma^{-1} & O \\ O & \frac{1}{2}D_G'(\Sigma^{-1} \otimes \Sigma^{-1})D_G \end{pmatrix}.$$

The Cramer-Rao Lower Bound

Inverting the information matrix gives the Cramer-Rao lower bound

$$I^{-1}(\theta) = \begin{pmatrix} \Sigma & O \\ O & 2L_G N_G (\Sigma \otimes \Sigma) N_G L'_G \end{pmatrix}.$$

These results were derived by Magnus and Neudecker (1980) though their approach using differentials to obtain the derivatives.

6.6 The Limited Information Model

6.6.1 The Model and the Log-Likelihood Function

The limited information model is the statistical model behind a single behavioural economic equation. In this model, it is assumed that all we have specified is this one equation, which presumably belongs to a larger linear economic model. The other equations in this model are not, however, available to us. Instead, what is given is that certain exogenous or pre-determined variables enter the reduced forms of the endogenous variables on the right-hand side of our specified equation.

We write the limited information model as

$$y_1 = Y_1\beta_1 + X_1\gamma_1 + u_1 = H_1\delta_1 + u_1$$
$$Y_1 = X\Pi_1 + V_1 \tag{6.10}$$

where Y_1 is an $n \times G_1$ matrix of observations of G_1 current endogenous variables, X_1 is an $n \times K_1$ matrix of observations on K_1 predetermined variables appearing in the equation, X is the $n \times K$ matrix of observations on all the predetermined variables appearing in the system, $H_1 = (Y_1\ X_1)$ and $\delta_1 = (\beta'_1\ \gamma'_1)'$. The second equation $Y_1 = X\Pi_1 + V_1$ is the reduced-form equation for Y_1.

We assume the rows of $(u_1\ V_1)$ are statistically, independently, and identically normally distributed random vectors with mean 0 and covariance matrix

$$\Sigma = \begin{pmatrix} \sigma^2 & \eta' \\ \eta & \Omega_1 \end{pmatrix}.$$

as always let $v = \text{vech}\Sigma$.

Alternatively, taking the vec of both sides of Equation 6.10, we can write the model as

$$y_1 = H_1\delta_1 + u_1$$
$$y_2 = (I_{G_1} \otimes X)\pi_1 + v_1$$

where $y_2 = \text{vec}Y_1$, $\pi_1 = \text{vec}\Pi_1$, and $v_1 = \text{vec}V_1$. Using this notation, we can then write the model more succinctly as

$$y = H\delta + u, \tag{6.11}$$

where $y = (y_1'\ y_2')'$, $\delta = (\delta_1'\ \pi_1')'$, $u = (u_1'\ v_1')'$, and

$$H = \begin{pmatrix} H_1 & 0 \\ 0 & I_{G_1} \otimes X \end{pmatrix}.$$

Under our assumption u has a multivariate normal distribution with mean 0 and covariance matrix $\psi = \Sigma \otimes I_n$, so the probability density function of u is

$$f(u) = (2\pi)^{-n} \det \psi^{-\frac{1}{2}} \exp\left(-\frac{1}{2}u'\psi^{-1}u\right)$$

$$= (2\pi)^{-n} (\det \Sigma)^{-\frac{n}{2}} \exp\left(-\frac{1}{2}u'\psi^{-1}u\right).$$

It follows that the probability density function of y is

$$g(y) = |\det J|\,(2\pi)^{-n} (\det \Sigma)^{-\frac{n}{2}} \exp\left[-\frac{1}{2}(y - H\delta)'\psi(y - H\delta)\right]$$

where J is the Jacobian matrix $\partial u/\partial y$. But from Equation 6.11, $\partial u/\partial y$ is the identity matrix so $\det J = 1$ and the log-likelihood function, ignoring a constant, is

$$\ell(v, \delta) = -\frac{n}{2}\log \det \Sigma - \frac{1}{2}\,\text{tr}\,\Sigma^{-1}U'U, \tag{6.12}$$

where in this function U is set equal to $(y_1 - H\delta_1, Y_1 - X\Pi_1)$.

6.6.2 Iterative Interpretations of Limited[3] Information Maximum Likelihood Estimators

It has been known for some time that mathematical manipulation of the first order conditions for the maximization of the log-likelihood function associated with an econometric model leads to an iterative interpretation of the maximum-likelihood estimator (see for example Byron (1978), Bowden and Turkington (1990), Durbin (1988), Hausman (1975), and Turkington (2002)). This interpretation is couched in terms of the econometric estimator developed for the parameters of primary interest of the model and is

---

[3] I should like to acknowledge my research assistant Stephane Verani for his excellent programming used in this section and the next.

often used as a justification for the econometric estimator. The econometric estimator can thus be viewed as the first step in an iterative procedure that leads to the maximum likelihood estimator. In terms of second order asymptotic efficiency, we know that for some cases at least the maximum likelihood estimator dominates the econometric estimator (see for example Efron (1975) and Fuller (1977)).

But what seems to have been overlooked in this literature is the iterative procedure itself. Several questions can be asked of such a procedure: How quickly does it converge from the econometric estimator to the maximum likelihood estimator? Does it converge if we start the iterative process with estimates obtained from inconsistent estimators, or if we choose any value as the starting point? In a statistical model, which is complicated in the sense that it has several sets of nuisance parameters, should we work with iterative processes derived from the log-likelihood function or from concentrated log-likelihood functions? That is, does further mathematical manipulations lead to more efficient iterative procedures?

In this section, as another application, we seek to investigate these matters using the limited information model, which is suited for this study as it has two sets of nuisance parameters. One then has the choice of deriving iterative procedures for the maximum likelihood estimators of the parameters of primary interest from the log-likelihood function or from two concentrated log-likelihood functions. The data used in this study is that associated with Klein's 1950 model. Klein's model and data are readily available in textbooks such as Theil (1971) or Greene (2010) and in the econometric package Gretl.[4]

In the log-likelihood function obtained in the previous section, the parameters of primary interest are contained in the vector δ_1. As far as classical statistics is concerned, what makes this function difficult to handle mathematically is that it contains two sets of nuisance parameters: those contained in the vector π_1, which are the reduced form parameters of the right-hand current endogenous variables, and those contained in the vector v, which are the unknown parameters in the covariance matrix Σ. Two sets of nuisance parameters mean that we are presented with a choice in the way we obtain the maximum likelihood estimator for the parameters of primary interest δ_1:

1. We can work with the first order conditions arising from the maximization of the log-likelihood function $\ell(v, \delta)$.

---

[4] Gretl is an open source econometric package developed by Allen Cottrell. It is available free of charge at http://gretl.sourceforge.net/.

2. We can use a step-wise maximization procedures, where we first maximize $\ell(v, \delta)$ with respect to the nuisance parameters v and form the concentrated log likelihood function $\ell^*(\delta)$, concentrated in $\delta = (\delta_1' \; \pi_1')'$. We then work with the first-order conditions for the maximization of this function.

3. Finally, we can start with the concentrated log-likelihood function $\ell^*(\delta)$ and maximize this first with respect to the second set of nuisance parameters π_1 to form the concentrated likelihood function $\ell^{**}(\delta_1)$ concentrated in the parameters of primary interest δ_1. We then work with the first-order conditions for the maximization of this function.[5]

All three procedures led to iterative processes, which can be interpreted in terms of econometric estimators. We now deal with each procedure in turn, again using the rules reported in Chapter 4 and the method for differentiating a log-likelihood function developed in Section 6.3.

Limited Information Maximum Likelihood Estimator As an Iterative Generalized Least Squares Estimator

The simplest iterative procedure is obtained from first order conditions

$$\frac{\partial \ell}{\partial v} = 0 \quad \text{and} \quad \frac{\partial \ell}{\partial \delta} = 0.$$

From Section 6.3, we know that

$$\frac{\partial \ell}{\partial v} = D_G' \frac{\phi \ell}{\phi \mathrm{vec} \Sigma}$$

and using the log-likelihood function written as in Equation 6.12, we have

$$\frac{\phi \ell}{\phi \mathrm{vec} \Sigma} = -\frac{n}{2} \frac{\phi \log \det \Sigma}{\phi \mathrm{vec} \Sigma} - \frac{1}{2} \frac{\phi \, \mathrm{tr} \, \Sigma^{-1} U'U}{\phi \mathrm{vec} \Sigma}.$$

Now,

$$\frac{\phi \log \det \Sigma}{\phi \mathrm{vec} \Sigma} = \frac{1}{\det \Sigma} \frac{\phi \det \Sigma}{\phi \mathrm{vec} \Sigma} = \mathrm{vec} \Sigma^{-1}$$

---

[5] There is one further possibility. First, maximize the log-likelihood function $\ell(v, \delta)$ with respect to nuisance parameters π and form the concentrated log-likelihood function $\bar{\ell}(v, \delta_1)$ concentrated in v, δ_1. An iterative process can then be derived from the first order conditions of the maximization of this function. However, this procedure did not easily lend itself to an interpretation in terms of known estimators and for this reason was not included in this study.

by Equation 4.4 of Chapter 4 and using the backward chain rule given by Theorem 5.2 of Chapter 5, we have

$$\frac{\phi \, \mathrm{tr}\, \Sigma^{-1} U'U}{\phi \mathrm{vec}\, \Sigma} = \frac{\phi \mathrm{vec}\, \Sigma^{-1}}{\phi \mathrm{vec}\, \Sigma} \frac{\phi \, \mathrm{tr}\, \Sigma^{-1} U'U}{\phi \mathrm{vec}\, \Sigma^{-1}} = -(\Sigma^{-1} \otimes \Sigma^{-1}) \mathrm{vec}\, U'U$$
$$= -\mathrm{vec}\, \Sigma^{-1} U'U \Sigma^{-1},$$

by Equations 4.5 and 4.16 of Chapter 4. It follows that

$$\frac{\partial \ell}{\partial v} = \frac{D'_G}{2} (\mathrm{vec}\, \Sigma^{-1} U'U \Sigma^{-1} - n \mathrm{vec}\, \Sigma^{-1})$$

which equals the null vector, only if

$$\Sigma = \tilde{\Sigma} = \frac{U'U}{n}. \tag{6.13}$$

The second derivative is by the backward chain rule and Theorem 5.1 of Chapter 5:

$$\frac{\partial \ell}{\partial \delta} = -\frac{1}{2} \frac{\partial u}{\partial \delta} \frac{u'(\Sigma^{-1} \otimes I_n)u}{\delta u} = H'(\Sigma^{-1} \otimes I_n)u.$$

Setting this derivative to the null vector gives,

$$H'(\Sigma^{-1} \otimes I_n)(y - H\delta) = 0.$$

Solving for δ gives and iterative interpretation for the limited information maximum likelihood (LIML) estimator $\tilde{\delta}$ as a generalized least squares estimator namely,

$$\tilde{\delta} = (H'(\Sigma^{-1} \otimes I_n)H)^{-1} H'(\Sigma^{-1} \otimes I_n)y. \tag{6.14}$$

This interpretation of the LIML estimator was first obtained by Pagan (1979).

Equations 6.13 and 6.14 form the basis of our iterative procedures, which is outlined as follows:

Iterative Procedure 1

1. Apply two-stage least squares (2SLS) (or another consistent estimation procedure) to $y_1 = H_1\delta_1 + u_1$ to obtain the 2SLSE $\hat{\delta}_1$. Apply ordinary least squares (OLS) to the reduced form equation $Y_1 = X\Pi_1 + V_1$ and obtain the OLSE $\hat{\Pi}_1$. Compute the residual matrices

$$\hat{u}_1 = y_1 - H_1\hat{\delta}_1, \quad \hat{V}_1 = Y_1 - X\hat{\Pi}_1.$$

2. Form the matrices

$$\hat{U} = (\hat{u}, \hat{V}_1) \quad \text{and} \quad \hat{\Sigma} = \frac{\hat{U}'\hat{U}}{n}.$$

3. Compute the GLSE

$$\hat{\delta} = (H'(\hat{\Sigma}^{-1} \otimes I_n)H)^{-1}H'(\hat{\Sigma}^{-1} \otimes I_n)y,$$

and compute $\hat{\hat{u}} = y - H\hat{\delta}$ and $\hat{\hat{U}} = \text{rvec}_n \hat{\hat{u}}$.

4. Repeat steps 2 and 3 with $\hat{\hat{U}}$ in place of $\hat{U}$.
5. Continue in this manner until convergence is reached. The LIML estimate of δ_1 is then the first component of the estimate thus obtained for δ.

LIML Estimator As an Iterative OLS Estimator

We have seen that maximization of the log-likelihood function $\ell(v, \delta)$ with respect to the nuisance parameters v gives $\Sigma = \tilde{\Sigma} = U'U/n$. If we substitute this into the log-likelihood function as given by Equation 6.12, we get the concentrated log-likelihood function, concentrated in $\delta = (\delta_1' \ \pi_1')'$. This function is, apart from a constant,

$$\ell^*(\delta) = -\frac{n}{2}\log \det U'U.$$

The first order condition for the maximization of this function is $\partial \ell^*/\partial \delta = 0$ and our iterative process is derived from the two components of this equation. We have using the backward chain rule and Equation 4.5 of Chapter 4

$$\frac{\partial \ell^*}{\partial \delta} = -\frac{n}{2}\frac{\partial u}{\partial \delta}\frac{\partial \log \det U'U}{\partial u} = nH'\text{vec}U(U'U)^{-1} = nH'((U'U)^{-1} \otimes I)u.$$

From the inverse of a partitioned matrix, we obtain

$$(U'U)^{-1}$$

$$= \begin{pmatrix} (u_1'M_{V_1}u_1)^{-1} & -(u_1'M_{V_1}u_1)^{-1}u_1'V_1(V_1'V_1)^{-1} \\ -(V_1'M_{u_1}V_1)^{-1}V_1'u_1(u_1'u_1)^{-1} & (V_1'M_{u_1}V_1)^{-1} \end{pmatrix}.$$

where $M_{V_1} = I_n - V_1(V_1'V_1)^{-1}V_1'$ and $M_{u_1} = I_n - u_1(u_1'u_1)^{-1}u_1'$. The first component of $\partial \ell^*/\partial \delta$ can be then written as

$$\frac{\partial \ell^*}{\partial \delta_1} = \frac{n}{u_1'M_{V_1}u_1}(H_1'u_1 - H_1'(u_1'V_1(V_1'V_1)^{-1} \otimes I_n))v_1 = n\frac{H_1'M_{V_1}u_1}{u_1'M_{V_1}u_1},$$

which is equal to the null vector when

$$H_1'M_{V_1}u_1 = 0.$$

Solving for δ_1 gives

$$\tilde{\delta}_1 = (H_1'M_{V_1}H_1)^{-1}H_1'M_{V_1}y_1. \tag{6.15}$$

In a similar manner, the second component of $\partial \ell^*/\partial \delta$ can be written as

$$\frac{\partial \ell^*}{\partial \pi_1} = n\text{vec}X'M_{u_1}V_1(V_1'M_{u_1}V_1)^{-1},$$

which is equal to the null vector when

$$X'M_{u_1}V_1 = 0.$$

Solving gives

$$\tilde{\Pi}_1 = (X'M_{u_1}X)^{-1}X'M_{u_1}Y_1 \tag{6.16}$$

Equations 6.15 and 6.16 form the basis of our next iterative process. Before we outline this process, it pays us to give an interpretation to the iterative estimators portrayed in these equations.

We have assumed that the rows of $U = (u_1 V_1)$ are statistically independently identically, normally distributed random vectors with mean 0 and covariance matrix

$$\Sigma = \begin{pmatrix} \sigma^2 & \eta' \\ \eta & \Omega_1 \end{pmatrix}.$$

It follows that we can write

$$u_1 = V_1\frac{\eta}{\sigma^2} + \omega$$

where ω is a random vector whose elements are independent of those of V_1. Similarly, we can write

$$V_1 = u_1\eta'\Omega_1^{-1} + W$$

where the elements of u_1 are independent of those of W. Consider the artificial equation,

$$y_1 = H_1 \delta_1 + V_1 \frac{\eta}{\sigma^2} + \omega,$$

and suppose for the moment we assume V_1 is known. Then, applying OLS to this equation gives

$$\tilde{\delta}_1 = (H_1' M_{V_1} H_1)^{-1} H_1' M_{V_1} y_1. \tag{6.17}$$

In a similar manner, write the second equation as

$$Y_1 = X \Pi_1 + u_1 \Psi + W, \tag{6.18}$$

where $\Psi = \eta' \Omega_1^{-1}$. Again, assuming that u_1 is known and applying OLS to this equation gives

$$\tilde{\Pi}_1 = (X' M_{u_1} X)^{-1} X' M_{u_1} Y_1.$$

What maximum likelihood estimation appears to do is to take account of the dependence of the disturbance terms u_1 and V_1, in the way previously outlined, and apply OLS. Of course, this interpretation is iterative as we have not really solved for Π_1 and δ_1 as $\tilde{\Pi}_1$ still depends on δ_1 through u_1 and $\tilde{\delta}_1$ still depends on Π_1 through V_1. Moreover, Equations 6.17 and 6.18 are artificial in that we have no observations on Π_1 and V_1 (if we did, we would not have a statistical problem!). But, our results clearly give rise to the following iterative process:

Iterative Procedure 2

1. Apply 2SLS (or some other consistent estimation procedure), to $y_1 = H_1 \delta_1 + u_1$ to obtain the estimate $\hat{\delta}_1$.
2. Form the residual vector

$$\hat{u}_1 = y_1 - H_1 \hat{\delta}_1$$

and

$$\hat{M}_{u_1} = I_n - \hat{u}_1 (\hat{u}_1' \hat{u}_1)^{-1} \hat{u}_1'.$$

3. Form

$$\hat{\Pi}_1 = (X' \hat{M}_{u_1} X)^{-1} X' \hat{M}_{u_1} Y_1,$$

4. Form the residual matrix

$$\hat{V}_1 = Y_1 - X\hat{\Pi}_1,$$

5. Obtain

$$\tilde{\delta}_1 = (H_1'\hat{M}_{V_1}H_1)^{-1}H_1'\hat{M}_{V_1}y_1.$$

6. Repeat steps 2, 3, 4, and 5 with $\tilde{\delta}_1$ in place of the original estimate $\hat{\delta}_1$.
7. Continue in this manner until convergence is obtained.

LIML Estimator As an Iterative Instrumental Variable Estimator

In obtaining our last iterative process, we conducted a stepwise maximization procedure where we first maximize the log-likelihood function $\ell(v, \delta)$ with respect to the nuisance parameter $v = \text{vech}\,\Sigma$ and obtained the concentrated log-likelihood function $\ell^*(\delta)$. We then maximized this function with respect to δ. But if our statistical interest is centred on δ_1, then π_1 should really be considered as a vector of nuisance parameters as well. Suppose now we continue with stepwise maximization and maximize the concentrated log-likelihood function $\ell^*(\delta)$ with respect to this second vector of nuisance parameters π_1. We then form the concentrated log-likelihood function $\ell^{**}(\delta_1)$ concentrated in the parameters of primary interest. In what follows, we show that the first order conditions of maximizing this function with respect to δ_1 leads to an iterative instrumental variable interpretation of the LIML estimator.

We have seen in the previous subsection that maximizing $\ell^*(\delta)$ with respect to π_1 gives

$$\tilde{\Pi}_1 = (X'\hat{M}_{u_1}X)^{-1}X'\hat{M}_{u_1}Y_1,$$

and hence

$$\tilde{V}_1 = (I_n - X(X'M_{u_1}X)^{-1}X'M_{u_1})Y_1.$$

It follows that

$$\ell^{**}(\delta_1) = -\frac{n}{2}\log\det\tilde{U}'\tilde{U}$$

where $\tilde{U} = (u_1\,\tilde{V}_1)$.

Before using matrix calculus to obtain the derivative $\partial\ell^{**}/\partial\delta_1$ it pays us to simplify this expression as much as possible. To this end, write

$$\det\tilde{U}'\tilde{U} = u_1'u_1\det\left\{Y_1'M_{u_1}\left[I_n - M_{u_1}X(X'M_{u_1}X)^{-1}X'M_{u_1}\right]M_{u_1}Y_1\right\}.$$

$$(6.19)$$

Consider now the artificial regression equation of Y_1 on X and u_1 given by Equation 6.18. Let $M = I_n - X(X'X)^{-1}X'$. Then, we know that the residual sum of squares from the regression of $M_{u_1}Y_1$ on $M_{u_1}X_1$ is equal to the residual sum of squares from the regression of MY on M_{u_1}. So, the determinant on the right side of Equation 6.19 is equal to

$$\det\left\{Y_1'M[I_n - Mu_1(u_1'Mu_1)^{-1}u_1'M]MY_1\right\}$$
$$= \frac{1}{u_1'Mu_1}\det\left[(u_1Y_1)'M(u_1Y_1)\right].$$

Furthermore,

$$(u_1\ Y_1)'M(u_1\ Y_1) = \begin{pmatrix} 1 & 0' \\ -\beta_1 & I_{G_1} \end{pmatrix}' (y_1\ Y_1)'M(Y_1\ y_1) \begin{pmatrix} 1 & 0' \\ -\beta_1 & I_{G_1} \end{pmatrix} \quad (6.20)$$

where the first partitioned matrix on the right-hand side of Equation 6.20 has a determinant equal to one. Therefore,

$$\det\left[(u_1\ Y_1)'M(Y_1\ u_1)\right] = \det\left[(y_1\ Y_1)'M(Y_1\ y_1)\right]$$

which does not depend on δ_1. Thus, the log-likelihood function $\ell^{**}(\delta_1)$ can be written as

$$\ell^{**}(\delta_1) = k^* - \frac{n}{2}\log\frac{u_1'Mu_1}{u_1'u_1} = k^* - \frac{n}{2}(\log u_1'Mu_1 - \log u_1'u_1)$$

where k^* does not depend on δ_1. Obtaining our derivative is now a simple matter.

Using the backward chain rule,

$$\frac{\partial \log u_1'Mu_1}{\partial \delta_1} = \frac{1}{u_1'Mu_1}\frac{\partial u_1}{\partial \delta_1}\frac{\partial u_1'Mu_1}{\partial u_1} = -\frac{2H_1'Mu_1}{u_1'Mu_1}.$$

Similarly,

$$\frac{\partial \log u_1'u_1}{\partial \delta_1} = -\frac{2H_1'u_1}{u_1'u_1},$$

so

$$\frac{\partial \ell^{**}}{\partial \delta_1} = -n\left(\frac{H_1'u_1}{u_1'u_1} - \frac{H_1'Mu_1}{u_1'Mu_1}\right) = n\frac{(H_1'Nu_1u_1'u_1 - H_1'u_1u_1'Nu_1)}{u_1'u_1u_1'Mu_1},$$

where $N = X(X'X)^{-1}X'$. The maximum likelihood estimator of δ_1 then satisfies the equation

$$\frac{\left(H_1'Nu_1 u_1'u_1 - H_1'u_1 u_1'Nu_1\right)}{u_1'Mu_1} = 0.$$

We now prove that this equation is the same as

$$\tilde{H}_1'u_1 = 0,$$

where

$$\tilde{H}_1 = X\left(X'M_{u_1}X\right)^{-1}X'M_{u_1}H_1 = (\tilde{Y}_1\ X_1) = (X\tilde{\Pi}_1\ X_1).$$

If this is the case, then the LIML estimator of δ_1 has an iterative instrumental variable interpretation given by

$$\tilde{\delta}_1 = (\tilde{H}_1'H_1)^{-1}\tilde{H}_1'y_1.$$

To establish our result, we expand $\left(X'M_{u_1}X\right)^{-1}$ to obtain

$$X\left(X'M_{u_1}X\right)^{-1}X' = N + \frac{Nu_1 u_1'N}{u_1'Mu_1}.$$

Then, after a little algebra, we find that

$$X\left(X'M_{u_1}X\right)^{-1}X'M_{u_1} = \frac{\left(Nu_1'Mu_1 - Nu_1 u_1'M\right)}{u_1'Mu_1}.$$

Thus,

$$\tilde{H}_1'u_1 = \frac{\left(H_1'Nu_1 u_1'Mu_1 - H_1'Mu_1 u_1'Nu_1\right)}{u_1'Mu_1} = \frac{\left(H_1'Nu_1 u_1'u_1 - H_1'u_1 u_1'Nu_1\right)}{u_1'Mu_1}$$

as we require.

Our results give rise to a third iterative process for finding the LIML estimator of δ_1, which is now outlined:

Iterative Procedure 3

1. Apply steps 1, 2, and 3 of iterative process 2.
2. Form

$$\hat{Y}_1 = X\hat{\Pi}_1$$

   and

$$\hat{H}_1 = (\hat{Y}_1\ X_1)$$

and obtain

$$\overline{\delta}_1 = (\hat{H}_1' \hat{H}_1)^{-1} \hat{H}_1' y_1.$$

3. Repeat steps 1 and 2 with $\overline{\delta}_1$ in place of the original estimate of δ_1.
4. Continue in this manner until convergence is achieved.

6.6.3 Comparison of the Three Iterative Procedures

The model and data used to compare our three procedures are those associated with the Klein (1950) model. This model consisted of three equations: a consumption equation, an investment equation, and a wage equation. For each equation, our three iterative procedures were started up with the following initial values:

1. The two-stage least squares estimates
2. The ordinary least squares estimates
3. The null vector
4. A vector of ones
5. A vector of arbitrary near values
6. A vector of arbitrary far values.

The arbitrary near values were obtained from a point arbitrarily chosen from the 95 percent concentration ellipsoid of the parameters obtained using the LIML estimators. Likewise, the arbitrary far values were obtained from a point arbitrarily chosen outside the 99 percent concentration ellipsoid of the parameters obtained from the LIML estimators. Each iterative procedure was run with each initial value until convergence was achieved or until it was clear that the procedure was not going to converge. Convergence was defined as taking place when the values obtained from the procedure all were within 0.000001 of the LIML estimates. No convergence was defined as taking place when this did not happen after 10,000 iterations. For each case, the number of iterations was counted for the procedure in question to move from the initial values to the LIML estimates. The programs were written in GAUSS. The results are presented in Tables 6.1, 6.2, and 6.3.

Focusing our attention on Tables 6.1, 6.2, and 6.3, we see that all three procedures converge when estimates are used as the initial starting values. Procedure 3 is far more efficient in terms of number of iterations until convergence than Procedure 2, which in turn is more efficient than Procedure 1. Moreover, it makes little difference whether the estimates used are derived from consistent estimators (2SLS) or inconsistent estimators

Table 6.1. *Consumption equation*

	Number of iterations until convergence		
Initial values	Procedure 1	Procedure 2	Procedure 3
2SLS estimates	829	559	6
OLS estimates	836	565	7
Null vector	712	No Conv.	6
Vector of ones	841	No Conv.	7
Arbitrary near values	825	514	6
Arbitrary far values	872	599	6

(OLS). For the other four sets of initial starting values, Procedure 1 and Procedure 3 always converge with Procedure 3, again being vastly more efficient than Procedure 1. Procedure 2 often would not converge. In the case where it did, it was ranked in efficiency terms between Procedure 1 and Procedure 3.

The message from these results seems clear. Iterative procedures based on the first-order conditions derived from the maximization of the log-likelihood function work, but are inefficient. More efficient iterative procedures can be derived by working with concentrated log-likelihood functions. But the most efficient procedure arises from the first-order conditions of the maximization of the log-likelihood function concentrated in the parameters of primary interest. Moreover, such a procedure seems relatively insensitive to the initial starting value. Concentrating out a subset of nuisance parameters can lend to a more efficient iterative procedure, but this procedure may become sensitive to initial starting values. Arbitrary starting values may not give rise to convergence.

Table 6.2. *Investment equation*

	Number of iterations until convergence		
Initial values	Procedure 1	Procedure 2	Procedure 3
2SLS estimates	135	75	4
OLS estimates	142	81	5
Null vector	129	86	5
Vector of ones	143	No Conv.	6
Arbitrary near values	139	No Conv.	5
Arbitrary far values	158	87	5

Table 6.3. *Wage equation*

Initial values	Number of iterations until convergence		
	Procedure 1	Procedure 2	Procedure 3
2SLS estimates	137	33	33
OLS estimates	137	34	34
Null vector	152	No Conv.	45
Vector of ones	167	No Conv.	48
Arbitrary near values	143	No Conv.	37
Arbitrary far values	120	37	37

6.7 The Full Information Model

6.7.1 The Model and the Log-Likelihood Function

The full information model is the statistical model behind a linear economic model. Assuming this model contains G jointly dependent current endogenous variables and k predetermined variables, we write the ith equation of the full information model as

$$y_i = Y_i\beta_i + X_i\gamma_i + u_i = H_i\delta_i + u_i, \quad i = 1, \ldots, G,$$

where y_i is an $n \times 1$ vector of sample observations on a current endogenous variable, Y_i is an $n \times G_i$ matrix of observations on the other G_i current endogenous variables in the ith equation, X_i is an $n \times k_i$ matrix of k_i predetermined variables in the ith equation, u_i is an $n \times 1$ vector of random disturbances, H_i is the $n \times (G_i + k_i)$ matrix $(Y_i\ X_i)$ and δ_i is the $(G_i + k_i) \times 1$ vector $(\beta_i'\ \gamma_i')'$. It is assumed that the u_i s are normal random vectors with expectations equal to the null vectors, and that they are contemporaneously correlated. That is, if u_{ti} and u_{sj} are the tth element and sth element of u_i and u_j, respectively, then

$$E(u_{ti}\,u_{sj}) = \sigma_{ij} \qquad \text{if } t = s$$
$$= 0 \qquad \text{if } t \neq s$$

Writing our model succinctly, we have

$$y = H\delta + u \tag{6.21}$$

$$E(u) = 0, \quad V(u) = \Sigma \otimes I, \quad u \sim N(0, \Sigma \otimes I)$$

where $y = (y_1' \ldots y_G')'$, $u = (u_1' \ldots u_G')'$, $\delta = (\delta_1' \ldots \delta_G')'$, H is the block diagonal matrix

$$\begin{bmatrix} H_1 & & O \\ & \ddots & \\ O & & H_G \end{bmatrix},$$

and Σ is a symmetric, positive definite matrix whose (i, j)th element is σ_{ij}.

A different way of writing our model is

$$YB + X\Gamma = U \tag{6.22}$$

where Y is the $n \times G$ matrix of observations on the G current endogenous variables, X is the $n \times k$ matrix of observations on the k predetermined variables, B is the $G \times G$ matrix of coefficients on the current endogenous variables in our equations, Γ is an $k \times G$ matrix of coefficients of the predetermined variables in our equations, and U is the $n \times G$ matrix $(u_1 \ldots u_G)$. Some of the elements of B are known a priori to be one or zero as y_i has a coefficient of one in the ith equation and some current endogenous variables are excluded from certain equations. Similarly, as certain predetermined variables are excluded from each equation, some of the elements of Γ are known to be zero. We assume B is non-singular.

The reduced-form of our model is

$$Y = -X\Gamma B^{-1} + UB^{-1} = X\Pi + V$$

or taking the vec of both sides

$$y = (I_G \otimes X)\pi + v$$

where $\pi = \text{vec}\Pi$, and $v = \text{vec}V = (B^{-1'} \otimes I_n)u$.

The unknown parameters of our model are $\theta = (\delta' v')'$ where $v = \text{vech}\Sigma$. Usually, δ is the vector of parameters of primary interest and v is the vector of nuisance parameters.

The likelihood function is the joint probability function of y. We obtain this function by starting with the joint probability density function of u. We have assumed that $u \sim N(0, \Sigma \otimes I_n)$, so the joint probability density function of y is

$$f(y) = |\det \mathsf{J}| \frac{1}{(2\pi)^{\frac{n}{2}} (\det \Sigma \otimes I_n)^{\frac{1}{2}}} \exp\left[-\frac{1}{2}u'(\Sigma^{-1} \otimes I_n)u\right],$$

with u set equal to $y - H\delta$ and where

$$\det J = \det \frac{\partial u}{\partial y}.$$

Our first application of matrix calculus to this model involves working out the Jacobian matrix $\partial u/\partial y$. Taking the vec of both sides of $U = YB + X\Gamma$, we have

$$u = (B' \otimes I_n)y + (\Gamma' \otimes I)x,$$

where $u = \text{vec}U$, $y = \text{vec}Y$, and $x = \text{vec}X$. It follows that

$$\frac{\partial u}{\partial y} = (B \otimes I_n),$$

and that

$$f(y) = \frac{|\det(B \otimes I_n)|}{(2\pi)^{\frac{n}{2}}(\det \Sigma \otimes I_n)^{\frac{1}{2}}} \exp\left[-\frac{1}{2}u'(\Sigma^{-1} \otimes I_n)u\right].$$

However, from the properties of the determinant of a Kronecker production we have $\det(\Sigma \otimes I_n) = (\det \Sigma)^n$, so

$$f(y) = \frac{(\det B)^n}{(2\pi)^{\frac{n}{2}}(\det \Sigma)^{\frac{n}{2}}} \exp\left[-\frac{1}{2}u'(\Sigma^{-1} \otimes I_n)u\right],$$

with u set equal to $y - H\delta$ in this expression. This is the likelihood function $L(\theta)$. The log-likelihood function, apart from a constant, is

$$\ell(\theta) = n\log|\det B| - \frac{n}{2}\log\det \Sigma - \frac{1}{2}u'(\Sigma^{-1} \otimes I_n)u,$$

with u set equal to $y - H\delta$.

An alternative way of writing this function is

$$\ell(\theta) = n\log|\det B| - \frac{n}{2}\log\det \Sigma - \frac{1}{2}\text{tr}\,\Sigma^{-1}U'U. \qquad (6.23)$$

Although this function has an extra term in it, namely $n\log|\det B|$, when compared with the corresponding log-likelihood function of the limited information model as given by Equation (6.12), it is far easier to manipulate mathematically than the latter. The reason for this is that this log-likelihood function contains only one set of nuisance parameters, whereas that of the limited information model contained two sets of nuisance parameters. However, this means that the log-likelihood function of the full information model does not lend itself to a variety of iterative processes. In the next subsection, we develop a single iterative process for the full information likelihood estimator (FIML).

6.7.2 The Full Information Maximum Likelihood Estimator As an Iterative Instrumental Variable Estimator

The term $n \log |\det B|$ of the log-likelihood function given by Equation 6.23 is a function of δ, but not of v. It follows that our derivative of the log-likelihood function with respect to v is the same as that derived in the limited information model and that the concentrated log-likelihood function for the model in hand is, apart from a constant

$$\ell^*(\delta) = n \log |\det B| - \frac{n}{2} \log \det U'U.$$

Now,

$$\frac{\partial \ell^*(\delta)}{\partial \delta} = \frac{n \partial \log |\det B|}{\partial \delta} - \frac{n}{2} \frac{\partial \log \det U'U}{\partial \delta} \tag{6.24}$$

so our first task is to express the matrix B in terms of the vector δ so we can evaluate the first derivative on the right-hand side of this equation.

To this end, we write the ith equation of our model as

$$y_i = Y \overline{W}_i \beta_i + X \overline{T}_i \gamma_i + u_i,$$

where $\overline{W}_i$ and $\overline{T}_i$ are $G \times G_i$ and $k \times k_i$ selection matrices, respectively, with the properties that

$$Y \overline{W}_i = Y_i, \quad X \overline{T}_i = X_i.$$

Alternatively, we can write

$$y_i = Y W_i \delta_i + X T_i \delta_i + u_i,$$

where W_i and T_i are the $G \times (G_i + k_i)$ and $k \times (G_i + k_i)$ selection matrices given by $W_i = (\overline{W}_i \ O)$ and $T_i = (O \ \overline{T}_i)$, respectively.

Under this notation, we can write

$$Y = (y_1 \ \cdots \ y_G) = Y(W_1 \delta_1 \ \cdots \ W_G \delta_G) + X(T_1 \delta_1 \ \cdots \ T_G \delta_G) + U.$$

It follows then that

$$B = I_G - (W_1 \delta_1 \ \cdots \ W_G \delta_G),$$

$$\Gamma = -(T_1 \delta_1 \ \cdots \ T_G \delta_1).$$

Moreover,

$$\text{vec } B = \text{vec } I_G - W\delta,$$

where W is the block diagonal matrix

$$W = \begin{bmatrix} W_1 & & O \\ & \ddots & \\ O & & W_G \end{bmatrix}.$$

Returning to our derivative now, clearly from

$$\frac{\partial \text{vec } B}{\partial \delta} = -W',$$

and as

$$\frac{\partial \log |\det B|}{\partial \delta} = \frac{\partial \text{vec } B}{\partial \delta} \frac{\partial \log |\det B|}{\partial \text{vec } B},$$

we obtain

$$\frac{\partial \log |\det B|}{\partial \delta} = -W' \text{vec}(B^{-1'}). \tag{6.25}$$

From our work on the limited information model,

$$\frac{\partial \log \det U'U}{\partial \delta} = -2 \frac{H'}{n} (\tilde{\Sigma}^{-1} \otimes I_n) u. \tag{6.26}$$

Now,

$$W' \text{vec } B^{-1'} = W'(\tilde{\Sigma}^{-1} \otimes I_G) \text{vec } B^{-1'} \tilde{\Sigma} = \frac{1}{n} W'(I_G \otimes V')(\tilde{\Sigma}^{-1} \otimes I_n) u. \tag{6.27}$$

Returning to Equation 6.24 using Equations 6.25, 6.26, and 6.27, we find we can write

$$\frac{\partial \ell^*(\delta)}{\partial \delta} = [H' - W'(I_G \otimes V')] (\tilde{\Sigma}^{-1} \otimes I_n) u$$

and $H' - W'(I_G \otimes V')W$ is the block matrix

$$\begin{pmatrix} H_1 - VW_1 & & O \\ & \ddots & \\ O & & H_G - VW_G \end{pmatrix} = \begin{pmatrix} (X\Pi_1 \ X_1) & & O \\ & \ddots & \\ O & & (X\Pi_G \ X_G) \end{pmatrix}.$$

Let $\overline{H}_i = (X\Pi_i\ X_i)$ and $\overline{H}$ be the block diagonal matrix where $\overline{H}_i$ is in the ith block diagonal position. Then,

$$\frac{\partial \ell^*(\delta)}{\partial \delta} = \overline{H}'\left(\tilde{\Sigma}^{-1} \otimes I_n\right)u.$$

Setting this derivative equal to the null vector and solving for δ gives

$$\tilde{\delta} = \left[\tilde{\overline{H}}\left(\tilde{\Sigma}^{-1} \otimes I_n\right)H\right]^{-1}\tilde{\overline{H}}\left(\tilde{\Sigma}^{-1} \otimes I_n\right)y \qquad (6.28)$$

where $\tilde{\overline{H}}$ is the block diagonal matrix with $\tilde{\overline{H}}_i = (X\tilde{\Pi}_i\ X_i)$ in the ith block diagonal position, $\tilde{\Pi}_i$ being the MLE of Π_i. Clearly, Equation 6.28 gives an iterative IVE interpretation of the FIML estimator of δ, where $X\Pi_i$ is used as an IV for Y_i. The iterative process arising from this equation can be outlined as follows:

1. Run three stage least squares (or some other consistent estimation procedure) on $y = H\delta + u$, to obtain the estimate $\hat{\delta}$. Compute the residual vector $\hat{u} = y - H\hat{\delta}$, $\hat{U} = \text{rvec}n\hat{u}$, and $\tilde{\Sigma} = \hat{U}'\hat{U}/n$.
2. Using $\hat{\delta}$ compute $\hat{B}$, $\hat{\Gamma}$, $\hat{\Pi} = -\hat{\Gamma}\hat{B}^{-1}$, and $\hat{Y}_i = X\hat{\Pi}\overline{W}_i$.
3. Compute $\hat{\overline{H}}_i = (\hat{Y}_i\ X_i)$ and $\hat{\overline{H}} = \text{diag}\hat{\overline{H}}_i$.
4. Compute

$$\overline{\delta} = \left(\hat{\overline{H}}'\left(\tilde{\Sigma}^{-1} \otimes I_n\right)H\right)^{-1}\hat{\overline{H}}'\left(\tilde{\Sigma}^{-1} \otimes I_n\right)y.$$

1. Repeat process with $\overline{\delta}$ in place of $\hat{\delta}$.
2. Continue in this manner until convergence is reached.

The Performance of Our Iterative Procedure

In this subsection, we use real data to investigate the efficiency of our iterative procedure. We wish to determine whether the procedure is sensitive to the initial starting values and if indeed any of these values result in non-convergence.

As in the previous section, the model and data used in this study is that of Klein (1950) model. The following starting initial values were tried:

1. The three-stage least squares estimates
2. The two-stage least squares estimates
3. The ordinary least squares estimates
4. The limited-information maximum likelihood estimates
5. The null vector
6. A vector of arbitrary near values
7. A vector of arbitrary far values

Table 6.4. *Full-information model*

Initial values	Number of iterations until convergence
3SLS estimates	107
2SLS estimates	108
OLS estimates	109
Null vector	108
Arbitrary near values	106
Arbitrary far values	105

As in the limited information case, arbitrary near values come from an arbitrary point chosen from the 95 percent concentration ellipsoid of the parameters of the model obtained using the FIML estimate; arbitrary far values come from an arbitrary point outside the 99 percent concentration ellipsoid. Unlike the limited information model, a vector of ones was not tried as initial values as this violates one of the assumptions of the full information model, namely that the matrix B of Equation 6.22 is non-singular. Again, the program was written in GAUSS, and the same definition of convergence was used. Our results are presented in Table 6.4.

Table 6.4 clearly indicates that this iterative procedure is insensitive to the initial values used in starting the procedures and that all initial values lead to convergence.

6.7.3 A Lagrangian Multiplier Test for Endogeneity

In this section, we develop a Lagrangian multiplier test for endogeneity in the full-information model. Our analysis calls on the work we did on twining matrices in Section 2.7 of Chapter 2.

Several of the matrices in the full-information model are in fact inter-twined matrices. The block diagonal matrix H', when we write the model as in Equation 6.21, is obtained by intertwining the submatrices of the block diagonal matrices

$$\overline{Y}' = \begin{pmatrix} Y_1' & & O \\ & \ddots & \\ O & & Y_G' \end{pmatrix} \quad \text{and} \quad \overline{X}' = \begin{pmatrix} X_1' & & O \\ & \ddots & \\ O & & X_G' \end{pmatrix}$$

so we can write

$$T\left(\frac{\overline{Y}'}{\overline{X}'}\right) = H',$$

where T is the appropriate twining matrix.

Recognising this relationship facilitates the mathematics required in applying classical statistical procedures to our model. To illustrate, suppose we want to test the null hypothesis

$$H_0 : \beta = 0$$

against the alternative

$$H_A : \beta \neq 0,$$

where $\beta = (\beta_1' \dots \beta_a')'$

The null hypothesis implies that the equations of our model contain no right-hand current endogenous variables and thus our model under the null collapses to the Seemingly Unrelated Regressions Equation Model, see Turkington (2005). Suppose further we want to develop the Lagrangian multiplier test statistic for this hypothesis and present it as an alternative to other test statistics that would be using to test endogeneity such as the Hausman test statistic (Hausman (1978)).

We are working with the concentrated log-likelihood function $\ell^*(\delta)$ formed by concentrating out the nuisance parameters v. The test statistic we seek to form is then

$$T^* = \frac{1}{n}\frac{\partial \ell^{*'}}{\partial \beta}\bigg|_{\hat{\theta}} \overline{I}^{\beta\beta}(\hat{\theta})\frac{\partial \ell^*}{\partial \beta}\bigg|_{\hat{\theta}}$$

where $\hat{\theta}$ refers to the constrained maximum-likelihood estimators (CMLE), that is, the MLEs formed after we impose H_0 on our model and $\overline{I}^{\beta\beta}$ refers to that part of the asymptotic Cramer-Rao lower bound corresponding to β. Thus, $\overline{I}^{\beta\beta}$ is the appropriate component of $\overline{I}^{-1}(\delta)$ where

$$\overline{I}(\delta) = -p\lim \frac{\partial^2 \ell^*}{\partial \delta \partial \delta}.$$

In forming $\hat{\theta}$, we set $\beta = 0$ so from Equation 6.21 our model becomes

$$y = \overline{X}\gamma + u, \tag{6.29}$$

where $\gamma = (\gamma_1' \dots \gamma_G')'$ and

$$E(u) = 0, \quad V(u) = \Sigma \otimes I_n, \quad u \sim N\left(0, \Sigma \otimes I_n\right)$$

which is the seemingly unrelated regressions equations model (Zellner 1962). An iterative interpretation of the constrained MLE of γ is then found by replacing $\tilde{\tilde{H}}$ and H by $\overline{X}$ in Equation 6.28 to obtain

$$\hat{\gamma} = \left(\overline{X}'\left(\tilde{\Sigma}^{-1} \otimes I_n\right)\overline{X}\right)^{-1}\overline{X}'\left(\tilde{\Sigma}^{-1} \otimes I_n\right)y,$$

where $\tilde{E} = \tilde{U}'\tilde{U}/n$, $\tilde{U} = \text{rvec}_n\tilde{u}$ with $\tilde{u} = (\tilde{u}_1' \quad \cdots \quad \tilde{u}_G')'$ and $\tilde{u}_i$ the ordinary least squares residual vector from the ith equation, that is, $\tilde{u}_i = (I_n - X_i(X_i'X_i)^{-1}X_i')y_i$.

This iterative interpretation regards the joint generalised least squares estimator (JGLSE) as the starting point in the iterative process to the MLE.

The constrained MLE of $\hat{\theta}$ (or at least the iterative asymptotic equivalent of this estimator) is $\hat{\theta} = ((0 \quad \hat{\gamma})'T'\hat{v})'$ where $\hat{v} = \text{vech}\hat{\Sigma}$ and $\hat{\Sigma} = \hat{U}'\hat{U}/n$, $\hat{U} = \text{rvec}_n\hat{u}$, and $\hat{u}$ is the JGLS residual vector, that is, $\hat{u} = y - \overline{X}\hat{\gamma}$. Notice that the twining matrix T is involved in the expression for the constrained MLE of θ.

Our twining matrix T comes into play again when we form the second component of our test statistic, namely $\partial\ell/\partial\beta$. Let $\Psi = (\beta' \quad \gamma')'$, then as $T\Psi = \delta$ it follows that $T\partial\ell/\partial\psi = \partial\ell/\partial\delta$ and that $\partial\ell/\partial\psi = T'\partial\ell/\partial\delta$. We can then obtain the derivative we want using

$$\frac{\partial\ell}{\partial\beta} = S\frac{\partial\ell}{\partial\psi}$$

where S is the selection matrix $(I_m \quad O_{m \times p})$ with $m = \sum_{i=1}^G G_i$ and $p = \sum_{i=1}^G k_i$.

In summary,

$$\frac{\partial\ell}{\partial\beta} = A\frac{\partial\ell}{\partial\delta} \tag{6.30}$$

where

$$A = ST' = \begin{pmatrix} (I_{G_1} \, O_{G_1 \times k_1}) & & O \\ & \ddots & \\ O & & (I_{G_G} \, O_{G_G \times k_G}) \end{pmatrix}.$$

Returning to Equation 6.24, we have that

$$\frac{\partial\ell^*}{\partial\delta} = \overline{H}'\left(\hat{\Sigma}^{-1} \otimes I_n\right)u$$

where $\overline{H}$ is a block diagonal matrix with $\overline{H}_i = (X\Pi_i \ X_i)$ in the ith block diagonal position. It follows from Equation 6.30 that

$$\frac{\partial \ell}{\partial \beta} = \begin{pmatrix} \Pi_1'X_1' & & O \\ & \ddots & \\ O & & \Pi_G'X_G' \end{pmatrix} \left(\hat{\Sigma}^{-1} \otimes I_n \right) u.$$

The third component of the quadratic form, that is, the Lagrangian multiplier test statistic, can also be expressed with the help of twining matrices. As $\partial \ell / \partial \beta = A \partial \ell / \partial \delta$, we have that $I^{\beta\beta} = A I^{\delta\delta} A'$. From our discussion in Section 6.2, it is clear that

$$\overline{I}^{-1}(\delta) = I^{\delta\delta}(\theta).$$

It is well known, see for example Turkington (2005), that

$$I^{\delta\delta}(\theta) = \left[p\lim \frac{1}{n} H'(\Sigma^{-1} \otimes N)H \right]^{-1},$$

where N is the projection matrix $N = X(X'X)^{-1}X'$. Moreover, $H = (\overline{Y} \ \overline{X})T'$ so we can write

$$I^{\delta\delta} = p\lim \frac{1}{n} ST' \left[T(\overline{Y} \ \overline{X})'(\Sigma^{-1} \otimes N)(\overline{Y} \ \overline{X})T' \right]^{-1} TS'$$

$$= p\lim \frac{1}{n} S \left[(\overline{Y} \ \overline{X})'(\Sigma^{-1} \otimes N)(\overline{Y} \ \overline{X}) \right]^{-1} S' \tag{6.31}$$

so in obtaining the part of the Cramer-Rao lower bound we want, we need the (1,1) block matrix of the inverse of Equation 6.31. That is,

$$\overline{I}^{\beta\beta} = p\lim \frac{1}{n} \left\{ \overline{Y}'\left(\Sigma^{-1} \otimes N\right)\overline{Y} - \overline{Y}'\left(\Sigma^{-1} \otimes N\right) \right.$$
$$\left. \overline{X}\left[\overline{X}'\left(\Sigma^{-1} \otimes N\right)\overline{X}\right]^{-1}\overline{X}'\left(\Sigma^{-1} \otimes N\right)Y \right\}^{-1}.$$

Evaluating the probability limit requires basic asymptotic theory. If from here on, we use the notation that $\{A_i'A_j\}$ stands for a partitioned matrix whose (i, j)th block is $A_i'A_j$, then

$$\overline{I}^{\beta\beta} = p\lim \frac{1}{n} \left[\{\sigma^{ij}\Pi_i'X_i'X_j\Pi_j\} \right.$$
$$\left. - \{\sigma^{ij}\Pi_i'X_i'X_j\}\{\sigma^{ij}X_i'X_j\}^{-1}\{\sigma^{ij}X_i'X_j\Pi_j\} \right]^{-1}.$$

The Reduced Form Parameters under H_0

Before we can evaluate our test statistic further it must be noted that both $\partial \ell^* / \partial \beta$ and $\overline{I}^{\beta\beta}$ involve reduced form parameters, and so we must investigate the nature of these parameters when we impose $\beta = 0$ on the model. Clearly, $\beta = 0$ implies that $B = I$, so $Y = -X\Gamma + U$ and Π is $-\Gamma$ and U is V. But, from Equation 6.29

$$Y = (y_1 \ldots y_G) = (X_1\gamma_1 \ldots X_G\gamma_G) + U.$$

Consider now the selection matrix Q_i such that $XQ_i = X_i$ for $i = 1, \ldots, G$. Then,

$$Y = (XQ_1\gamma_1 \ldots XQ_G\gamma_G) + U = X(Q_1\gamma_1 \ldots Q_G\gamma_G) + U,$$

so under the null hypothesis

$$\Pi = (Q_1\gamma_1 \ldots Q_G\gamma_G).$$

Moreover, as $Y_i = Y\overline{W}_i$

$$\Pi_i = (Q_1\gamma_1 \ldots Q_G\gamma_G)\overline{W}_i$$

under the null hypothesis.

Procedure for Forming the Lagrangian Multiplier Test Statistic

We are now in a position to form the LMT statistic. Taking the components $\partial \ell^* / \partial \beta$ and $\overline{T}^{\beta\beta}$, and evaluating these at the constrained MLE $\hat{\theta} = ((0 \quad \hat{\gamma})' T' \hat{v})'$ leads to the following procedure.

1. Apply JGLS to the equations $y = \overline{X}\gamma + u$ and form the JGLSE $\hat{\gamma} = (\overline{X}'(\tilde{\Sigma}^{-1} \otimes I_n)\overline{X})^{-1}\overline{X}'(\tilde{\Sigma}^{-1} \otimes I_n)y$, together with the residual vector $\hat{u} = y - \overline{X}\hat{\gamma}$.
2. Form $\hat{\Sigma} = \hat{U}'\hat{U}/n$ where $\hat{U} = \text{rvec}_n\hat{u}$, and $\hat{\Sigma}^{-1}$ is the $G \times G$ matrix whose (i, j)th elements is $\hat{\sigma}_{ij}$.
3. Form the selection matrices $Q_1, \ldots, Q_G$ and $\overline{W}_1, \ldots, \overline{W}_G$. Using these and $\hat{\gamma}$ form $\hat{\Pi}_i = (Q_1\hat{\gamma}_1 \ldots Q_G\hat{\gamma}_G)\overline{W}_i$.
4. Form

$$\frac{\partial \ell}{\partial \beta}\Big|_{\hat{\theta}} = \begin{pmatrix} \hat{\Pi}'_G X'_1 & & O \\ & \ddots & \\ O & & \hat{\Pi}'_G X'_G \end{pmatrix} (\hat{\Sigma}^{-1} \otimes I_n)\hat{u}.$$

5. Form

$$\overline{T}^{\beta\beta}(\hat{\theta}) = \frac{1}{n}[\{\hat{\sigma}^{ij}\hat{\Pi}'_i X'_i X_j \hat{\Pi}_j\} - \{\hat{\sigma}^{ij}\hat{\Pi}'_i X'_i X_j\}\{\hat{\sigma}^{ij}X'_i X_j\}^{-1}$$
$$\times \{\hat{\sigma}^{ij}X'_i X_j \hat{\Pi}_j\}]^{-1}.$$

6. To obtain the LMT statistic derive the quadratic form,

$$
T^* = \frac{1}{n} \frac{\partial \ell^*}{\partial \beta} \bigg|_{\hat{\theta}}' \ \bar{I}^{\beta\beta}(\hat{\theta}) \frac{\partial \ell^*}{\partial \beta} \bigg|_{\hat{\theta}}.
$$

Under H_0, our test statistic for large sample sizes approximately has a chi-squared distribution with G degrees of freedom so the upper tail of the distribution is used to get the appropriate critical value.

Symbols and Operators Used in this Book

With Respect to a Matrix A

$A_{i\cdot}\,,\,a^{i'}$ ith row of A

$A_{\cdot j}\,,\,a_j$ jth column of A

$(A)_j$ matrix formed by deleting the first j rows of A

$(A)^j$ matrix formed by deleting the first j columns of A

With respect to the Identity Matrix

e_i^G ith column of the $G \times G$ identity matrix I_G

$e_i^{G'}$ ith row of the $G \times G$ identity matrix I_G

With respect to Partition Matrices

Let

$$
A = \begin{pmatrix} A_1 \\ \vdots \\ A_G \end{pmatrix} \quad \text{and} \quad B = \begin{pmatrix} B_1 \\ \vdots \\ B_G \end{pmatrix}
$$

where each submatrix of A is $m \times p$ and each submatrix of B is $n \times p$.

$$
A \tau_{Gmn} B = A_1 \otimes B_1 + \cdots + A_G \otimes B_G
$$

$$
T_{G,m,n}\begin{pmatrix} A \\ B \end{pmatrix} = \begin{pmatrix} A_1 \\ B_1 \\ \vdots \\ A_G \\ B_G \end{pmatrix}
$$

255

$$A^{(j)} = \begin{pmatrix} (A_1)_{j.} \\ \vdots \\ (A_G)_{j.} \end{pmatrix}$$

$$\text{rvec}_m A = \begin{pmatrix} A_1 \dots A_G \end{pmatrix}$$

Let $C = \begin{pmatrix} C_1 \dots C_G \end{pmatrix}$ where each submatrix is $q \times n$.

$$C_{(j)} = \begin{pmatrix} (C_1)_{.j} \dots (C_G)_{.j} \end{pmatrix}$$

$$\text{vec}_n C = \begin{pmatrix} C_1 \\ \vdots \\ C_G \end{pmatrix}$$

Special Matrices

K_{mn}	commutation matrix
$\text{rvec}_n K_{mn}$	generalized rvec of the commutation matrix
$\text{vec}_m K_{mn}$	generalized vec of the commutation matrix

$$N_n = \frac{1}{2} \left(I_{n^2} + K_{nn} \right)$$

$L_n, \ L_n N_n, \ \bar{L}_n N_n, \ L_n, \ L_n^*$	elimination matrices
$D_n, \ \bar{D}_n$	duplication matrices
$T_{G,m,n}$	twining matrix
O	null matrix
0	null column vector

References

Byron, R. P. '*On the Derived Reduced Form from Limited Information Maximum Likelihood*', Australia National University Memo, 1978.

Bowden, R. and Turkington, D. A. 'Instrumental Variables', vol 8 of the *Econometric Society Monographs in Quantitative Economics*. New York: Cambridge University Press, 1990.

Durbin, J. 'Maximum Likelihood Estimator of the Parameters of a System of Simultaneous Regression Equations', *Econometric Theory* **4** (1988): 159–70.

Dwyer, P. S. 'Some Applications of Matrix Derivatives in Multivariate Analysis'. *Journal of the American Statistical Association* **26** (1967): 607–25.

Dwyer, P. S. and MacPhail, M. S. 'Symbolic Matrix Derivatives'. *Annals of Mathematical Statistics* **19** (1948): 517–34.

Efron, B. 'Defining the Curvature of a Statistical Problem (with Applications to Second Order Efficiency)', *Annals of Statistics* **3** (1975): 1189–242.

Fuller, W. 'Some Properties of a Modification of the Limited Information Estimator', *Econometrica* **45** (1977): 939–56.

Graham, A. *Kronecker Products and Matrix Calculus with Applications*. Chichester, U.K.: Ellis Horwood, 1981.

Graeme, W. H. *Econometric Analysis*, 7th edn. Pearson, N.J.: Prentice Hall, 2010.

Hausman, J. 'Specification Tests in Econometrics', *Econometrica* **46** (1978): 1251–71.

Henderson, H. V. and Searle, S. R. 'Vec and Vech Operators for Matrices with Some Uses in Jacobian and Multivariate Statistics', *Canadian Journal of Statistics* **7** (1979): 65–81.

Henderson, H. V. and Searle, S. R. 'The Vec-Permutation Matrix, the Vec Operator and Kronecker Products: A Review', *Linear and Multilinear Algebra* **9** (1981): 271–88.

Horn, R. A. and Johnson, C.R. *Matrix Analysis*. New York: Cambridge University Press, 1981.

Lutkepohl, H. *Handbook of Matrices*. New York: John Wiley & Sons, 1996.

Magnus, J. *Linear Structures*. New York: Oxford University Press, 1988.

Magnus, J. R. 'On the Concept of Matrix Derivative', *Journal of Multivariate Analysis* **101** (2010): 2200–06.

Magnus, J. R. and Neudecker, H. *Matrix Differential Calculus with Applications in Statistics and Econometrics*, revised edn. New York: John Wiley & Sons, 1999.

Maller, R. A. and Turkington, D. A. 'New Light on the Portfolio Allocation Problem', *Mathematical Methods of Operations Research* **56** (2002): 501–11.

Pagan, A. 'Some Consequences of Viewing LIML as an Iterated Aitken Estimator', *Economic Letters* (1979): 369–72.

Parring, A. M. 'About the Concept of the Matrix Derivative'. *Linear Algebra and its Applications* **176** (1992): 223–35.

Rilstone, P., Srivastava, U. K., and Ullah, A. 'The Second-order Bias and Mean Squared Error of Nonlinear Estimators', *Journal of Econometrics* **75** (1996):369–95.

Rogers, G. S. *Matrix Derivatives*. New York: Marcel Dekker, 1980.

Theil, H. *Principles of Econometrics*. New York: John Wiley & Sons, 1971.

Turkington, D. A. *Matrix Calculus and Zero-One Matrices, Statistical and Econometric Applications*, paperback edn. New York: Cambridge University Press, 2005.

Zellner, A. 'An Efficient Method of Estimating Seemingly Unrelated Regressions and Tests for Aggregation Bias'. *Journal of the American Statistical Association* **57** (1962): 348–68.

Index